Built Environments, Constructed Societies

Sidestone Press

Built Environments, Constructed Societies

Inverting spatial analysis

Benjamin N. Vis

This book is based on the original MPhil thesis supervised by Prof. Dr. Jan Kolen
and Alexander Geurds, PhD, written at the Faculty of Archaeology, Leiden University, Leiden, January 2009.

Committee in charge:
    Prof. Dr. Jan Kolen
    Alexander Geurds, PhD
    Prof. Dr. John Bintliff
    Prof. Dr. Huib Ernste
    Prof. Dr. Maarten Jansen

© 2009 Benjamin N. Vis

Published by Sidestone Press, Leiden
    www.sidestone.com
    Sidestone registration number: SSP38670002

ISBN: 978-90-8890-038-9

Illustrations, book design: Micha Meijer

"For the layman and scientist alike I would like to say I feel very strongly that we must recognize and understand the cultural process. We don't need more missiles and H-bombs nearly so much as we need more specific knowledge of ourselves as participants in culture."

Edward T. Hall 1959: 215

Contents

Preface	X

Introduction
    Biographic-calls   3
    Content-wise   6
    Subjectivist Objectification   11

Chapter 1 Axes of Developing Societies
    Epistemology   17
    Axis of Time - Absolute Time   18
    Axis of Time - Social Time   20
    Axis of Time - Subjective Time   23
    Axis of Human Action - Disciplined Humanism   25
    Axis of Human Action - Max Weber   26
    Axis of Human Action - Ludwig von Mises   28
    Axis of Human Action - Alfred Schütz   30
    Axis of Human Action - Michel de Certeau   35
    Axis of Human Space - Existentialism and Embodiment   39
    Axis of Human Space - Territoriality and Proxemics   41
    Axis of Human Space - Built Environment   45
    Axis of Human Space - Space Syntax   48

Chapter 2 Along Disciplinary Lines
    Foundations of Human Geography   57
    New Geography, New Archaeology   58
    Present and Future Discource   61
    Social Evolutionism   63
    Culture History, Culture Areas   67

Chapter 3 Processes of Becoming
    Time-geography and Structuration   73
    Introducing Allan Pred, Criticising Anthony Giddens   74
    Place and the Social   79
    Place beyond Structuration   81
    Towards Place as Historically Contingent Process   84
    What about the Built Environment?   92

Chapter 4 Theorising towards Datasets
    From Regionalisation and Culture Areas   99
    Towards Regionalisation and Culture Areas   102
    Constructing Detailed Systemisation   111
    Towards Built Environments   116

Chapter 5 Theoretical Integration for Datasets
    Some Fundamentals   129
    Social Positioning of Spatialities   133
    Spatial Datasets, Interpretive Issues   137
    Spatial Features   143
    Boundaries and the Macro Scale   148

Disputation of Potentialities
    Are Things Stirring in Archaeology?   155
    Basing a Theory   157
    Building a Theory   160
    A Methodological Turn   162
    Concluding Remarks   163

Acknowledgements   166

References   168

Preface

This book was originally written as a Master's thesis resulting from an academic programme in archaeology at the Faculty of Archaeology, Leiden University. Before the final publication of the thesis text some minor revisions regarding content and linguistics were carried out. During the writing process it soon became clear that through the focus of this study it could contribute to ongoing debates in archaeological theory. Some people strongly advised against getting involved with archaeological theory, often stressing the obvious pitfalls, highlighting the risk of getting detached from what practical archaeology is all about. Taking this advice to heart, it is still theory which is the primary topic of this book. However, care is taken to make a solid connection to essential characteristics of archaeological datasets. At the same time it was insurmountable that this study would not keep within archaeological discourse alone.

Since I have a lifelong fascination with big philosophical questions it is hardly surprising my research would fumble with the foundations of the discipline. Invested with the relative freedom of a young scientist, I allowed myself the audacity to get involved with significant aspects of various disciplines in the social sciences. The most important contribution was made by social geographical theory. Geography and archaeology were befriended for a significant period in their disciplinary formations, but chose diverting paths along the way. As demonstrated in this research, this proves to be a most unfortunate event. Approaching archaeological problems from a perspective derived from social sciences opened up opportunities for reasoning from a dissentient point of departure unrestricted by typical practice respected in current archaeological discourse. Therefore the ideas contained in this book are born from logical reasoning rather than concrete knowledge. That is also why its main arguments are based on closely-reasoned theories instead of empirical evidence. This type of approach asks for the reader to adopt a stance that diverts from usual discourse. My conviction that there is not one way to soundly conduct science is derived from my personal relativist and individualist worldview, much of which is explained in the Introduction to the book. Shedding the constraints of testing hypotheses, this study is the result of a search into what plausible academic solutions can be offered to certain inadequacies I noted in prevalent discourse. Rather than working from a comparative angle, this study follows a curiosity about the interpretive value of social scientific theory in its own right. In such effort theory may become both constitutive as well as a heuristic device. Next to the presented theory the interdisciplinary angle of the current book may still renew mutual disciplinary interests, which gives a sound basis for disciplinary advances in various directions.

Despite its firm basis in disciplinary and paradigmatic debates, the specific spatial interest of the research is no coincidence either. From my first introduction to field archaeology onwards I developed a strong interest in the spatial aspect of datasets. Maps, site lay-out and dispersion patterns all appealed to me. As I became acquainted with geophysical prospection and aerial archaeology during my first field seasons, I was immediately drawn to it. Perhaps, in the beginning it was a masculine affection caused by prospection's technological marvels rather than professionalism. Nevertheless, the great potential the future holds for these techniques, being a powerful source of information joined with the advantage of being non-invasive, could not escape my attention. Prospection produces increasingly detailed and good quality data of the spatial features of material remains. Space, however, is not merely a material feature. Its principal position in the archaeological discipline is particularly made explicit by the culture-specific interests I cherish.

The original incentive to start my studies in archaeology was a strong affection for the history of Mesoamerican cultures. My BA research treats the case of the Postclassic K'iche' Maya city of Q'umarkaaj in Guatemala, focusing on the utilitarian relationship between archaeology and (ethno)archaeology. The attention given to the relation between site lay-out and social organisation in Q'umarkaaj triggered my interest in particular. It demonstrates the distinct influence of urbanism and architecture as products of historical social processes. However, it also made me wonder about the rash use of terms like culture and society, especially considering the way they have determined the history of archaeology and still influence the subdivision of the archaeological world. The borders within Mesoamerica drawn on most maps, may seem to be clear-cut, yet they are far from uncontested. Hence, I was attracted to focus on the eastern border of the Maya culture area and beyond. The eastern Maya periphery and Intermediate/Chibchan/Circum-Caribbean area are poorly researched. Therefore they would make a great place to start to redefine the designation of cultural or societal labels from a truly social scientific point of departure. The application of such labels to spatial entities interferes with our understanding of regions and boundaries. Despite their differences the various research themes contained in these personal interests turn out to have more in common than expected.

Eventually it was decided that a culture-specific angle was too extensive to adequately address at this stage. Since the primary contribution of the thesis is theoretical, a secondary case study probably would not have been beneficial. Because of this decision the explicitly general and overtly theoretical nature is preserved, which now makes the research in this book widely applicable. I encourage the reader to use its ideas independent from the discipline it originated from.

Benjamin N. Vis
Leiden, October 2009

Introduction

Biographic-calls

Objective science does not exist. I realised this early on in my studies at Leiden University. Though many scholars will share this insight, few have used it as a constructive power in their academic practice. If objective science does not exist, consequentially it becomes essential not only to be aware of your own subjectivity, but make others aware of that subjectivity too. For both, neutrality will be abrogated as a frame of reference. One's personal subjective background, against which research is conducted, eventually affects the ways its outcomes are comprehended. This thesis is witness to the fact that science can explicitly concur with personal development. It contains several concise reproductions of potent theoretical assertions proposed by others. These represent a selective body of literature that variably appeals to my personal worldview, and thus acts as a theoretical mediator for basing arguments. Closing in the combination of themes presented in this work are the instantaneous result of the disciplinary interests I pursued over the past few years. My worldview, subscribed epistemological notions, and personal history largely comprise my subjectivity. They are often quite directly responsible for the questions that generated this research. In order to better appreciate its theoretically argued disputations, in addition to my conviction that science is not objective, I feel obliged to introduce this study slightly autobiographically.

Through accumulative interests in the past cultures of Native America, archaeological prospection techniques and theories of social archaeology, this thesis originally meant to set out focusing on the latter, whilst starting with the first. Slowly, however, cultural particularism disappeared into the background as I came to realise that the contribution I could make concentrated around theory, due to practical and intellectual reasons. Nevertheless, these three main ponderings eventually prompted the research objectives. These quickly came to concentrate around issues with the continually intertwined themes of time, space and sociality. The main problem focuses on the seemingly inferential inability to regard human space as socially meaningful without referring to stylistic fineries. It appeared problematic to me that archaeology starts with presumably objective measurable information on spatial data, in order to interpret the social. Therefore the first aim would be to find a theorisation explicating the way space becomes materialised by sociality. Associated questions regard the static character ascribed to space and place, following the lack of temporality in spatial analysis. Yet meaningful and variable concepts of time should connect inferential perspectives. Archaeology, both as a material and social science, apparently does not use its strength to explain socio-spatial phenomena by offering a time-space specific developmental view. (Throughout this study, time-space is used adjectivally to express that that notion pertains to time and space simultaneously, instead of 'interval' as its meaning in physics.) At the interface of space and society, temporal solutions need to be explored.

At the start there was my fascination with the south-eastern Maya neighbours in the small of Central America, which grew as I co-organised the European Maya Conference held in Leiden in 2005 and conducted the research for my Bachelor's degree. This part of the world in archaeology is alternately known as the Intermediate area (especially Willey 1971), the Isthmo-Colombian area with the inclusion of northern South America (Fonseca and Cooke 1993), the Circum-Carribean area excluding the Pacific Coast (John Hoopes; personal communication) or Chibchan Area (Constenla Umaña 1991, John Hoopes personal communication). The problem with its designation lies in the culture history approaches generally used towards the definition of culture areas. As the area is usually considered terra incognita, and the issue is nourished by the very limited understanding of its commonalities in virtually all fields of research. Besides the determinations of major culture areas bordering Central American cultures, like Maya or Moche, were often made in the same reductionist ways. The linguistically and anthropologically defined Lenca culture located in Honduras and El Salvador in particular caught my interest. Scholars assume the Lenca had the strongest ties with the monumentality of its Mesoamerican neighbours of all surrounding groups, providing portals and pathways for contact and trade with societies residing in the south. Subsequently, Wyllis Andrews' (1976) excavations of Quelepa, presumably the largest urban settlement outside of the Mesoamerican area, and the existence of substantial mounds in northern Nicaragua (Jorge Zambrana personal communication), broadened my horizons to the possibility of applying constantly improving prospection techniques in the area. Initially these methods could be used for detecting and mapping architecturally constructed sites from air and outer space, verifying and expanding the currently poor archives of archaeological sightings. Afterwards, more detailed techniques, such as LiDAR and geophysics, could be employed to produce spatial datasets. These rival the accuracy of excavation maps whilst operating on extensive scales. Most importantly, it could change the general tendency of archaeological research on space in the Americas that focused almost exclusively on datasets of elite architecture, obstructing a grasp of the full complexity of any indigenous society. The commonality between these two interests is found in their spatiality, though operating on different levels of detail. The primary source of information produced by prospection techniques is of a spatial nature, and so a theme started to develop. Despite my eagerness to get my hands dirty, even plans limited to the site of Quelepa proved perhaps overambitious for this thesis. In further exploring the Lenca culture I came across Andrea Gerstle's (1988) PhD-research on Copán. Gerstle's focus on the characterisation of its built environment to ascribe compounds to certain socio-cultural groups foreign to the Maya administration (Gerstle 1988) opened my eyes to the possibility of combining my three main interests from a theoretical angle.

This led to a rather sudden interest in theoretical advancements made in social geography. After all, this discipline explicitly featured all things spatial, informed by social theories. This consolidated especially when geography was tipped-off again as a promising source of inspiration in meetings with Rosemary Joyce and John Bintliff. Despite Gerstle's (1988) interesting line of reasoning she eventually based almost all social ascriptions on the basis of ceramic typologies. Similarly, her view of architectural traits at Copán was rather static also. Instead of using social theories to study spatial patterning, archaeology appeared to have its mind set on statistical pattern analysis, leaving social inference mostly to specific stylistic traits. Societies are thus reduced to mathematical formulas and hierarchical classifications.

This feels as if the socio-cultural interests of archaeology are mainly limited to the most voluntary, arbitrary and changeable stylistic aspects of material remains. In addition to the inductive and reductionist tradition of designating culture areas, restricting interpretive research by not taking into account the past societies inhabiting them, there appears to be no solid ground for a social theoretical vantage point. Despite repetitive postprocessual attempts to explore other approaches to social, cultural and perceptive inquiries with various contextualisations allowing for individualism, archaeology seems inadequately equipped to address big questions on the fundamental aspects of developing societies. Archaeology makes little use of its disciplinary abilities. The most important contribution to such grand themes was the postprocessualist endowment of discourse with everyday life.

Since archaeology's material records are basically comprised of usually measurable spatial and temporal properties (although it is recognised that all human production to various extents is a social affair), I think it will be helpful to attempt to formulate a truly social theory informing and perhaps changing its persisting current empiricist methodologies. This should avoid the obvious pitfalls marked by postpressualism. Change, as the most meaningful component of continuity, needs to be made intelligible. The most readily available way to do this would be to focus on performed processes, i.e. social processes. Development and process are also part and parcel of evolutionary approaches. The increased interest in biology, lateral to the approaches resulting from interpretive postprocessualism, thrives for obvious reasons in (fields of prehistoric) archaeology. However, Darwinian models of evolution often prove inadequate for the explanation of the variability in social expressions as well. Evolutionary thought stood at the cradle of the archaeological discipline, but early social adaptations have led to prejudicial political practices and consequentially fell from grace in archaeology, although their generalities still pervade archaeological discourse. The study of process was, of course, one of the main interests of processual practices following the New Archaeology movement of the 1970s. Reacting against previous traditions and inspired by the natural sciences, at the time it was not realised that their practice let earlier reductionist and classificatory methods prevail. Next to the use of biology, now archaeological research focusing on process is rather scattered and narrowly defined.

If a return to social processes is desired, I must take care not to be mistakenly categorised as a newborn processualist. Therefore, when applicable, I choose to use the word processive rather than processual here. Some initial investigations of theoretical literature on the humanisation of space brought me to anthropological interests in proxemics and associated embodied space. There, certain social geographical theories were mentioned. Upon reading, I strongly felt that such theories do not only incorporate everyday life, they put individuals to operate social processes in order to address cultural and historical questions on the regions and geographies these individuals both produced and inhabited. Moreover, I believe the way individuals are treated, takes in the full complexity of the processes that generate and meaningfully inform spatial datasets. Such datasets will be much like the ones we are able to produce in archaeology, especially taking into account the progressing opportunities offered by prospectional techniques. Rather than starting from reductionist classifications or hierarchies, geography appears to concentrate on the fundamental dealings of humans with space. What archaeology uncovers, are the results of its materialised transformation. So my mind was set on trying to establish the potential of such social geographical theories to inform our spatial records, and interpretively enable and reinstate the central big issue of developing societies. Archaeology should become better prepared to make assertions on socio-spatial identities.

Content-wise

The well informed reader will probably know that the disciplines of archaeology and geography have had a lot in common in the past. In fact, it is remarkable how similar the development of geography and archaeology was up to the present. After the emergence of postprocessualism primarily some phenomenological geography was imported. In the USA this occurred often through anthropology, where the meaning of place became a main concern. Specifically in England the New Cultural Geography of Dennis Cosgrove e.a. also was occasionally adopted, informing the concept of place in archaeology. Less specified, it could be suggested that archaeology almost lost sight of geography in favour of more particularist approaches.

Before exploring the possible potential of other perspectives developed by geography, the difference that grew between the disciplines needs to be understood. In spite of their comparable histories, geography never structurally noticed archaeology. Yet, more importantly, the question of why archaeology came to be selective in its interest towards its significant other arises. In the second chapter of this thesis, a short historical overview is given, where the advancement of human geography (of which social geography is a part) is discussed and joined with archaeology at the moment the major movements of New Geography and New Archaeology respectively claimed their voice. In contrast, the advancement of archaeology as a discipline in the light of social evolution and culture history is then elaborated upon separately. Both disciplinary lines are followed until the theoretical point on which the disciplines clearly diverge. In this way, it will be demonstrated why archaeology's inferential deficiency could potentially be complemented by an adaptation of the theoretical choice made by human geography.

The disciplinary developments in chapter two contextualise the fundamental theoretical reasoning previously presented in chapter one. Departing from the position of archaeology, none of the theoretical objectives and questions are well informed without the distinct building blocks resulting from archaeology's interest in the development of societies. The building blocks consist of specific notions resulting from specific, yet various disciplinary ideas formed about the general themes of time, human action and human space. The represented interests have an interdisciplinary character, thus the chapter embeds the fundamental notions epistemologically. As such, there is no escaping certain philosophical foundations that are briefly touched upon at times. The order the general themes are discussed in functions accumulatively, leading to connect the theory directly to the material world. The interconnected notions in the themes comprise them as three axes along which societies develop. Being inherent to developing societies, they lay the basis for the complex theories that follow, whilst cohering the material counterpart through which archaeological empirical analysis may operate. The intelligibility of these notions does not only serve archaeology. Due to the broad appeal of such terms, I hold no pretentious illusions about this study. Given the limited space available, severe selections had to be made as to which notions are most essentially contributing to the line of argument for the theory to be built.

Time has been coarsely divided into absolute time, social time and subjective time, composing theoretically capable temporalities. Included is a very compact discussion of important theories informing the intrinsic temporal character of archaeology, amongst which the Annales School of historiography and the making of subjective time through phenomenology are most significant for interpretive purposes. Subsequently, human action is placed against a background of humanist thinking, before closing in on four prominent thinkers on human action: sociologist Max Weber, economist Ludwig von Mises and social philosophers Alfred Schütz, and Michel de Certeau. Their ideas have been highly influential for the emergence of following action theories, which are contained in geographical theory later on. Furthermore, they are historically tied together, since von Mises was a fierce criticaster of Weber. In turn, Schütz was an apprentice of von Mises. Michel de Certeau's contributions are slightly more recent, yet connected to phenomenological notions as in the work of Schütz. Then the facilitating component of the performance of action, human space, is initially explored through existentialism and embodiment. This is complemented by more specified human spatial expressions. First the essential notion of territoriality in proxemics of anthropologist Edward Hall is discussed, then the meaning of and treatment of the built environment by architect and archaeologist Amos Rapoport, followed by the very sophisticated computerised methods of space syntax, analysing potentialities for the use of space in the complicated built environments of cities. Space syntax as a set of analytical tools was proposed by architectural morphologist Bill Hillier and colleagues in the 1970s, but is still progressively growing more refined. Especially the uni-directionality of inferential arguments concerned with spatial datasets demonstrated in the section of human space is insatisfactory as an accumulative result of the building blocks in the axes. This provides a principal reason for addressing the development of human society in archaeology from a social perspective instead of material. In effect, this would mean an inversion of analytical theory. Therefore, this last section is provided with more commentary then the others, as it is from here that the adaptation of the following social geographical theories is launched. This empirical archaeological turn is better appreciated with the disciplinary appropriations of chapter two.

The notions that file past in chapter one are selected because of their relatively pure theoretical stances, some of which have acquired iconic qualities for certain types of discourse in various disciplines. An extreme example of this is the almost annoyingly consistent construction of (economic) society by Ludwig von Mises. At the same time, such perspectives logically hold greater value for building theories because of their uncorrupted nature. Alternatively, as is the case for the approaches to the built and urban environment, approaches have been selected because they particularly serve archaeological methods. Preference is given to perhaps less strictly related ideas, rather than symbiotic adaptations which often corrupt notions, because they construct the following arguments on a more fundamental level instead of particular details. Therefore, the ideas presented in chapter one theoretically contextualise chapter two, while the paradigmatic chapter two disciplinarily contextualises chapter one. As a whole, it serves as a large introductory treatise, representing the background used and elaborated upon in the consecutive chapters containing more specific directions followed by others and myself. Moreover, this extended context emphasises the issues for which potential solutions are developed.

The rest of the thesis is divided into three chapters: bridging, building and operationalising theoretical necessities following from the presented issues. Chapter three introduces the geographical theory developed by Allan Pred in the 1980s. His work acts as a bridge between the epistemology of the first two chapters and the geographical immediacy of the next. Since he was specifically influenced by the Annales School, time-geography and structuration theory, the symbiosis represented by his work offers a perfect base. Pred made this thought applicable as concrete microgeographies of everyday life, especially significant in the ways change is enabled by social processes in history. The general scope of his theoretical contributions readily indicates the opportunity it provides for studying the big issue of developing societies. As a geographer, space was inextricably connected to social organisation in his research. Nevertheless, it was the concept of place that had his undivided attention in this potent early work, in which some phenomenological ideas are evidently present too. Pred saw processes as processes of becoming, and in his theory he placed them within a historical flow of time and operating in the natural environment. So he combined time, human action and space in a manner that appears closely related to what could be archaeologically adapted. This chapter critically appropriates the current potential of this approach.

Of course there are recent additions to such theory also. In the light of their potential for archaeological research objectives, two directions will be shortly discussed in chapter four, represented by Benno Werlen and Adreas Koch respectively. In their ability to assess scalar differences in detail, they fill in the blanks left by Pred's generality. Their successive importance is characterised by the equivalence of time and space, which is also an intrinsic part of Pred's theory. Whereas Werlen works on the scale of regionalisation and borders, Koch works at a scale that is easily translated into micro scale built environments. It counts for both that through a focus on generative processes, these concepts lose their static nature. Quickly passing over performance, regions and network theories, conceptualisation grows increasingly complex here. One of the side effects, as might be suspected, is the distance they create to archaeological empiricism again. These recent developments in geography and the divergence they could cause once more, give a more concrete form to the issues we are confronted with when attempting to continue such theoretical considerations into the scope of archaeological methodologies. Although their idealised theories seemingly distance themselves from actual situations, on the other hand, they force a focus on features of meaningful potential that are also present in archaeological datasets. The inferential opportunities such datasets comprised of idealised features offer consequentially needs to be conceptualised. Both an integrating adaptation of the presented theories for archaeological purposes and this conceptualisation are part of chapter five. Themes like place, region, culture area, borders and social evolution are thusly revitalised through theorisation.

Given the coarse nature of archaeological data, a fairly high level of detail is needed to comprehend the meaning bearing social processes producing the data. This implies a dataset that reflects most activities and societal relations produced by sociality, preferably within a holistic kind of selection. Hence an argument will be made for using data from urban environments embodying the most complete degree of physical consolidation and mediation expressed in a built environment. The main concern of such a dataset is its ability to address inferential problems by employing archaeological methodologies to increase insight in the underlying social processes. Through the aforementioned geographical theories, certain aspects of the spatial record will be suggested as being specifically informative on interactional processes. Here it will be asserted there are specific localities where significant social positions are negotiated. These localities are invested with elevated social meaning by this systemic negotiation, both producing the built environment and being mediated by it. The cues that follow from such theoretical considerations will be of a more fundamental nature than the stylistic traits which have overshadowed most culturally particular studies so far. Recognising spatial signatures on the basis of theoretically selected cues should lead to an appropriation of the socio-spatial identity of places based on a practice of socially positioning spatialities as interspatial relations grew over time.

Dealing with datasets of the built environment and past cities comes with some proper problems and is currently dominated by generally accepted assumptions dichotomising inference. Michael Smith (2007) excellently indexed most of these in his comparative article on early cities. The most obvious problem is the flawed datasets acquired by archaeology. Due to the degenerative condition of material remains, details are lost over time and previous developmental stages are superimposed or demolished. Also, datasets are restricted by sheer scale, rendering archaeology inevitably selective. There are simply practical and financial inhibitions to covering sites extensively or completely, despite the efforts that have been made. Moreover sites should not be analysed as isolated cases, which questions the very geometrical definition of a site. These practical problems cannot be overcome.

Secondly, the theoretical implications will cast doubt on some general dichotomies. Smith (2007) most notably signals the false dichotomy of planned and unplanned cities (or planned and organic growth), ignoring the rejection of cross-cultural comparisons for interpretive purposes. In addition, I will challenge the traditional dichotomy of continuity and change, especially the conceptualisation of change as events or short-lived revolutions. Here specifically the proposals of Michel de Certeau (1988) offer a persuasive perspective, allowing for a reappropriation of change. As will be shown, the continual dialectic processes of structuration actually intrinsically incorporate both the long and short term. The concept of stratigraphy may help to detect structural changes consolidated in the built environment. Connected to this is the dichotomy between micro and macro scales, which will be theoretically captured in the same process for both time and space. Questioning these dichotomies leads to a less isolated dealing with inquiries on sociality in time and space on the basis of archaeological data. Also, it should put archaeological inference in a socio-cultural position to enlighten knowledge of the past, which helps a better appreciation of our own current position in such way that this insight can be used for future endeavours in our dealings with space.

Nevertheless, this study does not promise any certainties, well-defined methodologies or clear-cut answers. Along the various themes addressed, it hopes to raise an interest for alternate lines of reasoning and establish the potential of social geographical theories and stimulate the use of technological data acquisition. As a whole it might better be taken as an incentive, setting the agenda, rather than an answer to hopes and prayers.

Subjectivist Objectification

As might have become clear in the above, I envision archaeology as a discipline with a strong and meaningful relation to the present and future, contributing significant knowledge on societal problems we are both currently confronting and are yet to be faced with. The traditional attitude towards archaeology as primarily looking at the past by working from empiricism, because of our inevitable ties to material remains, should better be left behind. Despite its inability to offer definite solutions or complete, fully-fledged methodologies, this study attempts to explicitly take into account our material condition upon which empirical inquiries are based. In order to facilitate a more direct comprehension of the assertions made in my writing towards archaeology, I should discuss the subjectivism derived from my personal views that permeates this epistemology and theory. Therefore I end this introduction by mentioning some of the prominent perspectives undoubtedly seeping from my worldview into this research.

During his lifetime, philosopher and founder of phenomenology, Edmund Husserl already remarked that contrary to practice then, the inner world of human being should not be studied with the same methods used by the researchers of nature (the outer world) (Cloke e.a. 1991). On the basis that we are human beings studying our own species, I concur with that. The greater distance that exists between human beings studying other species allows us to accept the role of observer. As illustrated by anthropology, initially this role of observing and describing was common practice in research on other cultures. Eventually some anthropologists decided to submerge themselves in another culture in order to better understand its traditions and beliefs. Phenomenology, however, shows us the unique position of each human being inhibiting an exact and true understanding of others' thoughts. Still, because of the reciprocal cognitive process of interpreting others by means of ourselves, the relationship between human beings is different from our relationship to other species. To me, this is the ground for the conduct of social science, which may strongly differ in conduct from natural science. Yet it remains dependent on it for the definition of our species.

Embedded in this assertion lies a very individualistic image of human being. The physical and phenomenological uniqueness of being human, permits in my view the existence of having original thoughts. The uniqueness of the cognitive process of perception, and the actions that may follow from that, account for continual change by the hands of man. Original thought, for me, is clearly illustrated in the process of learning. Learning consists of roughly two parts: memorising and understanding. Memory is flawed and phenomenologically proper. It directs the perception and eventually conception of phenomena in each mind in similar ways, but in reproduction it therefore contains individually unique views. Understanding is the cognition of a process previously held in the mind of another. Still this is unique, since it is filtered by individual experience. True understanding of another's reasoning means reproducing an original thought in reference to one's self. Moreover, human beings have continuous disposal of free will, envisioning a result and a free choice to act according to their ordinal expectations of its consequences. This free will is only constrained by material, biological and physiological reflexes and impossibilities, although acquiring (technological) abilities will increase the amount of possibilities. This perspective essentially puts human beings as free agents in the world, capable of self-determination and understanding the natural and social world self-referentially.

Furthermore, epistemologically I am moderately relativistic. That indicates that I generally accept all others' logic. Nevertheless, that does not mean all individual worldviews are of definite value to academic advancement. In this I have been inspired by Hillary Putnam's epistemology, which entails that any argument can be true when consistently applied within a specific conceptual framework (Putnam 1981). This notion has been interchangeably termed pragmatic realism, internal realism and conceptual relativism. Basically, such epistemology allows for subjective science, as mentioned before, only if the researcher stays loyal to his theoretical framework and this is communicated. This too was suggested by Putnam before (idem). Additionally, it immediately permits the lateral existence of plural scientific truths. For me, this means that conducting research from a socio-cultural perspective does not cause the rejection of natural scientific approaches. They can exist side by side, both producing their own truths. Moreover, the knowledge they produce should be seen as complementary. Inhibitions contained in natural scientific insights will sharpen the focus on understanding socio-cultural variations. The long term debate on the uniqueness of *homo sapiens sapiens* as a species separated from animals is irrelevant to me (cf. Corbey 2005) and therefore not a part of this thesis or the definition of the built environment (cf. Ingold 2000). Human beings are a product of biological evolution and understanding of it steadily increases. Thus, essentially all things human are a product of biology, including the socio-cultural. However, the development of the socio-cultural does not necessarily follow the rules of biology and may interfere (fenotypically) in the evolutionary process. In short, I argue that it is in the relational difference in our academic position to our species that an alternative analytical (or social) method is justified. This attitude to social and biological approaches I tend to call pragmatic naturalism.

On the basis of all this, it is hardly surprising that I chose to take a point of departure for archaeology defying its materially bound condition. This aprioristic social theoretical approach (cf. von Mises 1998, Werlen 2005) will be experienced as troublesome for many archaeologists, especially as I have chosen not to exclude explicit material cases to illustrate my assertions. Comparable to the way Max Weber's classificatory theory ought to be used and how Allan Pred argues for the value of his notions, this theory building will prove to be of mainly inferentially informative use rather than offering direct answers to specific questions. Moreover, the theory requires specific types of data and forces data acquisition accordingly. Altogether this indicates that presenting particular examples here will cause misunderstandings instead of clarifying theoretical potentials. Fortunately, in geographical literature Benno Werlen in his work on everyday regionalisations has argued for a similar point of departure for the spatially bound geographical discipline. "[My perspective] exists in contrast to all approaches that begin with regions, borders, spatial patterns and other spatial phenomena and work toward an analysis of social structures, rather than the other way around." (Werlen 2005: 47) This, in a nutshell, is the kind of background against which this research should be read.

Chapter 1 *Axes of Developing Societies*

Epistemology

Big themes are nothing to be scared of. They are a challenge that any academic discipline should be happy to accept, despite its implication of big questions followed by big issues. The main interpretive issue in archaeology is the question how human societies developed. Unfortunately, the prejudicial results of early ponderings about this particular big issue, especially those originating from evolutionary infusions, have led to various degrees of rejection in the development of the archaeological discipline, as is briefly demonstrated in chapter two. This has obstructed opportunities for more nuanced adaptations of evolutionary thought, specifically those fit for addressing social processes that produce society.

Social inquiries are usually treated in narrowly defined and restricted fields of research, rendering knowledge asunder. Moreover, archaeological discourse, due to its materially bound character, tends to work from material objects rather than social arguments informing analysis. The study of society in itself is a complex composite of knowledgeable elements. Adding to that the requirement of a physical counterpart to enable the empirical research methods employed by archaeology, even more elements need to be considered, distributing the big issue over many topics. Since all these elements have been made part and parcel of several disciplinary interests, knowledge about them is even further dispersed, complicating the acquisition of an overview of theoretical notions separately developed in those disciplines. Archaeology will oscillate through all parts of this study, while philosophy, sociology, history, anthropology and geography occupy their respective places. The challenge of being able to address and position such a theme is not only down to archaeology, but needs an epistemological bringing-together explored in this first chapter.

Here I will initially explore interdisciplinary thought on developing societies along three main constitutive axes conceptualised as fundamental components playing important roles in the composite of society. In doing so, it first establishes knowledge of the most essential ideas, rather than adaptive complementarily inclined discourses, comprising the societal theme in archaeology. These axes are represented by time, human action and human space. This chapter will be far from exhaustive on the plethora of disciplinary notions relating to the axes that have been formulated over time. Instead it chooses to examine several notions associated with certain prominent scholars. To some extent these illustrate my personal point of departure, which embeds the more particular theories that will be discussed later, and make explicit the connections that tie the three axes together. As will be demonstrated social and subjective time are a constitutive background to the action theories of Max Weber, Ludwig von Mises, and Alfred Schütz, which in turn imply a human environment conceptualised as physical space by embodiment and the built environment. Taking a slightly different angle,

Michel de Certeau's reappropriative action will shortly be discussed also.

The first chapter will easily converge with the second, offering a context of relevant perspectives on a selection of sequential intervals of disciplinary history. These academic developments are silently present in the preceding discussion of the three constitutive axes. The historical overview will focus on the disciplines of archaeology and geography, exploring their former epistemological junctions and the present distanciation. In most cases, the perspectives and notions discussed will have a philosophical background generally referring to humanism, existentialism and phenomenology. This historical overview will allow a better appreciation of the lateral positioning of comparable notions in the axes of the societal composite. Also, it will now explicitly uncover the reasons for the potential entailed in repeating the disciplinary junction once again, further embedding the following chapters that lean heavily on the combined informative arguments of these two chapters.

Altogether this first part of the thesis will move back and forth in time in order to reach the same theoretically suggestive destination at several occasions by following the constitutive axes and disciplinary developments. In the mean time it informs both the reasons for the presumed potential of the social geographical theories presented in later chapters and shapes their contexts. The aim is not to write a compelling philosophy or epistemology in its own right, but to provide the knowledge necessary to comprehend the current situation obstructing adequate assessments of the big issue of interpreting societal development in archaeology. Consequentially, this part introduces the requirement of changing our theoretical angle to equip a fundamental treatise of this big issue. For this, spatio-temporal data will prove to be the most readily available source of information. The axes presented here will inform the reading of the social geographical theories for future conduct, as well as make an attempt to overcome traditional pitfalls resulting from the social evolutionary and culture historical approaches presented in chapter two and their still prevalent discursive echoes.

Axis of Time - Absolute Time

As the study of human development on the basis of material remains, the discipline of archaeology exists by grace of the passage of time. Nevertheless, the discipline saw a neglect of this fundamental condition in its discourse over the past decades, despite the early overview on time in archaeology by Geoff Bailey (1987). An extensive follow-up, edited by Tim Murray (1999), bundled a wide array of articles dealing with all conceptions and empirical implications of time. Hereafter it was the compelling book of Gavin Lucas (2005), *The Archaeology of Time*, that recently laid a definite foundation for the recurrence of the topic. Some of his findings will concisely be reproduced here.

The traditional dealing of archaeology with time incorporates quite static terms, most fundamentally captured in the concept of chronology. Chronology is divided in two sets of concepts: firstly, absolute chronologies, and secondly, relative chronologies. Absolute chronologies are clearly linked to the archaeological method of calendrical dating, which allows our datasets to be precisely situated on a timescale. They provide us with valuable information and measurable facts that can be reproduced at will. Relative chronologies relate to the interdependence of selections of data, which, through methods of classification, lead to periodisations and stratigraphies (Lucas 2005). "[Not] all archaeologists would necessarily agree with this categorisation […], in many ways, the distinction between absolute and relative time is mostly one of scale and regularity. All chronologies are ultimately based on events that incorporate time into their very structure." (idem: 8) Note that these rather methodologically embedded takes on time concentrate on positioning static categories detected in archaeological data.

This character of time follows from the problem, also noted by Lucas, that time is conceptualised as a uni-linear sequence. This affects archaeological interpretation. As applied to typologies and stratification, the way time is dealt with also reflects on the social and the spatial as a framework of inference. Despite its informative value, it is actually a more abstract notion of time that is of interest here: time in a processive, evolutionary or historical sense. In archaeological discourse it is the degenerative process in the progression of passing time that leaves us with material remains, making material remains temporal. Most importantly, however, passing time enables the analysis of human development as a process, making the social temporal also.

With this notion (specifically in periodisation) time moves into a debate on evolution. Influenced by the teleological nature of biological advancement in the theory of evolution, researchers like Lewis Henry Morgan in the 19th century and Vere Gordon Childe in the 20th century expanded the so-called three age system, further elaborated by revolutionary pivots. This resulted in a tradition of research called social or cultural evolution, in which societies were seen as developing from barbarism and savagery towards a civilisation or state. Implications of such approaches which will be discussed in chapter two. As will also become apparent here, Foucault's view on chronology is actually quite insightful, despite maintaining an emphasis on periodisation: "Each periodisation is the demarcation in history of a certain level of events, and conversely each level of events demands its own specific periodisation, because according to the choice of level different periodisations have marked out and, depending on the periodisation one adopts, different levels of events become accessible. This brings us to the complex methodology of discontinuity." (Foucault 1980: 67)

The discontinuity of Foucault cleverly includes and elaborates on what in social evolution eventually was also recognised: the assumed uni-directional, teleological development was not going at the same pace everywhere (Lucas 2005). This indicates that time is not only absolute, it is also situational thus relative. In this sense it might be better to speak of temporalities rather than time. "[Temporality] is not chronology (as opposed to time), and it is not history (as opposed to chronology). [...] In the mere succession of events there is no time, as nothing does. [...] Temporality entails a perspective that contrasts radically with the one [...] that sets up history and chronology in a relation of complementary opposition." (Ingold 2000: 194) In order to form temporalities, Ingold takes the complementary A and B-series of McTaggart. The B-series entail actions or events seen as isolated succeeding happenings, frame by frame. In the A-series "time is immanent in the passage of events [... encompassing] a pattern of retentions [corrig.] from the past and the protentions for the future. Thus from the A-series point of view, temporality and historicity are not opposed but rather merge in the experience of those who, in the activities, carry forward the process of social life." (idem: 194) These activities taken together compose Ingold's *taskscape*, which bears temporality within. Temporalities thus allow for differing rhythms, durations, etc. in activities according to the context and experience of time. Alternatively, as Bourdieu has put it: "time derives its efficacy from the state of the structure of relations within which it comes into play" (Bourdieu 1977: 7), though he simultaneously believed in intelligible objective structures produced by history, laying the foundation for structuralist relationships in time. A specific aspect of the interpretive activities of archaeology should be concerned with the understanding of various temporalities. In order to produce a clear perspective on temporalities, the notion of social time emerges.

Axis of Time - Social Time

There are several scholars who have contributed considerably to the characterisation of social types of time. Advanced thinkers like Norbert Elias (1997) and Tim Ingold (1986) have proposed that the 20th century rejection of studying long term developments of social life by the deconstruction of evolutionary theories, is an impoverishment of understanding human activity and confuses the oppositions of agency and structure in temporal contexts (Dunning and Krieken 1997). Ingold introduced the distinct temporality of social life and social evolution (Ingold 1986), which concisely entails the contrast of the real time of social life and the abstract time associated with social or cultural evolution. This differentiation tends to inform or reconstruct influential distinctions made in historiography.

Adverted by Henri Berr, Lucien Febvre, Marc Bloch and Fernand Braudel, the Annales School in history emerged in France. In his extensive article on Braudel, Hexter already noted that "against considerable odds [a structure resulting from the mentality change (focusing on social and economic history) of historiography] has taken over historical studies in France, at the same time winning for those studies worldwide admiration." (Hexter 1972: 483) This influence did not remain restricted to the historical discipline, but was quite readily applied in many of the social sciences. Hexter's own criticism, leading to an alternative view, has never become as widely accepted.

The temporal concepts of historiography, most importantly propagated by Braudel, have been concerned with a non-linear history and operated on distinguished temporal scales. In contrast to anthropology and sociology, historiography has been confronted with the need to understand the nature of social time (J. R. Hall 1980). The Annales School is concerned with the relativity of multiple scales of objective time. The Annales historians focused on processes that moved beyond individual's intentions and texts, a type of structuralism that coincides with the work of Emile Durkheim (J. R. Hall 1980, Lucas 2005) and Bourdieu (1977). The work of Fernand Braudel is essential for the focus on temporal scales. He proposed three temporal scales: *les temps courts* or *l'histoire événementielle*, *la moyenne durée* or social history, and *la longue durée* or an ecological or geographical history (J. R. Hall 1980, Santamaria and Bailey 1984, Bintliff 1991b, Lucas 2005). Braudel does stress that these scales are not to be taken separately. All scales interrelationally influence each other, and he even holds that all scales have their own cycles and rhythms functioning within them. However, eventually there is only one (objective) time of history that they all adhere to (J. R. Hall 1980), which is similar to Bourdieu's structure of objective history. Yet Braudel was mostly interested in the longue durée, where he placed the processes of geo-history and (changing) mentality: an underlying current by which, in a way, everything is connected. Archaeology naturally found itself directly applied to this long term history. Therefore, little attention has been given to the events of les temps courts or the socio-economical and demographic processes of the conjunctures in la moyenne durée. In archaeology, the Annales School also has received considerable attention in various contexts, but most elaborately in the volume edited by John Bintliff (1991a), *The Annales School and Archaeology*. This book places structural history in the perspective of the archaeological paradigms of processualism and postprocessualism, arguably making them complementary instead of opposing positions (Bintliff 1991b) (see chapter two).

Despite the fact Braudel acknowledged his scales to be part of a whole, the arbitrary division has proven to be quite useful for ordering analysis. For the greater part, it has been used for applications in archaeological data in this fashion. This has led to interpretations on different temporal levels. Firstly, recognising events that had profound effects following from (short lived) traumas, that are also called contingent catalysts. On the second level, analysing processes of cultural and economic change, which is where social evolution could probably be placed. Finally, reaching the relationship between the environmental and people, which moves at the slowest rate (J. R. Hall 1980, Bintliff 1991b, Lucas 2005) and appears most applicable to our discipline. Interpretations following from this analysis reinstate Braudel's arbitrary division rather than reaching the point of integrating different temporal scales, a possibility that he actually did enable.

The tendency of social sciences to look for structures and patterns in order to understand behaviour could be served by incorporating some other elements of Braudel's concepts. In the first place, he notes that all structures are defined by duration and subsequently their effect on human behaviour. Secondly, his notion of simultaneity, which indicates the combined presence of the past, present, and future (Santamaria and Bailey 1984), is applicable to assertions and objects of study in many disciplines like history, archaeology and anthropology. This implies there is only the present, with retentions from the past and protentions for the future, an idea developed by phenomenologist Edmund Husserl, but continued upon by Tim Ingold (2000) (see above). As such, in the study of the past only present moments and direct inference of the past exist. The phenomenological stance to time is thus essentially a-historical, because the past and the future continuously fuse together in unique compositions in the present (Kolen 2005). The implication of the search for structures is that researchers are not only imprisoned by a notion of time as duration and measurement, but they are also concerned with the history of sociologists that studies the constraints on the possibilities of human action (Santamaria and Bailey 1984).

Here Santamaria and Bailey introduce us to an uneasy dichotomy in Braudel's concept of duration that juxtaposes formal (mathematical, exogenous, objective) time that measures his tripartite division, and material (internal, subjective) time that realises those in terms of geographical, social, and individual time. This contradiction is based on the problem that the formal division of time envelops all scales by one another, while the material times, derived from concepts of other disciplines, do not. Braudel asserts that subjective variable concepts of time, revealing the relationship of social action and the processes of history, detach themselves from objective time and thus attempt to escape historical time. This has been opposed by phenomenology which holds that irreversible objective time is undeniable, but actually synthesises the multiplicity of subjective temporal experiences (J. R. Hall 1980). It is this understanding that is of particular interest to this study, since the irreversible objective flow of time (cf. Husserl's temporal flux (Lucas 2005) in the section on Alfred Schütz below) is just the philosophical or academic vehicle situating temporalities in the larger framework of continuous developments.

The assertions phenomenology reacted to deny the possibility of analysing concrete phenomena and the non-chronological meaningful character of actual social life. This was exercised by the structuralist philosophy of Althusser and later Balibar, who inhibited reconciliation of their theory with the concrete by not incorporating subjective and intersubjective temporal concepts. Their investigation of social life required that subjectivist concepts of time were transformed into the structuralist edifice (J. R. Hall 1980). This can easily be projected back to the deficiency that the Annales School has had defective attention for the theorising of the event as a present moment.

The event was seen as determined by the past and future, leaving inadequate space for the contemporary, rather using the subjective interpretations of a period (Santamaria and Bailey 1984). The Annales School also lacked a theory of social change, or the shift from one historical entity to another. The event cannot stand alone, but is redirected to the moyenne durée for any understanding of it. It seems that this is the consequence of the lack of inquiry into the effects of action on the creation of structures (idem). It is also comparable to Althusser's notion that individuals are only those who enact the determinate structure (J. R. Hall 1980). This is because the longue durée as a structure is superimposed on the other temporal scales. In order for change to happen an event should exceed the limits or obstacles defined by the structure of the longue durée, thereby the issue of its creation is avoided (Santamaria and Bailey 1984). This means that in order to reach an understanding of long term developments, we need to move beyond structuralist objective time towards an understanding of individual subjective time in an intersubjective temporal world. Socio-temporal meaning is produced on occasions, as Hall argues: "Each social occasion has subjective temporal locations keyed to the pasts and anticipated futures of the persons involved [...]; they are enmeshed in non-sequential subjective contexts of meaning, which give an extra-chronological character to unfolding social life." (J. R. Hall 1980: 124-125)

Axis of Time - Subjective Time

This brings us back to the aforementioned distinction of the time of social life and social evolution (Ingold 1986). The social life takes place in real time, while social evolution, which is created through contingent social life, can be labelled as taking place in an enlarged, abstract time. Also, compare these notions with Ingold's take on the A and B-series mentioned before, arriving at the temporality of taskscapes that operate social life (Ingold 2000). Overall, Ingold ties different types and experiences of time intricately together into a 'continuous state' of present. Strongly influenced by phenomenologist experientialism, featuring the temporal occasions of individuals, Ingold further elaborates on the concept of the present in his book *The Perception of the Environment*. The present is the scale in which évenements take place. In doing so he actually provides a plausible theses for what the utilisation of the Annales School was missing. Following assertions made by phenomenologists like Merleau-Ponty and Gell, he conceptualises the present as a unique moment that incorporates a vista of the past and the future that only is available for that specific moment and no other. Rather than being delimited to the past or the present, it gathers the past and the future into itself, enabling it to move (in time) without crossing temporal boundaries (idem). This makes a good context for events to operate in and take on specific meanings according to the subjectivities of time.

Subjectivist historians have ignored subjective time, while phenomenological analysis of time has remained a-historical. To resolve this hiatus phenomenological approaches must be applied to the empirical tasks of interpretative sociology and historiography (J. R. Hall 1980). For investigations along these lines, Husserl's phenomenological analysis of essential structures of time-consciousness can be used to derive alternative concepts of time, using them to enrich sociological concepts and analyse specific historical developments. This applied phenomenology recognises four idealised types of subjective temporal orientations, based on Husserl's a priori possibilities of time-consciousness: *synchronic* (referring to the intersubjective temporal orientations the 'now' is the locus of individual and collective attention, fully consciously 'lived time'), *diachronic* (de-emphasises the 'now' in favour of reproduction of the past and anticipation of the future), *strategic* (exclusive emphasis on the anticipation of the future, goal directed, determining actions in the 'now' with the past only constraining possible actions), *eternal* (deriving meaning from a mythical past, preceding any diachrony, attaining a character of timeless recreation) (idem). Especially this last temporal orientation is also where one could locate certain cultural specific ideas on time. Many cultural (mythical) concepts of time have been developed, varying from Lévi-Strauss' and Leach's structuralist oppositions in temporal components (Lucas 2005) to the more rich and complex concepts as primordial and circular time, elaborated upon by Mircea Eliade (Eliade 1959). However culturally enticing, these ideas do not directly contribute to the more fundamental character of time at stake here.

The application of phenomenology, actually a form of Schütz's constitutive phenomenology (Cloke e.a. 1991), could establish Husserl's life-world as the zone of sociological analysis, and subjective time as the basis for meaning, social action, complex fields of social action, and history. Hall remarks that many events happen in realms of activity, which are not essentially tied to any location on the objective time scale, while objective time in different ways remains more or less important. They have their meaning in the content of social life (J. R. Hall 1980). This indicates that if the event, despite having a duration in objective time, is not tied to specific locations in that time, we have successfully replaced the need for chronology without losing touch with objective time. The relations within subjective time are more meaningful than substituting it with the consecutive nature of events in chronology. In such temporal interconnectedness it suffices to say that the temporalities of processes are objectively tied (rhythms and time-spans), yet their exact position in objective time in itself does not hold inferential value. Their operational force as a cog-wheel in the progression of social life does. The scale of objective temporal change may transcend the individual's consciousness, but the phenomena themselves embody subjective temporality. "If we are to avoid a kind of abstraction which obscures the nature of these phenomena, we must insist that every concept of social time […] be based in part on reference to temporal subjective acts of consciousness." (idem: 126) Due to social life being dependent on events (or occasional opportunities for happenings), subsequently interconnected with an abstracted timescale extended into social evolution, the long term concern becomes separated from that objective framework as well. The subjective temporality issue is now conceptualised as momentarily specific perception of the past and the future (the present of events) in the context of social life. Both subjects and researchers adhere to that, so subjective time effectively becomes an all inclusive notion. If temporalities are causative of the operation of social life, they must be inhabited by human beings, leading to the awareness that human actions are events. It is against this backdrop that the interpretive potential of temporalities in the study of developing societies should be appreciated.

Axis of Human Action - Disciplined Humanism

Human action eventually depends on the ability of a human being to perform that action. Since not only action, but physiologically speaking, also human beings are finite (thus temporal), a conceptualisation of human beings necessarily takes into account the given precondition of the flow of time and the existence of temporalities. There have been many disciplines at various periods that developed their own manifold definitions of 'man', but it would serve no purpose to be exhaustive here. Most important for this study are those views that, directly or indirectly influenced by humanist thought, place human beings in the context of their actions. In addition, existentialist philosophies have thoroughly situated human beings in their environment and separately influenced many disciplinary approaches. Man is an acting being. Since both man and his actions are temporal, man as a facilitator for action with physically preconditioned abilities and potentially enabled by free will is most significant here.

In the first place, human beings have traditionally become the focus of anthropology. The position of this discipline is special due to its twofold character, internally uniting the natural scientific approach of physical anthropology with the social and cultural characterisation of man and his environment. This twofold character is seconded by archaeology which has been heavily influenced by anthropological thought, in the United States in particular. Before converging the physical human being with its social counterpart in specific details, going back to the cradle of positioning human being centrefold to academic analysis will be most informative for the understanding of both past and present theories of human action. Many of these have been significantly influenced by the history of humanist thought.

In the volatile trends of human thought in history, humanism has had formative voices in classical Greek philosophy, the medieval Islamic world and subsequently in the Renaissance. This era effectively established the human individual as something indispensible to human thought and action, able to attain knowledge of external and internal worlds. Galileo proposed the mobilisation of the human senses in a supposedly objective and empirical method for his scientific humanism, in which the cosmos consists of an order of laws. He used human rationality to understand the natural world. René Descartes then introduced Cartesian rationalism (*je pense, donc je suis*), which inverted this argument by casting doubt on existence through an existential doubt about being. Hence science became the tool for knowing the world. Both the ideas of Galileo and Descartes have been criticised for dehumanising science, opposing Renaissance humanism to academic humanism which takes humanity as the measure for academic inquiry (Cloke e.a. 1991).

A humanism paradigm was subdued till the 19th century, when the term humanism was reintroduced, principally in the United States. While humanism now usually entails an opposition of arts and sciences, noting significant deficiencies in traditional science, in the Renaissance it incorporated all sciences and arts. Since the 19th century many different branches can be discerned, most notably secular and religious directions of humanism. From the early 20th century onwards humanist thought regained interest in academic discourse. Philosopher F. C. S. Schiller (member of the German idealist tradition, with the likes of Hegel and Kant) has had a large influence in the re-establishment of academic humanism. His definition of humanism is effortlessly grasped: "Humanism is really in itself the simplest of philosophic view points: it is merely the perception that the philosophic problem concerns human beings striving to comprehend a world of human experience by the resource of human minds. [Furthermore he insists on] leaving in the whole luxuriance of individual minds." (as quoted in: Cloke e.a. 1991: 59) Humanism yielded the preoccupation with the fact that reality can only be understood through the human mind, rather than studying human beings (humanity) in particular worldly circumstances. It nourishes intellectual activity on the 'realities' of life, coupled with the reciprocal goal of improving such realities.

Axis of Human Action - Max Weber

One of the most prominent thinkers who has put human action, and thus a theory of action, to the fore, is Max Weber (1864-1920). His theses have been extensively discussed by Campbell (1981). A selective summary of which forms the following brief treatise that introduces and contextualises the purposeful notions for the axis of human action in Weber's work.

Weber's version of human action entails both emotion and values, as well as rational calculation and includes *value-free* social science. This coincides with his personal duality, as he both admired the achievements of modern society, while appreciating different cultures as a sociologist. In his view, sociology attempts the interpretive understanding of social action in order to explain its cause and effects. Value-free signifies that a scientist detaches himself from personal values, since these cannot be deduced from empirically observable facts. However, the scientific approach should neither be a compromise of theories when interpreting or explaining social phenomena. Such value compromise is not made, he holds, when choosing phenomena to study. This is done before scientific investigation itself, as long as one shows that these choices have been made. Furthermore he held that in order to understand and explain behaviour, one must enter the mind and mood of social actors. Put differently, this would be like the empathy employed by anthropologists like Boas, Durkheim, Lévi-Strauss and Geertz. However, Weber says it is not necessary to endorse actor's thoughts and feelings, but one should be restricted to demonstrate their means (Campbell 1981).

For Weber, social action is not the same as behaviour. For example, movement is only action when it involves meaning for the actor. This requires awareness (analysed in terms of the experience of intentions), motives and feelings, detached from movement without intentional reference. Action is social insofar as the meaning attached takes into account the behaviour of others. He excludes actions against things, unless they have significance for the actions of others (e.g. arts and crafts production). It does not require mutual awareness, but at least one individual giving meaning to the action in terms of subjective experience. Understanding social action (intellectually, empathetically and assumptive) requires evidence of the social meaning given to it by actors, requiring a total understanding of the complex of meaning the actor uses to explain his reasons. Therefore knowing the symbols (usually language) is necessary. There is a difference between understanding and explaining action in causal terms. Sociological understanding of action is based on standard meanings of typical social actions that can be expressed in common symbols. Therefore, understanding an action is recognising it as a type of activity characteristic to that society. The actor has to recognise it as fitting a type. The researcher needs to hypothesise a type of conduct common to individuals in such situations (idem).

In this almost causal generalisation Weber's most important concept already appears: the *ideal type*. Ideal types adhere to the split of understanding an objective causal explanation. They are meaningful simplified models of social activities used in the interpretation of human behaviour. Ideal pertains to having value free ideas of action, extrapolations of selected aspects of action that form an intelligible complex in which we can understand actual behaviour. Weber suggests ideal types are not causal generalisations in themselves, but can be utilised to empirically classify and to draw connections between social phenomena. Also, they provide explanations of empirical correlations to see meaningful connections between values and observable sociological facts. Such ideal types are not complete representations, but selective oversimplifications to promote understanding of the nature of social phenomena (idem).

Weber's theory of man is comprised of four ideal types of human action. 1) Rational conduct: the most effective means to achieve an end in particular circumstances and side-effects of these means to his other purposes. 2) Value-rational conduct: unconditional value of the activity and the means to achieve the valued objectives. 3) Affective or emotional action: dominated by feeling, thus irrational. 4) Traditionalist, habitual conduct: established practices and respecting existing authority, which are only partially conscious and rational. These ideal types act as ways to give meaning to action. Together they compose a picture of any individual according to their behaviour and values. People vary according to this composite and the values they choose. However, people are free to choose their values, which will influence their actions not adhering to a universal set of values. In his notions on universalism, Weber was clearly influenced by Nietzsche's existentialism. People are influenced in their choices by their social relationships and prone to follow authoritative structures. As such, the theory of man is entangled with the theory of society. The composite pictures of individuals based on the ideal types of action are the building blocks of society captured within ideal types of social interaction. He developed ideal types of such phenomena in order to contrast traditional and rational (often contemporary) types of society, reducible to meaningful patterns of interaction e.g. social relationships (idem).

What we may take from Weber's theory is primarily his focus on action and the significance of action in the context of constituting society. Discursively, his notion of the ideal type is also of interest. It allows aprioristic definition without necessitating existence of its representations in reality. Aprioristic reasoning is also the basis for Ludwig von Mises' idealist theory of society.

Axis of Human Action - Ludwig von Mises

In the light of human action and Weber's ideas, it is a logical continuation to take into account the work of economist Ludwig von Mises (1881-1973). Although his entire theory of human action and society had the aim of providing a thorough theory for economy, his very pure notion of human action is not only very comprehensible, but also theoretically persuasive for later specifications in social theory. In his insightful and provocative book *Human Action* (originally published in 1949), he gives a very clear definition: "Human action is purposeful behavior." (von Mises 1998: 11) As he eloquently argues, this definition should not need further explanation, but could be elaborated with many clarifying assertions, which may prevent misinterpretation. As purposeful behaviour, human action stands in sharp contrast to unconscious behaviour, i.e. mainly reflexive physiological actions. For von Mises *praxeology*, the general theory of human action, is the basis. Praxeology is not concerned with how actions cognitively came about, which is in the realm of psychology, but truly focuses on the actions themselves. Actions as purposeful behaviour have a teleological character. They are aimed to an end and have a (rational) meaning for the actor performing the action. Action is not just giving preference. This is also done in unavoidable situations or belief. "He who only wishes and hopes does not interfere actively with the course of events and with the shaping of his own destiny. But acting man chooses, determines, and tries to reach an end. Of two things both of which he cannot have together he selects one and gives up the other. Action therefore always involves both taking and renunciation." (idem: 12) If thoughts are expressed referring to actions (annunciation, recommendation, rejection), this should not be confused with action. Action is real, not the things not realised. However, that is not to say that action is not extended into the world of speech, as action can entail choosing to talk or not to talk, or consumption and enjoyment as well as abstaining from them. There is no distinction to be made between an active or passive mentality, for the choice not to act is also action as it may affect the course of events. "Wherever the conditions for human interference are present, man acts no matter whether he interferes or refrains from interfering. [...] Action is not only doing but no less omitting to do what possibly could be done." (idem: 13) Slightly tautologically, one could say that action is the manifestation or product of man's will or choice. Action and its meaning depend on the freedom of choice. Put into a social setting, man is not empathetic, but understands another by means of himself. The same ordinal decision process takes place in actions bearing social consequences as those performed entirely for the benefit of oneself (idem).

Von Mises is said to be one of Weber's severest critics and follows his theory through in a pristine way, as opposed to what could be said of Weber. The difference is that von Mises was not concerned with the inference of actual situations, but rather was building an idealised world that functions in a completely logical way. Therefore there was no need to take into account deviations that might occur in the application of his ideas, as the preconditions would not be met in actual situations. He works in a truly aprioristic way. In spite of being detached from actuality, his pure theoretical notions can be informative in the same way Weber's ideal types can be. Actual situations may be contrasted against his assertions and ways of (economic) improvement may be set out upon the insight that is produced. Note, however, that von Mises' purposeful rationality is not an ideal type in the sense of Weber, since the way to act would not be universal. Despite this difference, von Mises recognises in his praxeology that at an abstract level there are underlying rules to action that are universal. There are commonalities in action that through research can be found as valid for all people of all eras, races and social classes (idem). This partially universalistic tendency of von Mises can be compared to Hodder's use of Wobst's models of cross-cultural generalisation in stylistic traits as messages coupled to the size of social units or the visibility of artefacts. Hodder intended to stress cultural differences on the basis of these generalisations, providing opportunities for comparison (Hodder 1986). The universalism of social processes here, however, should not so much lead to discerning cultural differences, but rather afford cultural changes.

Von Mises' work provides us with one of the most compelling, uncorrupted definitions of human action and this is what we should keep in mind, though further developed reasoning on the basis of human action might elaborate or change its nature. Also, von Mises' individualistic and self-referential view of social man is a strong, yet concise vantage point for continued explorations into societies. Although many sociologists, philosophers and anthropologists would argue against it, I am convinced by the existence of free will and the freedom of choice. Conformist actions are still a choice and express that the consequence of resistance or abstinence will have been envisioned as less favourable. Michel de Certeau examines such notions in some detail, but extends his research into cognition and the invisible behind it. A self-referential understanding of the world is part of phenomenological views on perception, man and his environment. Still the idealistic theory of von Mises rests unaffected in all its purity, positioning action centrefold in developing society.

Axis of Human Action - Alfred Schütz

In sociological advancement of social theorising, one of von Mises students has become most influential: Alfred Schütz (1899-1959). He was not concerned with economy but sociology, and found himself strongly inspired by the phenomenological ideas of Edmund Husserl. His ideas came to be known for introducing phenomenology to sociological thought. He set the first step in seeking to clarify Weber's sociology in terms of Husserl's phenomenological philosophy. This phenomenological sociology exposed otherwise obscure philosophical ideas, and in doing so supported understanding of what he called the social world. Founding phenomenology, Husserl had conceptualised the 'stream of internal time-consciousness' as the source of meaning, thereby giving a profound critique of Weber's subjectively meaningful action (J. R. Hall 1980). This primordial, pre-reflexive idea of time is derived from an idea of the heterogeneous continuum of time defying a definition in lived experience. This he expressed as the *temporal flux* (Lucas 2005).

Such concept of time demonstrates that Husserl's phenomenology is a metaphysical one, influenced by Cartesian rationalism. This idealist rationalism entails the existence of the truth of the world or objects, before science or human subjectivity could mingle with it. In his pre-reflexive or pre-scientific (i.e. before conceptualisation takes place) time, there is a slight positivist tendency concurring with his metaphysics. Nevertheless, it came as an opposing reaction to positivistic researchers ignoring their own involvement. Husserl was not an adversary of the prevalent naturalist attitude of science. Actually he stressed that humanist thinkers needed to develop a philosophy that entailed distinctive methodologies to be able to understand the inner humanity. Therefore he found that, as was the practice at the time, the inner world of human being should not be studied with the same methods used by the researchers of nature (the outer world). Positivistic science fails in dealing with the disposition and behaviour of 'things' because of an a priori conceptualisation of essences that are viewed simultaneously as explanations. A philosopher should penetrate into the essences of things to explain the way things act. For Husserl these essences of things will be the truth of knowledge about them. The essences of science do not reside in the object under study nor the human researchers, but in the relationship between these objects and subjects (Cloke e.a. 1991, Eberle 1984). This foundation indicates that in archaeology phenomenology was wrongfully adapted as a vehicle for producing personal and idiosyncratic perspectives of the world. This is illustrated by the great impact Tilley's *A Phenomenology of the Landscape* (1994) and Shanks' *Experiencing the Past* (1992) have had in archaeological discourse, whose earlier papers also demonstrated a lack in the conceptualisation of time.

Husserl's followers, including Schütz and Merleau-Ponty, proposed alternatives in existential and constitutive phenomenologies that do not attempt to transcend the everyday, but study the everyday meanings particular to peoples, societies or cultures. Still others turned back to a type of psychology deprived of Husserl's transcendentalism (Cloke e.a. 1991). Schütz took an examination of the temporal character of meaningful action as his starting point. With this he also provided a descriptive phenomenology of the temporal structures of the *life-world*, a(n) (individual) world of paramount reality. The life-world is what humans act in or upon, by means of our animate organisms. He only described the a priori temporal structures of the life-world, which are invariant and essential, and never used them for historiographic purposes of describing empirical variants of these temporal structures (J. R. Hall 1980). This lies very close to the way Braudel's tripartite division of time should be used in academic analyses.

As a progressive alternative to Weber's subjective individuals and inspired by von Mises, Schütz's phenomenology returns to the social actor. His theory of society is based on the analysis of the individual's social experience, in which social life is an internal reality constituted by the subjective experiences of actors. This resulted directly from Husserl's examination of the inner life, the stream of consciousness comprised of experiences of phenomena. Schütz avoids ontological inquiries into 'reality', as opposed to Husserl's Cartesian conduct. He assumes that experience is not a given, but intentional in that the actor directs attention towards objects that are perceived according to past experiences and acquired knowledge, which compose his experience. This process he calls *apperception*: the spontaneous attribution of meaning to what is perceived. All consciousness is consciousness of objects, thus constructs made by the individual directing attention to objects in his consciousness (Campbell 1981). Note that here Schütz gets involved with cognitive processes that were not part of von Mises' human action, whilst maintaining that the directing of attention is intentional (purposeful). This means that attributing meaning through experience is at least partially a process of free choice in the ability to direct one's attention, despite the actual attribution of meaning being spontaneous. Experience (the subjective life-world) is comprised of various elements that can be removed by reflecting on experience. One does not really see something specific, but refers to things as specific sets of objects in one's experience. Where Husserl hoped to arrive at the basic elements and underlying structure (the essence) of our experience, Schütz focuses on the process of phenomenological reduction. In so doing, he attempts to reach a point where, derived from theoretical preconceptions, the meaning of phenomena can be analysed as experienced. He prefers not to filter out all empirical elements, including those directed by the individual consciousness, as Husserl's search for essence demands (Campbell 1981, Eberle 1984). This reduction places Schütz in a position between Weber and von Mises, since it lets phenomenology arrive at levels of abstraction within ideal types. These should not be seen as rules, but rather commonly present contingencies. At this level there is a need for empirical analysis of reason, sense and motives (Eberle 1984). With this he pushes interest beyond the objectives contained in the notions of both Weber and von Mises.

Schütz's concern lies at the topic of social experience and discovering the elements of social life. He reflects on social experience as interacting individuals or as the intention of social life. Again this inhibits the presuppositions about the reality of the world, c.q. the reality of social life outside our experience (Campbell 1981). Weber's theory of society places individual action at the centre of argument. Social interactions are meaningful for the participants. One can understand the complex of social relations making up a society by understanding the subjective aspects of interpersonal activities of members of that society. Similarly, von Mises lets action be meaningful in the eye of the beholder, placing individual subjectivism as an inherent part of human reason. For von Mises individual subjectivism entails that actions depend on the ordinal value of the consequence that follows the action. In social interaction this means that empathy does not exist as a motivator for action (von Mises 1998). This strength is continued by

Schütz in that he avoids speculative empathy in the explanation of how we understand the lives of others, but focuses on our own experiences of ourselves to understand others (Campbell 1981). Both the ideas of von Mises and Schütz in this way insist that one understands another by referring to his identification of himself. In social interaction there is an inter-subjective mutual understanding, which incorporates a sense of belonging. The inter-subjectiveness of mutual understanding as a part of individual subjectivism makes societies intelligible by the analysis of various types of human action.

Schütz asserts that individual subjectivism is not possible in real time (present), but only for past events that can be analysed in terms of the referential objects by which we can make sense of the world. Understanding action and interpreting it is only possible in reflecting on our past behaviour, because it necessitates the division of action into discrete acts with distinguishable objectives. This observed learning process of grasping the meaning of our actions cannot take place while we are engaged in that behaviour. Vivid experience is flawed by memory. In some reflexive cases the individual is active, but intentional experience involves spontaneous activity. "Everyday life is […] a pragmatic orientation to the future." (Campbell 1981: 202) The activity of human beings is therefore a unity, which becomes separated through reflection in memory. Yet because it belongs to one person, it remains a unity that is inseparable from the experience of activity itself (Campbell 1981).

This results in tracing back the problems of social sciences to the fundamental facts of conscious life. Although this seems an idealist individualistic method of explaining social life through the lived experiences of the individual, social experience is actually anchored in the community. Human consciousness presupposes the reality of other people and its experiences are mediated through past social relationships (idem). Here Schütz deepens the interest of von Mises to understand the tendency for social relations in human action. Schütz's theory of human being is mainly restricted to "the essence of the human condition in the subjective experience of acting and adopting attitudes towards the everyday 'life-world'. For Schütz this is a world of practical activity." (idem: 200) One can discern human capacities analysing the elements of practical consciousness. The continuous action performed to achieve a goal enables us to see life in terms of the projects pursued. As his tutor already asserted: all action is meaningful, because it is always consciously directed towards an end, which the actor imagined in his mind, a purpose (von Mises 1998). In this process the individual must identify his situation by contrasting it to a common *stock of knowledge* that he developed through his own experiences and social inheritance. The situation that sets the possibilities for purposeful action thus becomes determined through *biography*, the personal history of experiences, within the context of his society. The goals themselves are also dependent on identifying the situation the actor is in and therefore affected by his biography (Campbell 1981, Eberle 1984).

The stock of knowledge, utilised to define situations, presupposes the ability to think in abstract classificatory terms. It entails connected classifications that enable the recognition of situations as a type, thus setting the possibilities for action by permitting a view of the world as meaningful configurations (Campbell 1981). Somehow the inherited part of the stock of knowledge seems to adopt the character of Weber's ideal types and the typifications of those who followed, but Schütz's stock of knowledge is more complex. The individual distinguishes his everyday world in domains of relevance, the primary of which pertains to all things he can immediately perceive, requiring detailed knowledge. Depending on his interests and desires, domains of relevance are distinguished according to classifications, also permitting him to change his situation by action. He imagines potential projects and by taking the situation into account, defines the actions able to fulfil that purpose. This is *rational activity*, the motivated lived experience at the centre of subjective awareness. Actors explain themselves according to their projects, rational activities and their biographies. It is in this composed 'in order to' motivation for action (including inheritance and biography, i.e. determination and spontaneity, envisioning a goal, comprising various types of relevance) that strictly discerns Schütz from his predecessors. The actor always acts freely, oriented towards the future (cf. von Mises). Only in retrospect does action appear determined. Man is social, as is his everyday consciousness (idem).

To this point the phenomenological sociology of Schütz has introduced some of the most apt building blocks for a social theoretical take on the processes of development and meaning in societies. His work moves on to specify social relationships in society and goes further than what is captured in the concise space dedicated to it here. Notions like the stock of knowledge, rational activity, biography, and a socially bound inheritance will become increasingly important in the arguments to follow. In his work, just as for most phenomenologists (most notably Merleau-Ponty), he emphasises the relationship between man and his environment. This relationship has been named the *bi-implication* of human being, a mutually influencing relationship of man and world, which replaced the preceding unidirectional causal analysis of this relation. This aspect of phenomenology will be significant for the following, but also has had great influence on the work of the aforementioned Tim Ingold and other researchers (cf. Ingold 2000, Kolen 2005).

As a note of critique, I think the notion of inheritance within the common stock of knowledge needs to be carefully addressed. The common stock of knowledge can never be an exact transference of experience held within a community or society. Firstly, no single participant of society holds an exact 'copy' of the common stock of knowledge, due to the affective condition of his own biography. Furthermore, any new member learning the common stock of knowledge will do so in an individually subjective way. This makes and influences selections of it, because the common stock of knowledge will only become part of the participant's biography. Through choices, selections and the direction of attention, following their own line of logic, all individuals hold a personalised version of the common stock of knowledge. Only in long term continuous participation in societal activity will more commonalities be invested in the individual. Vice versa, increasingly more influence of the individual biography will find its way into the common stock of knowledge. This may imply that its conceptualisation is redirected to a level of academic constructs or analytical idealist formalisation. The researcher or observer is the one who abstracts these aspects of common experience, much like Weber's ideal types.

In general Schütz's theory is potent, since it leaves open possibilities for long term developments and rapid changes by informing the fundamentals of human action. In this, the phenomenological nature of his theory includes the individual life-world, stressing the bi-implication of man and world. Man is directly spatial and temporal. By the vehicle of his body actions are interactions. He carries his personal biography individualising his meaningful activities and perception of the world. He influences his own learning process, creating his own stock of knowledge. This means one should adopt a critical stance towards the so-called common stock of knowledge, which is better utilised as an ideal type for academia. We could learn from the steps Schütz takes to include parts of the cognitive process in perception and decision making. This may enrich our concepts of action and interaction, whilst the uncorrupted performed human action of von Mises can be maintained. Acting man remains a free agent, although it would be better to use the term subject from here on. The strong individualist subjectivity of phenomenology panders to radical relativism (i.e. exclusively personalised perceptions of the world) in scientific discourse. Although I tend to philosophically adhere to this, as said in the introduction, one should better be and make others aware of one's subjectivity in order to enable a means of informative translation of one's work.

Axis of Human Action - Michel de Certeau

Mentioning Michel de Certeau (1925-1986) amongst these action theorists, is mainly caused by the intrinsic value he ascribes to human action in his most influential book, *The Practice of Everyday Life* in 1984. De Certeau was a philosopher and social scholar exploring ethnology and history. This currently leads to the application of his ideas in disciplines as economy, sociology and anthropology.

The practices of everyday life are simply ways of operation, distinct because of their repetitive and partially unconscious nature. De Certeau introduces the examination of the practices of everyday life specifically not as an implied return to individuality, the individual as an axiom in social atomism. A (social) relation determines its terms, not the reverse. The individual is only a locus in which a plurality of such relational determinations interact. Therefore his study concerns schemata of action and not directly the subject itself. His aim is to show the systems of operational combinations which also compose a culture and the models of action that users adhere to, whilst being dominated in society concealed as consumers. "Everyday life invents itself by poaching in countless ways on the property of others." (de Certeau 1988: xii)

His ideas are influenced by the manifestations of modern society and mass production, perhaps making many archaeologists reluctant to its use in the often non-modern, non-capitalist cases of the past they are confronted with. De Certeau explored the everyday activities of productive and consumptive society. Yet he was also very receptive to the idea of colonisation as imposing entire prefabricated sets of products to new consumers. This is a scenario that many archaeologist face, especially those concerned with the New World. It is necessary to determine the use of representations of a society and its modes of behaviour by groups or individuals. What does a subject do with a representational product during the time it takes to consume it? What does the cultural consumer make of it (in terms of production or creation)? Systems of production define the areas consumers use, so they can no longer indicate what they made of the system's products as the system leaves no place for that. Consumption is an elusive kind of production, manifested through its ways of using products imposed by an economic order (idem).

The colonisation of the New World leads de Certeau to say that colonisation imposes a system of representations and laws that indigenous people use without major alterations. They do not reject them, yet use them with completely other ideas than those internal to the imposed system they had no choice but to accept. In their procedures of consumption of the system they diminish the dominant power, which they could not challenge. In this way they still escaped (idem). This argument on colonisation can also be extended to migrant populations. In archaeology, much thought has been given to this, especially in the paradigm of New Archaeology, focusing on cultural dispersion and invasion. Burmeister (2000) has proposed to look at the differences between the internal and external domains, i.e. the private and the public actions spheres of migrant populations. He reasoned that people now living in a different environment or culture would still act in ways that are common practice in the culture they originate from, increasingly so in the private sphere. Only rarely will an artefact category of their original culture find its way into the new cultural environment. Many of their subconscious actions will be carried out using the products of the new culture, making them archaeologically unrecognisable in the process. Burmeister suggests that in order to find migrant populations, we should start looking at the way objects are used (Burmeister 2000). In other words, the differentiating actions of individuals and groups producing the everyday practices varying in the private and public domains, which also includes the subconscious use of objects in ways deviating from the system producing them.

In modern society, migrant populations and the results of colonisation are more commonplace, perhaps changing the proportions of meaning between the producing and consuming cultural systems. De Certeau stretches this difference to the ordinary everyday practices in societies, making them ambiguous by distinguishing common consumers (users) of a culture (objects) from the 'elites' producing and imposing the culture. "The presence and circulation of a representation [...] tells us nothing about what it is for its users. We must first analyse its manipulation by users who are not its makers." (de Certeau 1988: xiii) Hence, the process of using is a secondary production. Just as in language the utterance (performance) of a sentence constructed by a subject is not reducible to the knowledge (competence) of the language. Speaking is a reappropriation of the language, "establishing a *present* relative to a time and place and it posits a *contract with the other* (the interlocutor) in a network of places and relations." (de Certeau 1988: xiii) This reappropriation de Certeau recognises in all everyday consumptive actions. From this follows that he opposes the privilege given to power and discipline as exercised by Foucault (e.g. Foucault 1982). Foucault's microphysics of power concentrates on the production of discipline. Since discipline is continuously growing more distinct, it becomes important to see "how an entire society resists being reduced to it, what popular procedures [...] manipulate the mechanisms of discipline and conform to them only in order to evade them, and finally, what 'ways of operating' form the counterpart, on the consumer's [...] side, of the mute processes that organize the establishment of socioeconomic order. These 'ways of operating' constitute the innumerable practices by means of which users reappropriate the space organised by techniques of sociocultural production." (de Certeau 1988: xiv) De Certeau acknowledges that this is analogous with Foucault in that it also studies the miniscule operations within structures and deflecting their functioning through tactics performed in the details of everyday life. On the contrary, it opposes Foucault in that it does not show how the violence of order becomes a discipline, but emphasises the submerged tactical creativity of groups or individuals that are already caught in discipline. These activities of consumers compose the network of an antidiscipline or resistance (idem).

Use and consumption of society, culture, or goods as a reappropriation that is seemingly conformist, yet silently resisting the producing order, is a potent approach to action related to social organisation and societal change. In regard to change, it enables a creative potential in the by discipline apparently subdued subjects. Although this concept diverges from the uncorrupted human action of von Mises in including subconscious practices as well, consuming commonalities becomes empowered, which again elaborates the freedom of choice. It is necessary to differentiate both the action that the system of products effects within the consumer, and the room left by the system to manoeuvre by the situations in which consumers exercise their 'art'. "Culture articulates conflicts and alternately legitimizes, displaces, or controls the superior force. [...]The tactical consumption [...] in which the weak make use of the strong." (de Certeau 1988: xvii)

Due to the partial subconscious nature of everyday human consumptive action, they follow wandering paths obeying their own logic, called *trajectories* by de Certeau. Although composed and subordinated by opportunities or syntax, these trace out things that are not determined by the systems in which they develop. Statistics remains ignorant of trajectories, because it only grasps the material of these practices, not their form. Statistics determines the elements used, not the phrasing produced by creativity and the combining of elements. It uses self-defined units and reorganises these according to its own codes, therefore it only finds the homogenous. Its power lies in the ability to divide, but this fragmentation obscures what it claims to represent (idem). I am happy to stretch these arguments over the imposition of classificatory and taxonomical inferential research methods. Trajectory suggests a movement and is also a tracing for acts, but should not be reduced to this. Therefore, one must recognise the difference between strategies and tactics (idem).

Strategy is defined as a force-relationship, enabled when a subject of power can be isolated from an environment. It has a proper place from which it generates relations with a distinct exterior. Tactic is defined as having no proper localisation, nor border that distinguishes the other. The place of tactics belongs to the other (cf. Bourdieu's (1977) habitus). It poaches on the other place fragmentarily, without affecting its entirety and without the ability to keep distance. The proper is a victory of space over time, on the contrary tactics have no place and thus depend on time. "It must constantly manipulate events in order to turn them into 'opportunities'." (de Certeau 1988: xix) This is achieved in moments where users are able to combine heterogeneous elements synthesised, not as a discourse, but as the way an opportunity is seized. Many everyday practices and ways of operating are tactical, arriving at the aforementioned use of the strong by the weak (idem).

Despite de Certeau's work being situated in and applied to modern societies of mass production, systems of production (either societal or material) and consumption or use were just as much operational in any era. Social and material production started well within ancient prehistory. Although its significance increases with the rise of administrative, centralised or formalised traditions of production, de Certeau's theory of action as resistance may offer socially founded directions of analysis for archaeological remains. It can shed light on otherwise 'statistical outliers', as well as making strong arguments for periodic and paradigmatic shifts. I subscribe to his potent arguments on the ignorance of statistics as an explanatory tool. In de Certeau's fashion, changes become simultaneously tied to systems of order and the freedom of individuals, whilst put into a relative temporal perspective. The differences in the time-space characteristics of strategy and tactics are also potent notions for the way change occurs geographically, a link which will explicitly be repeated in chapter four. In this way, the constitution of societies and radical changes are both part of everyday practices, rather than situated in the realm of isolated extraordinary revolting moments.

Axis of Human Space - Existentialism and Embodiment

The axis of human space so far has only been implicitly present. Quite simply due to the fact that man exists in his body, there is an intrinsic spatial component to human being. Most significantly, existentialist philosophy and anthropological embodiment conceptualised this spatial component of being. As noted before, the physical or biological condition of human being causes him to be temporal. Here the emphasis will be on how this condition makes human being and human action spatial. The spatial component is of paramount importance to archaeological discourse, because it is the property that makes actions explicitly material. Human temporality and action, without the physicality of the body mediating opportunities of material interaction with the world, do not readily have a physical counterpart in themselves. That is not to say that time has no physical implications both in processes in the past and the presence of the past in the present. For its effect on material remains and deposits, one should only read the compelling book by Michael Schiffer on the formation processes (cultural and natural) in archaeological records (Schiffer 1987). The relevance of time and action here is bound to the physical domain by the human body, which basically boils down to various notions of space. Space generates archaeological data in many ways, producing clear-cut facts by their very existence. Moreover, physical space is measurable. Nevertheless, one requires a connection to meaning attributing processes shaping such spaces for interpretation.

Man as a physical being exists within space by means of his body. This body not only conditions how human beings are within space, it also conditions all (inter)actions within space. The physical condition of the body makes that we have a specific delimited locality within our surrounding physical environment. All human actions are initiated within and performed by the body. However, actions are performed in, or in relation to and mediated by the physicality of the environment. Through modes of perception, as in the phenomenological theories above, the body, its environment, and its position in the environment are conceptualised through experiences, often generated by the actions chosen to perform. As in Schütz's phenomenology, the situation as understood through the stock of knowledge and the memory of one's biography, the perception of the environment affects the choice and execution of actions within that environment. "External physical action always involves confrontation with specific environmental elements, personal contacts, influences, or information in general, as well as emotion and feelings that otherwise would not have been experienced [and] requires internal mental activity." (Pred 1984: 286) Over time, practices of performed action will construct the direct surroundings of the body according to the degree of satisfaction with the way past actions turned out in regard to the material and social environment. The way the material condition and the proximity to the body are experienced individually results in an individual sense of territoriality, which is continually shaped by the actions performed in the environment. The perception of the environment through actions becomes a part of one's identity (cf. Ingold 2000). Social and material forms of interaction are a continuous renegotiation of space which, through physical transformations, dynamically constructs surrounding territories within a community or society, making constructed spaces arguably social expressions of identity.

This assertion has been elaborately explored in anthropology, through discourses concerned with *embodied space*: the location where human experience and consciousness take on a material and spatial form, the construction of localities. It exists, related and lateral to phenomenological perspectives, spatial orientation and linguistic dimensions (Low and Lawrence-Zúñiga 2006). In the sense of existential philosophy, embodied space coincides in virtually all aspects with the notion of 'being-in-the-world' that has been pursued following Heidegger's (1972) philosophy. Existentialism resulted from the philosophical assumption that man is what he makes of himself, and especially Sartre's assertion that essence follows existence. Hence there were questions formulated that specified the relationship between humans and non-human things, which culminated in Heidegger's being-in-the-world. This incorporated structures founded in the primordial temporal and spatial relationships between human beings and non-human things in the world, as well as their intrinsic condition of mortality (Heidegger 1972, Cloke e.a. 1991). 'To be' (*Dasein*), through its structural linkages, refers to being in the world. We need a world to be in, otherwise we cannot exist (Heidegger 1972). The world, on the other hand, does not stand apart from us and our actions, but depends on our being in. Through our actions we create the world in which we are, we create to be in our creations (Richardson 2006).

Archaeological adaptations of existentialism have been given body by the significant contributions to landscape archaeology made by Julian Thomas (1996, 2001), integrating the temporal also. In geography, phenomenological existentialism was specifically introduced by Yi-Fu Tuan. He asserted that the essential meaning of world is man, and therefore to know the world is to know oneself (cf. the bi-implication of phenomenology). He did not search for order, but for meaning in space. There are several essential ways in which people inscribe and derive meaning from space. The meaning he attached to the organisation of space was often connected to psychological experience, feelings and the human body (Tuan 1977, Cloke e.a. 1991). Tuan's theory also finds its way into archaeological discourse on certain occasions.

The human body is at the basis of all existentialist approaches, as it takes into account that humans have and are bodies at the same time. The body exists both biologically and individually, and can best be conceived as a multiplicity of social and physical aspects or derivations from that. Starting with the body itself, the experience of the body results in *body space,* which has been characterised in many different ways. Body space has been assessed in psycho-analytical manners, stressing the internal psychology of each human being, in metaphorical and symbolical manners emphasising its relation in myths or as an anthropomorphic form in cultural life, or as locations in a social web, a site of action and agency (Low and Lawrence-Zúñiga 2006). Primarily both the cultural and social aspects are stressed in anthropological discourse. More holistic approaches refer to philosophy, or can be found in the work of Pierre Bourdieu (1977). His concept of *habitus*, which locates the means for structuration, incorporates embodied experience with a social counterpart. "An individual's habitus is structured by the social rules and institutions in which they exist and interact with others in their social environment. Thus social engagement at the level of the individual is an embodied experience dialectically inextricable from society writ large." (Wynne-Jones and Kohring 2007: 7) It is not hard to imagine how this also can be made applicable to the material domain in space. In archaeology, Bourdieu's ideas are still of considerable importance, especially when approaches within the agency and structure debate are concerned (Last 1998, Dobres and Robb 2000b, Ingold 2000, Barrett 2001, Bintliff 2006).

Axis of Human Space - Territoriality and Proxemics

The most apparent element of social space is interpersonal distance as an extension to the way human beings organise space. Irving Hallowell's work introduces, as the organisation of space is intrinsically human, culture can be found in spatial orientation. A worldview which supersedes personal experience. He regarded distance in technical terms, especially how it was measured in different cultures (Hallowel 1955). Zoologist Heini Hediger was the first to describe personal and social distances in operational terms, developing *proxemics* in animal behaviour, typifying various situational distances. In demonstrating that those distances are so precise they can be measured in centimetres, he inspired anthropologist Edward T. Hall to work on a human or social adaptation (E. T. Hall 1959, E. T. Hall 1968, E. T. Hall 2006). He took this idea and truly started to study the perception and use of space as an aspect of culture. In doing so, he established the field of proxemics, which studies the behavioural complex of activities, ethologically known as territoriality. The subconscious setting of spatial distances between individuals stands centrally in this field of research. Proxemics is an invented term which generally tries to capture the contents of this specific research and substitutes descriptions like 'social space as bio-communication' and 'micro-space in interpersonal encounters' (E. T. Hall 2006). An easy definition of his proxemics is as follows: the study of the cultural, behavioural, and sociological aspects of spatial distances between individuals. Human being, embodiment, and action in the context of social relations come beautifully together in Hall's insightful ideas on territoriality.

As early as 1959, Edward Hall already poses that besides the physical boundary that delimits all organisms (the body) "[a] short distance up the phylogenetic scale […] another, non-physical boundary appears that exists outside the physical one. This new boundary is harder to delimit than the first but just as real. We call this the 'organisms' territory'. The act of laying claim to and defending a territory is termed territoriality. […] In man, it becomes highly elaborated, as well as being very greatly differentiated from culture to culture." (E. T. Hall 1959: 187)

This innate boundary is a precondition for how social contact takes place, depending on the social relation that already may exist and the situation. This makes the territorial boundary situational and personal, but it is also embedded in the spatial aspects of culture that were learned by the actor. For the larger part, the boundary exists subconsciously or implicitly and only becomes explicit for the actor when the boundary is violated, usually when the actor comes into contact with another culture (E. T. Hall 1968, E. T. Hall 2006, Low and Lawrence-Zúñiga 2006). People can only be vaguely aware of their own culture in the absence of a direct encounter with another. It therefore becomes more important to observe what people do instead of what they say or elaborate upon when questioned, as this pertains to the conscious mind. The things that are difficult to consciously control are most significant. Also, one should distinguish between several levels of awareness within a culture, since these will affect the behavioural patterns (E. T. Hall 1968, E. T. Hall 2006). Hall separates two extreme types of awareness: the formal and the informal. The formal is a very explicit conscious treatment of cultural values (often traditional), while the informal is expressed almost entirely subconsciously. Nevertheless, these aspects of culture are never truly hidden, as long as one knows how to look for the eloquent signs (E. T. Hall 1959). A third level, technical awareness, only emerges when activities are fully explicated and analysed (E. T. Hall 1968, E. T. Hall 2006). Hall differs in his dealing with awareness from the conscious human action conceptualised by von Mises and Schütz. However, I doubt it directly opposes to them, as the informal level appears to pertain to historically learned social practice that results in patterns of action, thus is an expression of the common stock of knowledge.

Hall himself clearly notes a difficulty in phenomenological approaches that stress an elaborate level of universalism, as they assume that "experience is what men share and that it is possible to bypass language by referring back to experience in order to reach another human being. [This] is based on the assumption that when two human beings are subjected to the same 'experience', virtually the same data is fed to the two nervous systems and the two brains respond similarly. Proxemics research casts serious doubts on the validity of this assumption, particularly when the cultures are different. People from different cultures inhabit different sensory worlds. They not only structure spaces differently, but experience it differently, because the sensorium is differently 'programmed'." (E. T. Hall 2006: 52) The experience learned from society or culture, as well as the biography in Schütz's phenomenology take away this problem. Hall continues that the body forms the means for interacting with others and the environment in various ways following the patterning of the senses, which determines spatial experience. Data (e.g. architecture) is selectively admitted and rejected through a screening or filtering carried out by the senses that shut things out (E. T. Hall 1968, E. T. Hall 2006). There are no universal values to measure behavioural aspects of spatial experience, they are culture or people specific. The questions that should be raised regard the senses and psychology and therefore need other disciplines to be answered (idem).

In a rudimentary way, Hall stresses some important things in his cultural specific territorialities. In social interaction, distance setting contributes strongly to the establishment of an identity, which lies at the basis of the development of society. He introduces the notion of infra-cultural bases to provide ways cultural specifics can develop. Here the influence of biology is clearly notable: "There is no break between the present, in which man acts as a culture producing animal, and the past, when there were no men and no cultures. There is an unbroken continuity between the far past and the present, for culture is bio-basic, rooted in biological activities. [...] Territoriality is an example of an infra-cultural activity." (E. T. Hall 1959: 60) The development of culture is an evolutionary process that takes place outside the body. Hall labels this composite process 'extensions', which forms a new dimension. To this cultural dimension man is in a state of dynamic equilibrium that, *to a certain extent* (my emphasis), replaces nature. Man, therefore, is able to determine what kind of organism he will be (E. T. Hall 1968, 2006). Hall acknowledges particular elements that help actors understand cultural differences in the use of space. These he calls spatial cues, which communicate our territoriality. Territoriality differs from culture to culture. The way people use space determines how we see those people. In different cultures distances between people's places or division of space are elements that can determine the character of social relations (E. T. Hall 1959). For the researcher the relationships between actors and their territoriality, held within the communication processes informed by spatial cues, have inferential potential.

The continuous processes of proxemics make a connection that is of considerable archaeological interest. Cultural values are learned, whilst being passed on both subconsciously into the subconscious, as consciously into the conscious. Repetitive enactment establishes daily practices in certain ways by people adhering to a culture. This will lead to structuring, and eventually physical construction of a culture in its environment according to this spatial experience. Thus embodied man, through the performance of actions in his environment, becomes tied to physical transformations in that environment.

Despite this potential, proxemics has found little grounds in archaeological discourse. It is probable that its focus on levels of communication, especially bodily communication and gestures, proves futile in dealing with archaeological records. Only when or if these communications lead to constructed consolidation in a physical sense could proxemics be an informative theory. Although his complex conceptualisation of territoriality is useful, Hall also can be criticised for taking an essentially ethological stance to his research objectives. Similar to the metaphysical character of Husserl's phenomenology, Hall proposed a foundational infra-culture (inspired by infra-language) (E. T. Hall 1959), again a level of universalism that can also be associated with von Mises or Wobst models in Hodder's *Reading the Past* (1986). The goal was to develop comparative angles of analysis, coming down to noting culturally specific differences. For this, Hall placed himself as a researcher outside or separated from his objects of study, looking down on people's behaviour. Otherwise it would not have been possible to remark the different culture specific sensory worlds people inhabit. Anthropology soon came to take a hermeneutic turn in which such reasoning was no longer accepted. Naturally, I do not directly adhere to this positioning of the academic either. It is especially his study on constitutive territoriality, placing the making of space in the realm of individual perception, adjusting distances to interpersonal satisfaction, that is of interest. It directly allows people to construct the spaces around them according to perception, which may entail phenomenological knowledge, whilst interpersonality (cf. intersubjectivity) pulls it into the social depending on their relation to a culture or society.

For illustrative purposes, I will finally dedicate some words to the deficient attention proxemics has been given in archaeology. In his 1996 article Jerry Moore explicitly stretches proxemic processes into the realm of architecture, stating: "such approaches [archaeological proxemics] consider constructed spaces as architectural arenas that shape and are shaped by social interactions partly structured by modes of human communication." (Moore 1996: 798) Ritual as a theme is gratefully chosen by Moore. It is group-specific and its repetitive execution is bound to reflect in the lay-out and size of the plazas. Yet it misses an attempt to understand the nature of the activity that conclusively shaped the plazas. Moreover, the societal element is isolated from socially environmental action by utilising the presupposed classification of ritual and plaza traditions. Similarly, Ronald Fletcher (2006) notices that in the built environment the use of raw material is not functionally determined, which leaves room for the internal operational character of behaviour within the community. This behaviour is nourished by communicative traditions, hence proxemics comes into play. "*A priori* [it] would seem unlikely [that communicative traditions create spatial order], as social action and verbal declaration are famously non-correspondent. The built space is, of course, a consequence to what they did to make the material form. However, it is an unwarranted but easy elision to assume that the verbal description people apply to their social life, fully describe those actions." (Fletcher 2006: 120) He goes on to conclude that forms of communication (declaration) are just one aspect, and do not capture the full complexity, of the material patterning of space. There can be no deterministic link between material features and the active components of social life. "The key implication of consistency and the heritage effect is that human space is patterned by internally coherent suites of tacit, spatial messages unique to a community. [A methodology must be developed to represent the] material spatial messages composed of the visual distances carried by structures and the location of entities. [...] [As] the issue is to explain how a suite of visual distances comes to constitute a settlement." (Fletcher 2006: 125)

Thus a problematic relationship between human action and communication is uncovered, moving closer towards the meaning of the built environment. The specific processes of the production of this built environment, however, are still obscure. Alternatively, there have been many methods for interpreting architecture and the built environment that started with the material record itself. One of the most influential of these has been the study of architect (and anthropologist) Amos Rapoport (1982).

Axis of Human Space - Built Environment

In anthropology, Rapoport's work has been readily received because of its focus on the humanity of urban forms and the ways spatial cues (cf. E. T. Hall) encode sociality (Pellow 2006, Richardson 2006). It follows from the anthropological idea that people are not only anchored in space, but in claiming it also develop it (Pellow 2006). Rapoport's central thesis posits the dichotomy of planned environments and its users interpreting its meanings. As opposed to much work on the meaning of architecture, which focused on the meaning for the planner, Rapoport is interested in the meaning it holds for its inhabitants and users in order to understand how spaces can be transformed to communicate specific information to its users (Rapoport 1982). This is not the still lacking knowledge of how social processes produce constructions or architecture. As Ingold notes, the interest somehow has turned around in disciplinary discourses from the activities of building, cultivation, and construction as practices in inhabiting the world (dwelling), to positioning such activities into a world already built. "Where before building was circumscribed within dwelling, the position now appears reversed, with dwelling circumscribed within building." (Ingold 2000: 185) This he criticises, following Heidegger, because it inhibits an understanding of dwelling activities, e.g. material construction, as belonging to the way we are (idem). In reaction to the approaches presented here, for the same reasons an inversion of discursive interests will be argued for below.

Rapoport is concerned with what has been labelled the built environment. Lawrence and Low (1990) give a neat definition of this term. They say this abstract concept is used to describe the products of human building activity. It refers to physical alterations of the natural environment through material construction by human beings. This includes built forms, which entail building types and defined spaces that are bound, but not necessarily enclosed (often infrastructure). Also, it might hold landmarks and sites that do not enclose activity. Finally, built forms may refer just to specific features, elements or divisions of the options stated above. The built environment should accommodate all 'types'.

For his studies, Rapoport uses datasets of specific buildings, building plans, phases, and styles. Architecture has concentrated on the *manifest functions* of buildings, which refers to the instrumental functionalism, rather than the *latent functions* of buildings, which refers to their expression and meaning. Rapoport stresses the importance of the moveable (decorative) elements in delimited parts of the built environment, because they can explicitly be meaning carriers. By them, personalisation of space may be achieved, while the elements that do not affect personalisation could be used for the framework of spatial design (Rapoport 1982). There is a strong relationship with studies of privacy, e.g. accessibility of rooms and intervisibility. The more private spaces are, the more individualised configurations of space become. To me this means that only to a certain extent the general privacy pattern is indicative for a generalised meaning of space from a specific group identity. The degrees in which personalisation may occur is (inter)related to both internal and external meanings of space. It is important that those moveable elements as spatial cues be noticed, i.e. represent noticeable differences, which is necessary for deriving meaning from them (idem). This coincides with Schütz's phenomenology in the fact that observed objects need to be contrasted to elements held in the stock of knowledge of the individual. But Rapoport also distinguishes between perception and association of spatial cues. In short, this means that the built environment is experienced, while in this experience it is associated with possible meanings. He argues that residential settlement systems are often more associational than perceptual, since through associated meaning this system becomes significant and informative for its users. This association is also called the *affective responses* to meaning, and its operation seems comparable with the spontaneous attribution of meaning of Schütz. Nevertheless, both the perception and association of space are principal factors (idem). It seems that the function a building has is recognised in Rapoport's perception, while the (social) significance it carries is established through associated meanings. Decoration, even to the level of colour, and its associated perception can influence the way space is used. To illustrate his assertions, Rapaport often uses examples of monuments. I feel one should take notice of the fact that monuments are intrinsically extravagant, just as large private properties can be due to their privacy. Therefore, their importance to the spatiotemporal relations in the social everyday life is limited. Yet in archaeology architectural (often monumental) style has been equally important to distinguish buildings of foreign origin within sites. This is applied to residential areas just as well, e.g. Teotihuacano presence in Tikal (Laporte 2003) and Lenca presence in Copán (Gerstle 1988).

Rapoport's focus on the meaning of urban environments deviates from the way abstracted elements of these fit in formative processes developing those spaces. Emphasising voluntary moveable elements and stylistic cues, his focus is less fundamental to built space. Especially where concurring with proxemics, Rapoport's anthropological methodologies are insufficient. Anthropological techniques, like interviews, are simply impossible with archaeological data, which means our discipline requires a direct connection between causal actions and consequential spatial cues.

As Smith (2007) also noted in his comparative cross-cultural approach to early cities, Rapoport's built environment consists of message carriers in their standardisation. He seeks to single out the (spatial, stylistic) cues that non-verbally communicate those messages. Rapoport assumes that social organisation and culture provide fixed sets of rules for the built environment that make people behave appropriately. Cues become legible through the process of enculturation, consolidating cues through consistent use (Rapoport 1982). In this, his ideas find connection with Henri Lefebvre (1991), who emphasises the symbolic meaning and significance of spaces, the enculturation of spaces, and the ways culture is spatialised.

Rapoport's meaning-carrying cues can be indicators of how everyday social life took place, and assess how this is culture, community or place specific and changes over time. Despite this possibility, both Rapoport himself and Smith recognise that in the approaches to the interpretation of the built environment, there has been a consistent lack of a temporal concept (Rapoport 1982, Smith 2007). Rapoport's levels of meaning search to distinguish how cosmology or ideology (identity or status) channels and interacts with behaviour and movement. In most cases an integration of all options can be expected. The middle-level meaning pertains to form, size, and location of structures to infer power, labour control and place of commoners. This is irrespective of the high-level rulers, builders, or religious motifs and usually consist of the political realities derived from formality and monumentality. The low-level meaning pertains to the recursive relationship between behaviour and architecture (Smith

2007). Rapoport approaches the low level from architecture, instead of from man producing it. Essentially, that is a top-down approach instead of bottom-up. Other difficulties with the use of Rapoport's ideas include his static concept of architecture and not completely reflexive users or actors by assuming learned culture. (Cf. e.g. Ingold (2000) arguing that acculturation is a two way process. See chapter three on participation.) The latter point is perhaps related to his dichotomy of the user and the (cue) planner, whereas historically these concepts merge: users become planners through transformative and constructive actions (see chapter five). Moreover, his concept of appropriate behaviour implies universal perception, interpretation, and subsequent action. Through bottom-up analysis, the cues that are meaningful to Rapoport are deliberately placed. Although that possibility is important, the cues from a bottom-up approach have been developed by social actions altering the natural environment. They become meaningful through the performance of the actions that caused them.

Human action, use, accessibility, visibility, and movement, can be placed at the low level of meaning. In computational science, some impressive contributions have been made in the modelling of human behaviour within built spaces in urban contexts. The greatest assembly of methods in this direction can be found in *space syntax* analysis. One of the most important researchers advocating and progressing these theses is Bill Hillier.

Axis of Human Space - Space Syntax

In the last decades space syntax has become an important player in the analysis of the layout of space in buildings and cities. It develops quantitative and descriptive tools by which space is studied. It is particularly applicable to the built environment, since it originated in architecture. Centrefold is the question of how space influences behaviour, often expressed in patterns of movement (Hillier and Hanson 1984, Hillier 2006). In space syntax, two basic ideas coincide. First, as also has been explored in existentialism, space is intrinsic to human activity and experience. This includes the linearity of movement and the convex character of human interaction (all participatory points in space need to be observable). The spaces in buildings and built environments (e.g. urban environments) are experienced as variously shaped visual fields. Eventually, there is a natural geometry to human activity by which space is shaped. Secondly, space syntax recognises that space does not only function for people due to its properties, but also because of the relations between all spaces making up a layout. The movement of people will be affected by the configuration of the layout that offers sequences and various intelligible choices. Understanding how layout affects movement requires the ability to make reasonably consistent descriptions of layouts as spatial configurations. Linguistics is proving difficult, as only basic spatial relations have articulated terms, while such complex spatial relations remain undefined. This could be caused by the intrinsic character of their existential cognition, which is discrepant with consciously thinking of space (Hillier 2006). Thus, space syntax combines two important inferential positions for working with the built environment: space is intrinsic to our being, but also maintains a geometric component in the experience of it. Moreover, the interpretation of delimited spaces should not be done in isolation. By accepting these positions, spatialities become part of a relational configuration of space, making them interrelationally meaningful.

These spatial relations are principal elements of focus in space syntax, where they take the form of degrees of access, facilitating movement and viewsheds, amongst others. This provides hypotheses about characteristics of spaces related to political control or ritual exclusion. Additionally, it can produce distinct patterns referring to social differences of class structures. These hypotheses are connected to the ways people experience and use the built environment, or e.g. political processes at play in the built environment (Hillier and Hanson 1984, Smith 2007). For research in urban contexts, space syntax supplies tools for analysing cities as the networks of space, following the configuration of spaces as in their locality, cluster, and orientation. It provides manners of observing the relationship between functional patterns of the utilisation of space (e.g. movement, differentiation, land use, migration, or social hierarchy and distress) and their part in the network of space. Furthermore, it formulates theories about the mutual affective relation between cognitive factors and space networks (Hillier 2007). Space syntax focuses on the way the extracted spatial laws mediate the social construction of urban space.

In visualising its results, space syntax analysis uses the generally known composition of elements and relations to produce axis maps, the main difference being the level of detail in which these elements are incorporated to compose a map of high complexity and various levels of information (Hillier 2002, Hillier 2007). The different types of *all-to-all* relations of elements or segments in urban space, are roughly divided into *to-movements* (accessibility potential) and *through-movements* (potential in all pairs of segments). They are assigned calculated, weighted values on the basis of *metric* (shortest paths) distances, *topological* (fewest turns) distances, and *geometrical* (least changed angles) distances. Such calculation can be made from each segment for each value, enabling us to see the city at various levels of functioning and scales. The apparent strength is that Hillier assumes that the grid and axis syntactic models resulting from the calculations capture the self organising logic of cities (Hillier 2007).

One of the problems space syntax is confronted with is understanding cultural differences and the appearance of invariant elements that emerge from the processes generating cities. A possible direction for a solution for this, is the socio-cultural imposition of local geometries on local constructions of urban space, whilst invariants, such as physical and socio-economic inhibitions and necessities, gain importance in the developmental growth of cities (Hillier 2002, Hillier 2007). These aspects create generative laws by which the city develops, such as the organisation of city spaces in blocks and groups with linear spaces connecting them (Hillier 1984, Hillier 2007). Space syntax research has led to many more (increasingly complex) laws, involving many general features in built environments (Hillier 2007). Eventually, these mathematical laws should enable calculations producing a model for city growth.

As a way to do cross-cultural comparisons with datasets on both past and present cities, space syntax has proven to be a strong tool. Researchers all over the world have applied the analytical techniques to cities in all parts and regions (Hillier 2007). It has the advantage of providing various sets of detailed information on the basis of city plans, thus making it applicable to archaeological datasets as well. Archaeologists, following architects, interior designers and city planners, have slowly begun to realise that space syntax offers significant tools for analysing delimited spaces in larger spatial contexts. Especially in the all-to-all relations of segments in space. In his space syntax study of the Zacuala residential compound in Teotihuacan, Matthew Robb (2007) states that, in order to make hypotheses on Teotihuacan domestic spaces, one must take into account the larger urban order. An analysis of the Teotihuacan city plan already showed that, space syntactically, the Street of the Dead was poorly accessible and probably not a segment offering the possibility of a marketplace or easy travelling through the city. As a segment, it appeared relatively isolated within the city. This knowledge and other inferences based on space syntactic types of analysis produced a certain perspective on the socio-spatial identity of Teotihuacan. These take into account the general features of otherwise heterogeneous compounds and the indivisible relations between the architectural unit, the social inhabiting it and the conditioning of both by the state apparatus (Robb 2007).

In spite of the considerable level of sophistication in space syntax, there are some problems in using it as a tool for social inference. Just as with Rapoport's theory, the difference in the aims of the method from archaeological interpretations is causing most of the trouble. Space syntax produces in the first place information that could be used by architects and city planners to better accommodate the way humans use built spaces in future designs. Of course, in order to make a well-reasoned argument for new designs, one needs to understand the socio-spatial characteristics affecting this behaviour. Here a connection is made to socio-cultural inferences, because these characteristics could enable us to formulate arguments about a socio-spatial identity. Hillier believes in a certain degree of universality in man's dealing with space, inferring universality in the cognitive processes causing the generative laws that appear to let cities develop in certain ways. He does attempt to discern between experiential universalism and differing cultural characteristics; similar to the development of phenomenology that went from the search for essences to taking into account personal and societal differences. Yet Hillier's focus lies on reasoning from the outcomes of both universalities and cultural specifics, while the underlying social processes that generate material construction of space in their physical interactions with the environment is not given primacy. This means that eventually, socio-spatial identity is still inferred on the basis of technical representations of patterns in the dataset, sophisticated as they may be, rather than involving a social understanding of the formative social processes shaping them. Essentially, it remains a statistic method, providing a possible mathematical explanation for how the city could have grown into its now consolidated pattern of buildings. In its degrees of abstraction, the sociological phenomenology of Schütz does allow for some universality (Eberle 1984, Campbell 1981), although these are redirected to social theoretical processes. In their operation, these may feature a panoply of variable individual, historical, physical, situational elements and so forth, which allow the production of multifold outcomes inferred as social specific identities of the built environment. To an extent, both Rapoport and Hillier depend on knowledge about such perception of actual situations, rather than socially informed constitutive processes also. However, as is the case with archaeology and anthropology, one can never achieve the same perception as another, certainly not in going back in time. Von Mises, phenomenology and proxemics all agree upon the individually differing aspects of perception and human action.

For reaching their goals, Rapoport and Hillier work from the current existence and shape of the built environment, architectural specifics, spatial cues and layouts. Whereas Rapoport tries to come to an understanding of the perception of the built environment by singling out significant features of buildings and their associated meanings, Hillier attempts to attach mathematical formulas to the way the use and perception of space in their formative qualities generate cities. With space syntax, it is also so that its foundational reasoning works from a final stage of the outcome, thus working top-down to get to the people behind it. Both make assumptions about which characteristic aspects of the built environment or city layouts are of specific importance to base social inferences on. In doing this, they lack a sound social theory that argues for the significance and value ascribed to characteristics of segments and functional levels. Therefore the calculations that are based on such segments produce potential facilities of space, but remain detached from the social processes that inform such spatial facilities like accessibility.

Projecting space syntactic methods weighing these possible abilities back in time may shed light on how space might have facilitated certain flows of movements and types of use. It will not clarify how the urban environment came about, why it is the way it is, i.e. the social meaning the configuration of space carries. This can only be elucidated by focusing on formative social processes. If a theory of social processes interfering with the construction of space provides an argument for the focus on specific aspects of datasets, allowing empirical research, space syntactic calculations could improve their significance for socio-cultural inference (see chapter five).

One of the great contributions space syntax makes to archaeological discourse is the way it deals with detailed and extensive datasets. In urban space, the built environment demonstrates its most fully-grown shape, in which all social relations to some extent are mediated in built spatialities. Archaeology, however, lacks adequate processive and holistic theories able to deal with such extensive datasets, causing a restricted focus (e.g. activity area archaeology) or quite general levels of inference. Following an extensive magnetic survey of the Hellenistic and Roman site of Doura-Europos in Syria, Christophe Benech used Bill Hillier's space syntax to analyse the use of domestic space in Doura-Europos houses (Benech 2007). Benech demonstrated the use of space syntax to such satisfaction that he has already planned a follow-up. This time he will survey cities of various periods, and hopes to reach some level of diachronic understanding (Benech 2008). He recognised the great and rich possibilities of the study of space on the basis of geophysical maps. Benech expects that a map of a complete site would not only allow inference of the use of domestic space, but by including all dwellings and infrastructure enable a socio-cultural study to the cities dealing with public and private space (Benech 2007). I would like to add that if such potential exists for space syntax, it must also exist for any social theoretical alternative for interpreting the built environment. Together with Benech I believe that the geophysical map will quickly move beyond merely localising new places to excavate or the confirmation that something lays below the surface. A quantitative method and a social perspective could complement and inform each other.

Space syntax takes up the challenge of extracting information of generative processes out of material records of built space. What is required is an inversion of interpretive analysis which is able to make the processes of the interplay between social processes and the physical environment intelligible, so the development of the built environment becomes informed. As Edward Hall in 1959 already prompted: "I feel very strongly that we must recognize and understand the cultural process. We don't need more missiles and H-bombs nearly so much as we need more specific knowledge of ourselves as participants in culture." (E. T. Hall 1959: 215) As I mentioned above, Ingold proposed something very similar. There is no use for the study of pre-given architecture, since it is entangled in a continuous reconstruction and reappropriation contained in the dwelling activities of inhabiting the world (Ingold 2000). Moreover, I would like to stress that as Smith (2007) particularly drew attention to, in the treatment of early cities and the built environment in archaeological discourse there has been a remarkable lack of temporal concepts. In focusing on processes pertaining to human interaction, time is intrinsically present. All this is not to say that all studies on spatial and architectural cues are futile or have not struck important inferential aspects; rather, they lack significance without being established by perceiving, acting, using and constructing man, who constitutes his society.

The social and its incorporation in space is a combination centrefold to the discipline of human, or specifically social, geography. This discipline quite directly emerged out of humanistic thought. The development of the geographical discipline is of specific importance to us, because it partially concurs with the development of archaeology. Briefly tracing their histories will clarify how their recent advancements differ and why the social geographical theories explored later can potentially inform and help the proposed inversion.

Chapter 2 *Along Disciplinary Lines*

Foundations of Human Geography

In the discipline of geography, the heritage of humanism has found fertile ground. The branch of geography concerned with the study of human beings and their actions in spatial contexts became known as Human Geography, which is a general term incorporating virtually all types of geography primarily concerned with people. Philosophically, human geography tends to see Cartesian realism as dehumanising, although many philosophers argue against this position. According to them, Descartes did not dehumanise science as it distinguishes questions on the determined qualities of matter (outside world) and the free will of mind (internal world), thus resulting in philosophies of meaning that influence human geography (Cloke e.a. 1991). Taking this line of reasoning, Descartes already opened the way towards a conjunction of the social domain and its (physical) environment.

Geography was often used as a forceful component of humanist education. This education was concerned with the cultural and moral aspects of humanity. It also directed the focus of Cosgrove's recent geography towards understanding ourselves, others and the world we share. Early geographers, however, already had a strong interest in people in their writings. Amongst the ones most influential especially the *géographie humaine,* founded by Paul Vidal de la Blache (1845-1918), stands out. His assertions challenged environmental determinism, proposing a mutually influencing relationship of 'land' and 'life', in which nature was not conceptualised as rigid boundaries, but rather a margin for transformation situated within human power as an ongoing dialogue. This dialogue takes place between *milieux* and *civilisations,* and in its operations produced a world full of *genres de vie*, historically distinct to particular peoples living in particular places. Vidal, as well as Émile Durkheim in anthropology, contributed in their focus on the geographical differentiation of regional cultures and communities to the Annales school (as discussed above). The concept genre de vie has been given many interpretations, most of which appealed to Durkheim's assertion that social contingency is held in collective societal ideas. Genre de vie should not be mistaken for a theory of contingency, although it captured a stable view on regional ways of life, it would fundamentally alter by changes in its manners (Cloke e.a. 1991, Kolen 2005). In his theories Vidal emphasised thought and action and the human ability to control destinies. He held that the environment offers possible avenues for human development, while the choice remains human (though not necessarily taken consciously) (Cloke e.a. 1991). This interest in lived spaces led him to the notion of *possibilism* which influences the gradual development of geographical regions, which in turn affects the analyses of place (Rodman 2006, Kolen 2005). Vidal's work indicates determinism does not preclude the possibility of free will, kept within the genres de vie (Cloke e.a. 1991, Kolen 2005).

Vidal's work influenced many prominent geographers like Buttimer, who took his assertions as guidelines for humanistic geography, enabling questions on tensions between tradition and innovation. Its humanist tendencies, nourished by the interest in peoples' intentions, gave way to the notion that places came about by the discourse of its inhabitants, not only their narratives of it. The humanist component inspired geographers like Ley and Samuels, but also the aforementioned Tuan (1976, 1977). They came to play an important role in anthropological theorising of place (Rodman 2006). Specific questions on human thought were introduced by Wright's *geosophy*, although it did not necessarily incorporate subsequent actions. Because his geography had no philosophical concern for theorising thought per se, it became very influential in the discipline. Such geography now serves as a prototype for current human geography and gave rise to sub-disciplines as cultural, historical, and regional geography. However, as the discipline developed, many of these ideas first disappeared with the rise of spatial science (Cloke e.a. 1991).

New Geography, New Archaeology

Spatial science redefined geography as a science of spatial patterns and relationships, uncovering fundamental laws of spatial organisation in natural landscapes and human activities in these landscapes (Cloke e.a. 1991). By its obvious cartographic expression, basic geographical concepts as location, distance, space, accessibility, and spatial interaction came to dominate the analysis of spatial patterns (Knox and Marston 2003). It left no room for humanism as it narrowed down scientific discourse into attempts to capture a few fundamental explanatory spatial laws on human activity in space. In a way, this narrow approach to spatial patterns is echoed by Bill Hillier's space syntax, although the concepts become more all-encompassing and its explanatory aims were expanded.

In this shift of the 1960s, idealised laws and models were often borrowed from scholars like Christaller, Von Thünen, and the sociology of Max Weber. Contemporaneously, some spatial scientists recognised such idealisations as inadequate for explaining observed patterns in society, alternatively proposing more probabilistic or stochastic analyses incorporating chance and randomness distorting ideal patterns (Cloke e.a. 1991). Other geographers proposed a cognitive-behavioural approach designed to engage directly with thoughts and actions of human beings. Here two main directions were explored: behavioural location theory and the cognitive aspects of human beings perceiving and processing spatial-environmental stimuli. This moved disciplinary interest from human beings acting in the world to human beings simply reacting to it, founding behaviourism. These newly-developed angles roughly composed the so-called New Geography (idem).

During the same period in archaeology the call for a more fully grown academic discourse became stronger. Coming from a comparative, descriptive science discussing stages and influences of cultures on each other, archaeologists like Walter Taylor, Gordon Willey, and Philip Phillips expressed their dissatisfaction with the archaeological impotence to explain things. They proposed an emphasis on social aspects in studying the general processes at work in culture history (see below). Such interpretive approaches were brought together in processual archaeology. The optimistic view on the potential of archaeological evidence for addressing social issues in past societies was especially advertised by the young Lewis Binford. Their view of the discipline became known as New Archaeology (Renfrew and Bahn 2000).

This new archaeology can be characterised as a turn away from history towards a connection with anthropology. As said before; moving from descriptions to explanations and incorporating a focus on processes observed in the material record enabling cross-cultural generalisations. Furthermore, its methodologies had to be modelled on the hard (often quantitative and natural) sciences, while an interest in the laws of human behaviour changed into the formation processes of the material record (Shanks and Hodder 1998). The comparability to the shift of interests in geography is not only clear in hindsight. It was David L. Clarke's *Analytical Archaeology* that argued specifically for the integration of quantitative and computerised methods, which could be borrowed from geography and other sciences (Clarke 1968, Renfrew and Bahn 2000). Despite his willingness to learn and derive methods from other sciences, his whoop claiming that "archaeology is archaeology is archaeology" (Clarke 1968: 13) propagating archaeology as a justified independent science, became even more famous. Firstly, processual archaeology turned almost exclusively to functionalist explanations, undoubtedly inspired by Malinowski's functional anthropology, including ecological approaches. Such approaches were therefore termed functional-processualism afterwards. The ecological perspective was fed by the paradigm of natural science. Social elements were considered as a second nature. It was inspired by biology and used the models of systems theory for questions on subsistence. In more recent times the cognitive and symbolic aspects of society also came into play, now termed cognitive-processualism (Renfrew and Bahn 2000).

In geography social cognition was similarly not the concern of behaviourist geography. Behaviourism was inclined to ignore the mental processes between stimulus and response, reducing interaction between man and environment to mere cause and effect relationships. Much of geographical discourse in this fashion was conducted from a positivist perspective, although some were aware of the problem of working with unobservable phenomena of mind. It used statistics to detect patterns and law-like associations in the way spatial science introduced it (Cloke e.a. 1991). Such yearning for objective knowledge was also employed in archaeology. Processual archaeology was supposed to produce objective, neutral and timeless knowledge of the past. As such, there were facts of the past which would not change and could be built upon (Shanks and Hodder 1998). While processual archaeology changed its focus towards cognitive processes, in geography behaviourism was bartered for behavioural geography.

The difference between behaviourism and behavioural geography is indeed the turn towards a focus on cognitive processes or the phenomena of mind. Instead of restricted stimulus-response relations, behavioural geography introduced the reflexive character of human being. Despite this gain in nuances, it maintained a narrow conception of how human beings act and think subscribed to versions of behaviourism. Not as simple as stimulus-response relations, yet neither as diverse and complex as psychological relations. Unfortunately the positivist methods were also maintained, using statistics to detect patterns and law-like associations, rather like spatial science, instead of opposing it. Nevertheless, behavioural geography had a greater overlap with humanistic geography. Therefore it can indeed be seen as the bridge from peopleless spatial science to 'peopled' human geography (Cloke e.a. 1991). In its questions regarding the perception of the environment, mental mapping, and the everyday spatial preferences of people utilising space, behavioural geography is still very much present in humanistic geography. In the absence of treatment of people in spatial science and only partial dealing with people in behavioural science, self-conscious humanistic geography emerged after 1970, although not accompanied by a rejection of behavioural geography (idem). Behaviour in archaeology comparably focused on activities of social actors without associated agency or meaning. Although knowledge, rationalisation and motivation can be employed in rational processes or social norms that can be cross-culturally contrasted (Hodder e.a. 1998). Illustrative for their close relation, for the definitions discussed in Hodder's (1998) volume, reference is made to the wider application of similar terms in human geography as described in the Dictionary of Human Geography (Johnston, Gregory and Smith 1994).

As a critique on geography as spatial science and its reconceptualisation, self-conscious geography emerged in the 1970s. The direct cause was the failure of spatial science to deal with or even recognise real human problems. Therefore, many geographers started to adapt a behavioural perspective. Some, however, thought it necessary to challenge the entire philosophical foundations of spatial science and its behavioural adaptations. They strictly defined and criticised the positivistic practice of spatial science and replaced it with the alternative of humanist philosophies, e.g. phenomenology and existentialism (Cloke e.a. 1991). During the 1980s for archaeology again a comparable shift took place towards the paradigm that has been called postprocessualism. It was influenced by neo-Marxism, post-positivism, hermeneutics and existential phenomenology, which resulted in a plethora of often loosely defined theoretical positions (Renfrew and Bahn 2000). Archaeology thus followed geographical sentiments about a decade later.

At the early beginnings of the 1970s humanistic geography sprouted, forming a solid philosophical critique, though the term itself was only introduced by Yu-Fi Tuan a few years later. Researchers were dissatisfied with the objectified reduction of people to statistics, graphs or numbers. In other words, they felt human beings had been dehumanised in disciplinary discourse before. Furthermore, humanistic geography opposed the position of the researcher as an objective individual that leaves his humanity outside the research process, the core of positivistic epistemology (Cloke e.a. 1991). Postprocessualist archaeology also aimed its focus at people and the practice of interpretation. Archaeology is a material practice in the present, making sense of material remains of the past: an ongoing process producing an indefinite account of the past. Moreover, it indicates that the outcome of the interpretive practice is essentially plural. As opposed to behaviour, practice is conceptualised as meaningful routinised actions of knowledgeable agents (Shanks and Hodder 1998). Postprocessualists actually contextualised archaeological discourse in various ways. While humanistic geography rarely articulated its dissatisfaction with spatial science and behavioural geography, postprocessualist archaeology had considerable difficulty positing a firm theoretical base from which it launched its critique. Both movements involved a component reacting against the way previous discourse took place in their respective disciplines and reassessed the way their objects of study were addressed. Significant parts of the contributions of human geography and postprocessualist archaeology have focused on the position of the researcher, arguing against positivist epistemology. The humanist critique that conventional science fails to recognise its own biases which configure its practices in such a way that the research conducted is bound to confirm the social status quo (Cloke e.a. 1991), goes for both disciplines. Its philosophical criticism is concerned with researchers getting in the way of their own studies because of their blinding subjectivities: a perspective derived from the philosophy of phenomenology (idem). Postprocessualism and humanist thought still have a strong voice in archaeology and geography, but after the 1980s it appears the development of the two disciplines was largely disconnected.

Present and Future Discource

Phenomenology and structuration, in addressing research objectives on the social, were of paramount importance to both disciplines. Phenomenology offers great potential, as has been indicated above. Nevertheless, one should take notice that many archaeologists in part have produced simply false adaptations of phenomenology, reducing it to personal idiosyncrasy and often devoid of its rich temporal frameworks.

It is in phenomenology that most studies of landscape archaeology can be placed. Alternatively, there is the hermeneutic approach that focuses on the uniqueness of each cultural complex. This is the most relativistic of all approaches, emphasising pluralist interpretations, as well as the most contextually embedded approach. Although it shares the phenomenological base of Husserl and Heidegger, it continues with the differentiation between natural and social phenomena and their modes of acquiring knowledge, that is, the opposition of understanding and explaining. This has been elaborated upon by the German historian Dilthey and later by the concept of pre-understanding that constitutes the hermeneutic circle of Gadamer (Shanks and Hodder 1998). Structuration or systems theory, specifically by Anthony Giddens (1984) and the notion of habitus of Pierre Bourdieu (1977), have essentially constituted a postprocessualist focus on types of practice. In this, human actions in the sense of practice, along with concepts of actors or human agents, are studied as shaping social structure (for a good discussion of practice theory and its research agenda, see Pauketat 2000a). Yet structuration in archaeology paradoxically caused a strong interest in the individual, which in theoretical debates came to illuminate the concept of agency (despite Bourdieu denying his actors agency).

Identity and place in the everyday relations of individuals received increased importance in the use of phenomenology, agency, and structuration in archaeology and geography. The essential difference is that archaeology chose to follow the direction of agency and, in doing so, separated agency and the individual from its dialectic with society or structure as a process. As various archaeological scholars are now starting to notice, this separation either way is an impoverishment of our understanding of the past. As Joyce and Lopiparo rightly state, structuration constitutes traditions over the long term. "A focus on agency can, paradoxically, risk overlooking the evidence of agency in structuration." (Joyce and Lopiparo 2005: 366) While Wynne-Jones and Kohring note that in the attempt to avoid a repetition of culture history (discussed below), the debate moved away from the complexity of society towards agency (Chapman 2003, Wynne-Jones and Kohring 2007). Not wanting to discard as trivial the obvious merits the theorisation of agency in archaeology has brought us, evidence of which is the critically approached array of topics included in the volume by Dobres and Robb (2000a) (Chapman 2003), Wynne-Jones and Kohring wisely suggest that we need to revisit the structure and agency debate as Giddens sets out. We should infuse it with the knowledge we acquired of agency. Few scholars have taken that step, although special acknowledgement must go to Ingold's efforts demonstrating social landscapes (technological and interpersonal understandings as constructed by personal experiences) in socially created yet structuring environments (Ingold 2000). Wynne-Jones and Kohring propose that a focus on societal complexity should entail the return to the structure and agency debate in archaeology (Wynne-Jones and Kohring 2007). Fortunately, we do not stand isolated in the pursuit of such goals, as human geography has made some specific efforts focusing on a further continuation and elaboration on structuration theory, sustaining its full complexity. It learned to incorporate both spatial and phenomenological aspects of knowledge, which enriched the otherwise narrow empirical potential of Giddens' original structuration. So now, after a few decades, there is a reason to revive the close relationship in the advancements of the archaeological and geographical discipline.

The processes that operate between agency and structure are able to remove the stagnation of the temporal element in phenomenological adaptations and the theorisation of agency, enabling a more historical and developmental perspective, though theoretically better informed. So the exceptional position of archaeology to refer to the long term may be exploited again. Recent theories in human geography can help set out some potential pathways to achieve this. Currently archaeology has turned almost exclusively to ecological and biological evolutionary insights to maintain its developmental process oriented mindset. However, increasing numbers of shortcomings for the explanation of social phenomena come to light. A social theoretical alternative guided by geographical pioneers, as will be suggested here, should not be seen as a replacement for biologically acquired insights and inhibitions. Rather, they should exist laterally as complementary lines of equal explanatory value. Similarly, I feel human geography could be made compatible with spatial science, resolving problems that were generated by its own shortcomings, thereby enlightening and informing both points of departure. Traditionally human geography is a collective term for all types of geography concerned with the social realm (culture, history, regions, postcolonialism, etc.). As I mentioned earlier, the subdiscipline of social geography is not exercised everywhere, but specifically is the vogue with Germanic geography. The theories presented in the following chapters are so intertwined with social theory that the term social geography feels more applicable.

In order to better appreciate the archaeological position, we should yet again go back to some fundamentals in terms and theories. This time concentrated on the start of archaeology as a culture historical discipline, still casting considerable influence into archaeological discourse, obstructing a long term developmental focus on societies and those (physical) aspects that are connected to them through the interdisciplinary assertions made in chapter one.

Social Evolutionism

Chapter one started by establishing time as one of archaeology's main concerns. During the 19th century this concern mainly contributed to the rise of the archaeological discipline. Two 19th century concepts were of paramount important for this development: Darwinian evolution and the *three age system*, presented by the Dane Christian Thomsen. This three age system divided the European prehistory into a stone, bronze and iron age, a classification that was quickly adopted and further subdivided by John Lubbock and others. Divergent chronological terminologies had already been developed in disciplines like geology. Essentially this made archaeology into a study of chronology and periods. This was of mainly technological concern and helped arrange and categorise material. Together with Darwinian evolution, such ideas gave rise to the practice of making typologies in artefact research, producing chronological and developmental sequences (Pluciennik 2005, Lucas 2005).

Evolutionary thought, however, also brought about some ideas that were later condemned. For one thing, the evolutionary process on the basis of survival of the fittest kindled a politics of winners and losers. Early on this became connected to the question of race, which led to genocidal practices. Especially Herbert Spencer, a fanatical Darwinist, was criticised for nourishing such thinking in bringing the concept to a larger public and drawing an exclusively progressive picture of human development. His view of evolution was strongly necessitarianist and much his own rather than Darwin's. This was employed for imperialism, domination and harsh capitalist competition. Moving from biology to sociology, Spencer consolidated the idea that societies developed with an increase in size and the associated complexity of social organisation. This rendered value judgements on many types of societies in the world (Sanderson 1990, Pluciennik 2005).

With the ideas and practice of evolution and typology archaeology was founded as a comparative, classificatory science in a technical sense. It was from the perspective of ethnography that, most notably, Lewis Henry Morgan introduced a sequence of societal progress that became hugely influential. His teleological proposal entailed that human societies evolved from the state of savagery, through barbarism, to civilisations. These stages were still coupled to materialist notions, which led Morgan to include actually seven stages dividing up societal development (Sanderson 1990, Pluciennik 2005, Lucas 2005). His work brought evolution in classificatory terms firmly into the social realm; yet the focus remained on material and issues of subsistence. Morgan excluded linguistics and religion from his studies of the social, but included race again, claiming Aryan superiority on supposed material achievements. Morgan's early evolutionary ideas also had a significant counterpart in thinking about the built environment. Morgan himself conducted fieldwork on aboriginal house forms and inhabiting households. The built spaces were seen as an intrinsic part of the complex of traits and adaptations allowing the maintenance of social groups in their natural environment, as well as mirroring the cultures producing them (Lawrence and Low 1990).

The material counterpart of social progress had obvious empiricist archaeological interest. It was mainly in the United States that the concern was different. The difference was that America was constantly and immediately confronted with otherness, whereas for the European situation this usually was only the case in colonial areas. This bent interests, driven by the future of these native others, towards processes of acculturation, culture, and identity. All fields of American anthropology were concerned with the genesis of the Native. Direct historical analysis (or later the direct historical approach) led (regionally) to a view of archaeology and ethnology in a historical continuum. The concept of the 'frontier' was developed, the borderline between civilisation and savagery. Thus the 'Indian problem' emerged. The notions of social evolution directly implied certain societies as inferior, placed at a lower stage of development. They uncritically nourished all kinds of ghastly political practices (Pluciennik 2005).

Following the tendency for generalities in evolutionary thought, anthropologist Franz Boas' historical particularism provided the basis for much more detailed descriptions. He also propagated for classification systems for the Americas to be different from the Old World. His practice was maintained for a few decades before being rejected (Lyman, O'Brien and Dunnell 1997, Renfrew and Bahn 2000, Pluciennik 2005). In the 1940s and 1950s social evolution was strongly revived as neo-evolutionism, especially by the efforts of Gordon Childe, who quickly gained support from Leslie White and Julian Steward, each with their own ideas. Gordon Childe is specifically accredited for inserting the ideas of an agricultural and urban revolution between stages of social evolution. This referred to the production of a surplus of food acting as a social security enabling other activities, and the economic and social processes of enabling urbanisation (Sanderson 1990, Lucas 2005). Towards the 1960s Leslie White significantly contributed to the debate. His work was greatly permeated by Morgan's evolutionary stages. Most significantly, he distinguished two types of economic systems: primitive society (economy based on social relationships) and civil society (relationships between goods dominate social relations). The transition between these two he conceptualised as his own version of the agricultural revolution, leading to cultural consequences. His perspective on evolution is called cultural evolutionism (Sanderson 1990, Pluciennik 2005). Both Gordon Childe's and Leslie White's evolutionary assertions were aimed at generalities and parallels between cultures. Therefore their ideas, as well as the early evolutionary thought, were readily adopted by New Archaeology, since it enabled cross-cultural comparisons and social classifications.

Julian Steward's work on evolution is slightly more nuanced, though simultaneously less consistent with evolutionary thought. He differentiated three types of evolution: unilinear, universal and multilinear. Unilinear basically entailed Morgan's original ideas, which in his view should be abandoned due to factual inaccuracies. Subsequently, Steward fiercely argued against the universal evolutionism of Childe and White, who emphasised the generalisations intrinsic to Morgan's social evolution, refusing the allowance of divergences and local variations. Thus he proposed multilinear evolution, or "the search for laws dealing with significant regularities in cultural change." (Sanderson 1990: 91). These cultural parallels and generalities would be of a much more limited scope refrained to form, function and sequence with empirical validity. Steward's contribution is simply a compromise between particularist Boasians and generalists as Childe and White (Sanderson 1990, Pluciennik 2005).

Although most of these concepts have been rejected to various degrees, they still heavily influence much archaeological practice, mainly because of the somewhat unaware adaptations of them in processual archaeology. In the 1960s a further elaboration followed, proposed by Sahlins and Service. This too was originally a teleological and classificatory sequence based on the assumption of increasing complexity in social structures. Its terms have become widely accepted and used in anthropology and archaeology. Societies were seen to develop sequentially from bands, tribes and chiefdoms to states. The mechanisms typically pertained to environmental resources and political competition within their organisation (Pluciennik 2005, Lucas 2005).

This model of complexity is still largely in use, although it has been recognised that societies could regress and progress, and that the model would move at different rates in different situational regions. Modifications to accommodate current insights have been made by various researchers. Flannery's continuation of Service's model emphasised the importance of the difference in levels of decision making and hierarchy in simple and stately societies. More complex societies were thought to be further centralised and segregated, creating levels of decision making requiring greater processing of information. Flannery explicitly linked the level of social organisation of the state to the notion of civilisation (Flannery 1972, Chapman 2007). Flannery's paper inspired others to develop ideas on levels of decision making separating the sequence of Service's model, focusing on administrative capacities. Archaeologically it was decided that site size was the best way to distinguish levels of decision making. In processual fashion, through cross-cultural comparison, five levels of site size were distinguished (Chapman 2007). This also led to mathematical formulas of site size ranking associated with population size, which were developed to establish site hierarchies (Flannery and Marcus 2003, Kowalewski 2003) or the centralisation, tribute drawing and catchment indexes by de Montmollin (1989). Archaeological settlement analysis and settlement patterning was regarded as mathematically explanatory for ascribed levels of social complexity and organisation. Whereas the link between state and civilisation was consolidated after Flannery's paper, the link between class society and civilisation originated with Childe. Recently in large cross-cultural studies, others have argued similar positions (Chapman 2007). Such developments were made without necessarily changing the characteristic of these models, unfortunately featuring a rather universal concept of history.

Eventually all approaches entail degrees of a concept of time which presents a unidirectional and classificatory view of social development, thus remaining similar to chronologies (Lucas 2005). This does no justice to the open-endedness of Darwinian evolution in implying teleological processes. Processual archaeology, often utilising these ideas, found itself being rather deterministic also. An illustration of the lively debate that is almost constantly held on the differences between cultural or social evolutionary views and Darwinian evolution is the article by David Rindos (1985), which provoked many fierce comments by several authors. More recently the inequality of biological and cultural types of evolution is strongly argued for by Dwight Read (2006), on the basis that in Darwinian evolution selection operates from individual properties, which cannot be used for the evolution of culture as a mental phenomenon. The case of kinship terminologies shows this, since not the individual properties benefit from the knowledge of terminology as a trait, but the individual benefits from the properties of the social group sharing that terminology, therefore being their kin. He has taken this knowledge to build a predictive mathematical model for structured complexes of kinship terminology. A similar argument is explored by Douglas Erwin (2000), who holds that the level of macroevolution is more that the accumulation of biological microevolutions.

Culture History, Culture Areas

Next to the development of social evolution, the United States in particular have known a persistent practice for the better part of the 20th century called *culture history*. For the most part it entailed studies to discern traits in artefacts that together comprise specific material cultures. These were assumed to adhere to ethnic groups. Material cultures would bear within the characteristics of such ethnic groups, which is essentially an inductive approach, as opposed to the deductive character of later processual archaeology. Almost automatically this lays a strong emphasis on comparisons on the basis of classifications, this practice being centerfold to culture history. It defined temporal units, artefact typologies, geographical dispersion and seriations. Archaeological practice focused on stratigraphy, chopping up the history of a site into separated segments. These segments were treated self-referentially. Stratigraphy and typologies controlled time in such a way that it structured inference, so the researchers mistakenly came to believe that their classifications had meaning to the people of the past. From an original interest in the construction of chronologies research started to concentrate more on the definition of archaeological cultures. Cultures were thought to influence each other, transferring stylistic features of its (material) characteristics through contact in a number of ways, such as trade, migration, social ties, associated with aggression, invasion or colonisation. This contractual process of transferring traits is called *diffusion*. These influences would result in other behavioural patterns as the traits were adopted into the culture. Archaeologies of invasion and diffusion, just as stratigraphy and typology, cause a discontinuous view of change and development of society. Nevertheless, historical narratives were construed from these sources of information (Lyman, O'Brien and Dunnell 1997).

Just as with previous social evolutionary thought, much of culture history became integrated in processual thought and therefore is still pervasive in archaeological discourse. Culture history thus appears to have never truly experienced a demise. Apparent parallels are their interests in function, adaptation and analogies, as well as a focus on style and a rather universal view of history (Lyman, O'Brien and Dunnell 1997). It is an evolutionary interest they have in common. Lyman, O'Brien and Dunnell therefore proposed to give way to biological rules of evolution in archaeology. The Darwinian model will offer an angle through which cultural change and development can be placed as part of the continuum they are part of, instead of the discontinuous explanations produced so far. As said before, many have followed and biological evolution has become an influential way to reintroduce the process into archaeological discourse. Despite the progress, I have to agree with Bruce Trigger's (1998) comments on Lyman, O'Brien and Dunnell's book *The Rise and Fall of Culture History*. Evolutionary perspectives have a lot more to offer archaeological discourse, yet at the same time an exclusive focus on biology is rather reductionist. Evolutionary selection not only takes place externally, but involves significant culturally mediated aspects. Without a biologically reductionist notion, evolution could be made better equipped to consider social phenomena (Trigger 1998). As becomes clear in current debates, the Darwinian model as opposed to more culturally inclined models of evolution still evokes lengthy academic disputes. It seems that social evolution, culture history and processual archaeology all had the right interest, but lacked a yet to be formulated truly social embedded approach to societal development.

The designation of culture areas is associated with the debates on social evolution and culture history. Like culture history, traditional methods of naming culture areas are rather inductive. Many cultural terms only refer to a certain language, group of languages or even rather neutral geographical surroundings, leaning on an unfounded 'pars pro toto' principle. Culture history approaches emphasise the diffusion of populations and traits on the basis of which they try to define culture areas as archaeological horizons. This generates endless debates on the origins of traits and their adaptation by populations, and implies donor and recipient relations between groups. Despite contributing useful data, the link to situations and people in the past is not founded. Culture history approaches could definitely have merited from a more multidisciplinary perspective working with areas in diachronic fashion. They pretend to have put meaningful, analytically used entities on our maps as culture areas, which makes one doubt the value of this entire concept.

As is illustrated by the relative terra incognita in Central America known as the Intermediate or Chibchan area (after an academically troublesome linguistic family), traditional approaches lack the ability to make meaningful arguments for the cultural *boundaries* of the areas that determine analytical research questions (see chapter four and five). The culture areas shown on our maps define the way we interpret the supposedly correlated societies residing in that area. Archaeology needs to arrive at its own designated areas independently. As has been suggested, the spread of iconographic traditions in archaeological artefacts could indicate a shared belief system that is true to the people of the past. It can be said of the Chibchan area that advancements in linguistics and genetics show the persistence of population line that remained in situ for thousands of years (Hoopes and Fonseca 2003). Hoopes argues for positioning Chibcha-speaking societies in the broader contexts of such research, before casting doubt on the material relations within the area (Hoopes in press).

What an approach to culture areas from belief systems is trying to get at is similar to what a developmental perspective based on social processes could offer. We should take notice of the inferential implications a simple line on a map can have and be careful with the meaning carrying connotations of the terms imposed on areas. Although it would mean a rather ambitious project, involving huge amounts of extensive archaeological work over large regions and surfaces, the call for a social theoretical endeavour in an archaeology of processes is felt here too. The plea to release archaeology from the boxing-in practices that for so long have been typical of archaeological thought is now getting stronger. This also applies to the spatially delimited areas in which ancient cultures and societies are thought to reside. Thinking outside the box has become fashionable and can be recognised in the practices and theories of total archaeology, e.g. Dominic Powlesland's long studies on the Vale of Pickering (2003, 2006, personal communication). Such boxes have been constructed from the early introduction of evolutionary stages onwards, constantly consolidating the archaeological discipline as yet another type of classificatory practice. Archaeological discourse at present is slowly being bent towards analysing or characterising societies and their complexity in social terms, as evidenced by Kohring and Wynne-Jones' (2007) *Socialising Complexity*.

Once again we have arrived at the place in discourse we reached at several moments before respectively. Joyce and Lopiparo quite rightly note that "agency and structure are indivisible parts of a single process through which society is continuously created over time, everything that persists or changes in archaeological sites is evidence of agency." (Joyce and Lopiparo 2005: 365) Although I agree with this assertion, it is due to the debates in archaeology focusing on agency rather than structure that a breach in social intelligible inference has unknowingly been created. We will now turn precisely towards that gap. Departing from adaptations of structuration, poststructuralist human geography has made theoretical advancements involving the processes between agency and structure, whilst incorporating the environment and the spatial, opening empirical possibilities. In the following chapter the contribution made by Allan Pred is thoroughly discussed and its potential for archaeological discourse is explored. Consecutively, some succeeding continuations of this geographical direction are discussed in chapter four.

Chapter 3 *Processes of Becoming*

Time-geography and Structuration

Against the backdrop of spatial science Torsten Hägerstrand, a Swedish geographer, made an important advancement in geography. Mainly during the 1960s and 1970s he introduced the discipline to the idea of tying individuals to *life-paths* (from birth till death) consisting of a continuous and unique sequence of events in time-space. Models of the life-path concept were designed and schematically visualised a function of time and space in which a line, representing movement and events, was drawn. This way of representing (parts) of an individuals' biography is called a three dimensional time-space diagram. Life-paths could easily be divided into temporal segments as days, weeks or months. The time-space continuum both facilitates and puts constraints on individuals' actions. Especially the physical constraints were emphasised in its application (cf. the ecological emphasis in processual archaeology). Hägerstrand's concept grew to be very influential in geographical practice and became known in the 1970s as time-geography. It introduced a temporal factor to spatial science captured in the individual which thrived in the 1960s. The key to its success was probably the result of the combination of retaining an objectivist physicality and the individual (Hägerstrand 1970, Pred 1977, Giddens 1984, Hallin 1991). Prominent geographers such as Nigel Thrift and Derek Gregory were amongst the ones influenced by time-geography, through whom it found its way into regional and cultural geographies (e.g. Thrift and Pred 1981, Thrift 1983). Also, in existentialist phenomenological geography there was definite interest in the work of Marwyn Samuels (1979) amongst other contributors like David Ley (Ley and Samuels 1978) and Donald Meinig's (1979) volume on the interpretation of landscapes in the context of everyday life.

Outside of the geographical discipline the potential of time-geography for sociology was recognised by Anthony Giddens, whose most influential work *The Constitution of Society* (1984) mentions it on several occasions. Whereas Hägerstrand was the main founder of time-geography, Giddens laid the basis for structuration theory in social organisation. Giddens noticed that the work of geographer Paul Vidal de la Blache and his contributions to the French Annales School had particularly influenced Fernand Braudel. In that, the 19th century foundations for history, sociology and human geography largely coincide. According to him, sociology had just as much to offer human geography (specifically time-geography) as vice versa (Giddens 1984). The geography of Paul Vidal de la Blache also claimed a presence in the work on human practice by Pierre Bourdieu (1977). In particular Vidal's genre de vie and later Bourdieu's habitus became very important for the archaeological discipline. Together with prevalent phenomenology linked to Heideggers (1972) existentialism, the structuralism of anthropologist Lévi-Strauss and the interpretive approaches of Ricoeur and Gadamer amongst others, these concepts were joined in the landscape archaeology of Julian Thomas (1996) (Kolen 2005).

With the fall of spatial science in the 1970s for human geography and with the rise of postprocessualism in the 1980s for archaeology, many of these prominent thinkers found their way into respective discourses. Poststructuralism followed shortly, inspired by the philosophy of Michel Foucault, e.g. focusing on power relations within society. Progressively separated from the omnipresent quantitative approaches and the emphasis on environmental determinism, the social and the interpretive were integrated into academic discourse. The 1980s ushered in exciting times. The theory of Giddens and certain elements in the work of Bourdieu and Foucault are significant for this chapter, but will not be its main concern. There would be no way to do justice to the complexity of their thought in the space available here and many profound accounts of their work have been produced in the last decades. Repeating their notions would add little quality to the arguments made here. Still, both silently and at times explicitly, their ideas are present, because in combination with time-geography they paved the way for Allan Pred's theory of place.

Introducing Allan Pred, Criticising Anthony Giddens

Allan Richard Pred, who passed away just short of two years ago, left a great body of literature and knowledge that may offer as much to his own discipline, human geography, as to others, such as history. The aim here is to assess his work on the concept of place for use in archaeological discourse. He has written numerous articles and books from the 1960s to the 2000s, with increasing interest in political themes in geography like racism and terror, moving away from his initial focus on history towards issues of modernity and the present. Although he is rightly placed in the realm of human geography, combining his eclectic interests in the discipline, his social theoretical basis bridges the next step towards specific social geography as well. As he mentioned on his personal website at Berkeley, he took a critical stance towards human geography. Unconcerned with its disciplinary limits, he saw geography as an inevitable ontological reality. No doubt from this specific attitude follows that his studies can be informative to other disciplines as well. Concurring with my perspective on archaeology as being of value to the present and future, Pred was interested in making an historical geography of the present. Here the focus will be on his work of the 1980s, specifically the theoretical outlines explored in his 1981 and 1984 articles. The reading of the latter article is labelled plural and dependent on the discipline of the reader by Pred himself (Pred 1985). With this remark he appears to stress the potential to use his ideas outside of the geographical discipline quite literally. The theoretical outlines of 1981 and 1984 culminated in the extensive theory described in his book *Place, Practice and Structure* (1986).

With his attendance to the translation of Torsten Hägerstrand's dissertation in 1968, the foundation for the strong influence of time-geography in his work is already accounted for. Hägerstrand went on to develop time-geography in its own right, and Pred continued it into the historical and social processive objectives of human geography. In his 1981 article he explores the possibilities to take time-geography out of the mere conduction of accessibility constraint analyses, furthering it into the everyday life. On the basis of time-geography providing an effective device for describing behaviour and biography in time-space, he argues for an adaptation of the core concepts of *path* and *project* in dialectical formulations tying the individual and society together. He adds that this placement of time-geography into dialectic processes had originally not been done by Hägerstand himself (Pred 1981). In 1984 he explicitly continues the combination of time-geography and structuration, which is the origin of the dialectical processive concept. He works towards a concept of place as a historically contingent process. Places are a kind of historical micro-geographies, in which many individual territories interact and biographics collide. The crossings of behaviour and movement generate spatial transformations and localise social structures. The historical construction of place involves the appropriation and transformation of space as well as the reproduction and transformation of society in time and space (Pred 1984). The most important arguments are made by then, but in his extensive theoretical outline of *Place, Practice and Structure* he reaches a completion which serves as a foundation for a case study in 19th century Sweden.

Pred is clear about his sources of inspiration and gives a lengthy account of where his ideas originate from. As has been indicated above, Pred chose to combine several of the many trends in social science that were meant to serve as a middle ground between structure and agency: Giddens' structurationism, Hägerstrand's time-geography and Foucault's post-structuralism. Finding the middle ground had implications for the debate on the interaction of structure and human agency and the variable nature of both these situational parts, which led to a better understanding of the positioning of action in the totality of society in time and space. The approaches which followed from it represent the difficulty of constructing a theory of action which distances itself from both the determinism of structuralism and the idealist individualism of agency (Cloke e.a. 1991). Like geography, structuration nourished the structure-agency debates in archaeology, but it appears that structure's determinism has gradually been replaced with natural sciences and agency grew into a particularist take on individualism, rather than employing the individual or actor as an analytical unit, using a kind of *methodological individualism* (a term first coined by economist Joseph Schumpeter). In addition, the theory of structuration's founder, Anthony Giddens, was quickly criticised for obstructing the asking of empirical research questions. The aforementioned sociology of practice of Pierre Bourdieu was less problematic, especially in the way it contextualised action and avoided cognitive processes of intention within his actors. In his view, habitual practices do not need intention (Bourdieu 1977). Detached from invisible mental processes yet offering contextualisation was a better match for archaeological capabilities.

In geography at first, structuration was definitely not received as an all-encompassing grand theory, but rather as a series of core abstract propositions that were informed and reformulated by more specific inquiries. This led to considerable differences in structurationist thought (Cloke e.a. 1991). Giddens, however, presented his work on structuration as an ontology of human society, concentrating around issues of the relation between actors and social institutions. Such dualism (originating from structuralism) permeated his work, explicitly in the positioning of both time and space, and structure and agency, whose interdependent relationships should transcend the risks of either single issue approach, defying determinism in the proposal of dualistic processes. His agents were knowledgeable and capable subjects (not the previously non-reflexive specimens of structuralism) and he saw changes in social life as their accomplishments (Giddens 1984).

With Giddens' structuration and Bourdieu's practice, the uncorrupted concept of purposeful action of Ludwig von Mises (1998) is differentiated into more realistically bound concepts of acts, actions, practice and agency. For Giddens, acts are discrete segments of individual performance and action represents a continuous flow of individual involvement. Agency, on the other hand, is not just purposeful, but purposive, which requires self-reflexive monitoring (Cloke e.a. 1991). Self-referential understanding of the world was already part of von Mises' and Schütz's theories, yet in structuralism and for e.g. Bourdieu, actors were non-reflexive. Giddens' assertions thus partially concur with Schütz's constitutive phenomenology, although Giddens adds the possibility for subconscious and unconscious motivations for purposive actions. Rationalisation and accounting for actions is a conscious process. Therefore, subconscious or unconscious motivations can only become intelligible through self-reflection if the unconscious is made conscious (Giddens 1984, Cloke e.a. 1991). Self-reflection is based on knowledge and memory, so, just as for Schütz, the experience of the consequences of actions affect the reflexive process (Campbell 1981). Still, despite his interest in e.g. time-geography, Giddens' approach did not fully take into account the experiential and existential aspects of agency and polarised intentional and unintentional types of action (Cloke e.a. 1991).

The way Giddens established the interconnectivity of agency and structure, while enabling the characterisation of structure itself, is his greatest asset. Moving into the realm of Foucault's philosophy, he mainly identifies structures by their rules and power relations, restricted by and reproducing distribution of resources. Rules exist in the enactment of social practice, contrary to formally formulated rules that are codified interpretations of rules. Such social rules structure interaction, but are also modified by it (Cloke e.a. 1991, Giddens 1984). Human action in the practice of everyday life is interpreted as resistance against power constraints or rules by Michel de Certeau. It basically entails that in each action a resistance is taking place (de Certeau 1988). This could account for the plural forms of social rules as opposed to formulated rules. The structural properties of social systems (rules and resources) are both a medium for social practice and the end result of social practice, hence the duality of structure. Instead of social interaction, Giddens places the rules and resources of structure in social institutions, giving solidity across time and space. The duality of structure is contained in regularising institutions producing and reproducing action (Giddens 1984).

Giddens' dialectic systems of interaction are of definite value. However, de Certeau's resistance may challenge the notion of reproduction that implicitly asserts a repetition of the same. Also, the difference between social rules (as a process of enacted practice) and formulated rules in society, by which they would typically be identified, is prone to change because the enactment of practice plays a constitutive role. Eventually, formulated rules grow out of human action; human action constitutes the systems of interaction that in turn coherently comprise a structure. This structure, which results from human action, produces formulated and/or codified rules. Only then does a dialectic start, in which enacted practice (social rules) can be a process of interpreting formulated rules. Social rules are the interaction systems of human action, and thus human action is fundamental to both types of rules, while in enactment it may (re)interpret the same rules it constituted itself before. Both structure and formulated rules are thus temporal and changeable.

Constitution and change appear to be only implicitly present in the distance taken towards determinism. The theories drawn by existentialism, phenomenology and a more specific application of de Certeau indicate that structure should be understood by its source. That source is comprised of actions of intentional agents, actually expressing the same primacy Giddens allows his subjects.

The problem with Giddens' rules and restrictions is that they are not well defined, nor does he provide the necessary criterion for importance, for which he has been criticised. Also, his systems of interaction do not take into account external influences, like other social classes or alien forces purposefully entering the social process. Despite the difference they must cause in the reproductive mechanisms of society, structuration renders invasive disruptions into knowledgeable accomplishments of social action (Cloke e.a. 1991).

At a later stage Giddens continued his structuration or systems theory with very specific interest in time and space. He recognised that social systems are not only structured by rules and resources, but also situated in time and space. His conceptualisation of this mainly followed adaptations and critiques on time-geography and concurs with human geographical interests. It introduced notions of localisation, regionalisation and temporalities into structuration. Nevertheless, Giddens' concepts never grew concrete enough to address empirical problems. Also, it is against this background that the continuations of geographers like Nigel Thrift and Allan Pred should be placed. Before moving on to Allan Pred's words proper, a short recapitulation of this development is given here.

Giddens realised that social analysis is both restricted and constituted by time and space, while social interaction is comprised of presences and absences in time-space. Time-space *distanciation* occurs when spatial presence is no longer required. Agency and structure thus should also be conceived in terms of distanciation, the extent to which social systems are integrated in time-space. Social integration and system integration are recognised as distinct levels of integration. Structuration theory therefore becomes concerned with how present social interaction is affected by social relations belonging to another time and/or space. Distanciation entails stretching social relations over time-space. Social integration (through routinisation of agents) and system integration (through variable time-space distancing) lead to societal integration. The two meet in modes of regionalisation which channel and are channelled by the time-space pathways of individuals and institutions. Regionalisation occurs on different scales and with different properties as an expression of the structuration of social conduct across time-space. In classifying terms of form, duration, span, and character, regionalisation elucidates how time-space routine and time-space distanciation come together. Regionalisation contextualises or captures human agency as situated events in time-space. The processes of routinisation and regionalisation were used to characterise particular places (Cloke e.a. 1991, Giddens 1984).

Opposed to some criticism, Giddens holds that micro and macro scale sociology are interconnected in structuration, basically referring to the interconnectivity of free agents and the analysis of structural constraints (Giddens 1984). In the same way, the human geographical adaptations and critiques offer this vantage point. Through structuration processes, incorporating interconnected elements, there is not necessarily a restriction to stretching them over time and space. In this sense Giddens' ontological position is repeated, although he specifically argued against evolutionary (as in stretching processes over time) applications. In contrast, this ontological possibility is submersibly maintained in Pred's theory. The geographers drawing on Giddens' concepts were not explicitly critical, but implicitly modified, stretched, and bent structuration so it would fit their empiricist discipline. Pred, however, explicitly incorporates a transformational material component in his take on structuration. This makes his place as historically contingent process specifically interesting for archaeological purposes also.

Place and the Social

Since Pred's theory building in *Place, Practice and Structure* is very comprehensively constructed, I chose to follow its structure to a large extent in the compendium offered below. However, for the full geographical account one is kindly redirected to his book, since the line of reasoning here follows the eventual archaeological objectives pursued in this study. As mentioned before, Pred's assertions are deeply embedded in the negotiation of the social theoretical position between agency and structure. In spite of Foucault's work on power and Bourdieu's work on practice being significant for the building of Pred's theory, he mainly aimed for an integration of structuration and time-geography. The relationships between structure and agency were conceptualised as systems in structuration, hence the alternative name systems theory. Through his interest in historical geographies, Pred rather sees systems as processes of becoming related to the constitution of a place. The sense of place had already become a focus in human geography and this was soon seconded by anthropology.

Yu-Fi Tuan is mainly responsible for the concern of a sense of place in geography. He was influenced by existential philosophies and Paul Vidal de la Blache (Tuan 1977). Such a concept of place does not follow the materially bound designation of places or areas according to the research on archaeological sites. Places and areas in both archaeology and geography were usually arbitrarily demarcated by material or geographical (landscape) features, comprising static spaces that are preferably measurable by means of visibility. People were thought to reside there, or at least consistently make use of such features over time. Tuan attributed the perception of space to the conceptualisation of place, supposing (invisible, immaterial) meaning to be ascribed to its composite features (idem). Consequently either consisting of elements, artefacts assemblages, or localisations, places developed into static scenes for human action (Pred 1986). Despite this still unsatisfactory concept of place in Vidal's and Tuan's notions, notably genre de vie and experiential place, part of Pred's basic principles are present.

Looking at place through the filter of action theory, such delimited spaces should be constituted by the concept of human action. They would be bound to the functioning and changing of society in time and space, by the practice of its inhabitants or users. In so doing, the definition of place would relate to many different scales, basically representing what spatially occurs through human activity, rather than physical localities in the landscape. It would no longer be comprised of the geographical features that are supposed to be conceived in a certain way by its inhabitants. Place becomes tied to a rich concept of the activities taking place instead of a reduction to ascribed meaning in static pre-given properties. (Cf. the New Cultural Geography of Cosgrove, Daniels, Gregory e.a. with its conceptualisation of landscape resembling this struggle with place. In New Cultural Geography eventually there is no true material landscape, but landscapes only defined by the people, history or culture behind it (Cosgrove 1985, Kolen 2005).) The taking place of place, or constant becoming of place, moves away from the static concepts previously adhering to it.

The interpretation of place has to be related to the society inhabiting it and its members' individual biographies. These are, as Pred would have it, "never in frozen states of being, but always and everywhere in the process of 'becoming'." (Pred 1986: 5) "The assemblages of buildings, land-use patterns and arteries of communication that constitute place as a visible scene cannot emerge fully formed out of nothingness and stop, grow rigid, indelibly etched in the once natural landscape." (idem: 6) This also implies that essentially there is no fixed limit to the geographical extent of place. Place can refer to villages or metropolises, industrial complexes and agricultural areas, but it is always a human product. Thus the conceptualisation of place is just as much the conceptualisation of area or region, either experienced or unexperienced as an entity by its inhabitants (idem).

At this stage archaeology is put in an equally problematic position for the reference of sites to areas and places as for the definition of community or society. One of the clearest positions on the designation of societies is Parsons' proposition. He combined the action theory of Weber with Durkheimian functionalism, utilising the notions of social action and social role (status). His theory of society delimited society by the functional relations between its components in a twin idea of social structure and social function. Within Weber's social action systems there were stable patterns due to the social roles of the actors performing in them. Normative rules emerged from the social system of social roles, from which actors deviated in various degrees. Only when there is sufficient consensus on the normative rules there is a social system. If interlocking social systems reach a point of social self-sufficiency, they compose a society. Such total social systems need to hold all social action necessary to persist internally (Campbell 1981). Therefore a society is only recognised at a scale large enough to incorporate all social actions necessary for sustainability. Archaeologically this is problematic to argue for, since social systems analysed in terms of social actions need to be materialised to end up as discernable datasets. These datasets will not show which external social relationships are necessary for them to be socially self-sufficient. Only certain types of data are so interpretable that they might shed light on relationships between areas containing social systems.

Parsons sought to explain the capacity of a society to sustain itself in terms of internal boundaries, which enable the exchanges necessary for persistence through Durkheimian functionality (idem). Not only archaeologically, but in general is a society thus reduced to a functional or material level. Positing primarily functional requirements for self-sufficiency results in a characterisation of society by scale rather than social aspects. Yet persisting social dynamics may already occur at small-scale geographical areas. In a geographically delimited area a system may already occur at a very small scale.

In contrast, Pred argues that the participating actors in the becoming of place cannot be viewed in isolated roles and instances. Rather, they are integrated human beings that are objects and subjects at once. Thus they are not reduced through status and functionalism. Thoughts, actions and experiences are all simultaneous, as well as their relation to their own material continuity in addition to the natural and human-made objects that are used in time-space specific practices. His agents are plural time-space specific process participants (Pred 1986). In Pred's concept of place the possibility of the interconnectivity of systems at both small and large scales is maintained. Nevertheless, due to the inevitable selective nature of our research, the social systems theorised at archaeological sites will more readily allow inference of a community than society which is tied to a space. The type of space under investigation will more easily pertain to villages or production areas than regions. Yet the theoretical open-endedness, both temporally and geographically, allows more thorough contextualisation in their interconnected processive environments. In addition, as said before, Pred incorporates a formative interaction with our physical surroundings. This interaction is not singular like Parsons' functionalism, but plural and action-specific instead. To fully grasp these glimpses into the theoretical implications of Pred's arguments, we need to first go back to assess its constitutive elements.

Place beyond Structuration

At the basis Pred theorises an interwoven relationship between the individual and society which leans heavily on the embrace of structuration in the social sciences. It fundamentally concerns the uninterrupted dialectic reproduction and transformation or modification of features like agency and structure, through the operation of (historical) structuration processes. In structuration, Pred holds, structure usually exists only as structural properties which express themselves through the operation of routine and non-routine daily practices, simultaneously generating, reproducing and transforming those structural properties of the social system (Pred 1986, cf. Giddens 1984). In order to clearly state his perspective on this, Pred provides us with his own definition of *social structure*. He stresses that social structure is comprised of generative rules and power relations which are already built into a specific historical and human geographical situation or social system. Rules and power do not only constrain and enable, but also emerge out of human agency and practice. Rules are learned and humanly produced, so contexts determine activity and behaviour in particular. Depending on their temporal and spatial extents, structuration processes may simultaneously occur on multiple (spatial) levels (Pred 1986).

Pred's definition of social structure already reveals his specific concern with the becoming of structure and the historic geographical situations it is contained in. He includes concepts of transformation and change, caused by agency and practice that generate such structures. Existing social and geographical situations are intrinsically connected to formative processes. This repeats a geographical or spatial link to the social that already rudimentarily had been made by the study of anthropological proxemics and the setting of territories (E. T. Hall 1959, 1968, 2006). Proxemics did not typically focus on the processive relations that generate territoriality, but similarly sought an explanation departing from the individual in a social context. While anthropology observed real time (micro level) actions with proxemics, Pred's structuration directly connects those to their enabling and restricting conditions, putting such activity in a temporally stretched historical situation in which they have become practices (macro level). The historic geographical situations containing structures tie the real (social) time to enlarged temporalities of abstract time. Both actions as events and existing social or geographical situations are indivisible parts of generative processes (cf. Ingold 1986, 2000 on taskscapes and temporalities, and the Annales School).

Pred recognises that the relational elements operating in structuration processes are posing a difficulty to social scientists because they are theorised in a conceptual manner that cannot be tested following the generally empiricist methodology of western science. These processive relational elements are neither visible nor measurable. However, most structurationists do appreciate that social activities and practices become concrete as time-space interactions. Thus the structuration of social systems occurs in time-space. Through recognising the time-space relational character of human interaction, some of the processive relations may become apparent by analysis on a socially totalising level. Structurationists arguing for this realisation of structuration processes in time-space specific practices are often criticised for not being able to identify exactly how these practices are simultaneously rooted in the past and a potential basis for future time-space situations. They do not demonstrate how the functioning and reproduction of social systems is connected to the time-space specific actions and biographies of individuals, nor to the time-space flow of structuration processes. As suggested, these problems can be placed in the context of dealings with social and subjective time as discussed in the first chapter. Pred contends that time-geography incorporates fundamentals that may overcome these problems of structuration theory (cf. Giddens 1984), especially by integrating his own adapted concepts of *path* and *project* that were originally introduced by Hägerstrand (Pred 1986).

In time-geography the concept of path is defined as the consecutive actions and events making up an individual's existence in time and space. Therefore the biography of an individual can be conceptualised as a continuous life-path through time-space over any duration scale, subject to various constraints. Natural phenomena, artefacts and other living creatures can be similarly conceptualised. The concept of project is defined as the series of tasks necessary to intentionally reach a goal. Each of these tasks is equal to a coupling of paths of two or more people or of one or more persons, and one or more resources or tangible inputs in time and space. Projects can be individual or institutional, the latter involving more people *participating* to achieve an end. The practice of time-geography has produced various types of time-space diagrams which depict the operation of paths and projects (idem). Pred's conceptualisation of participatory subjects can be connected to the phenomenological bi-implication (man is temporal and spatial). Ingold also employed a refined idea of participation in which he saw learning and acculturation as a participatory process. This implies that both the subject and the process (here the project he participates in) are mutually affected by participation (Ingold 2000).

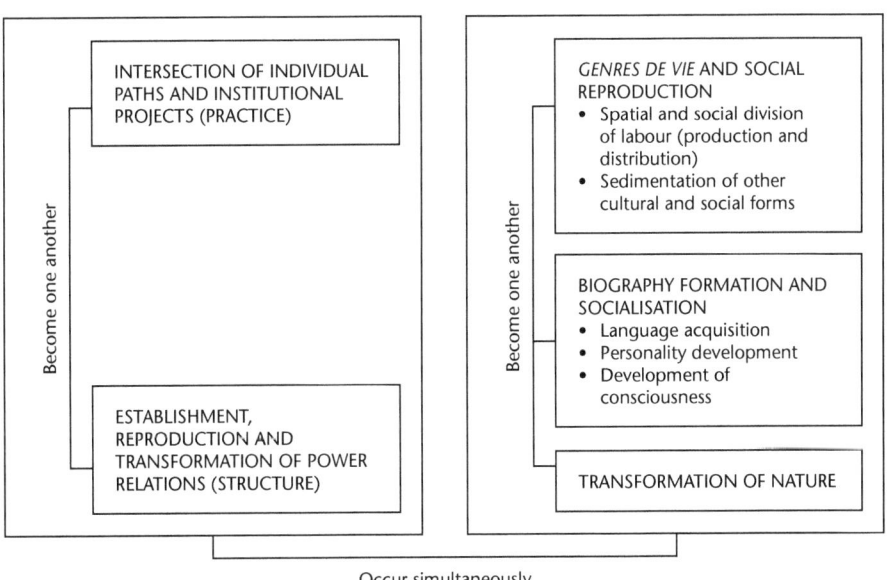

Table 1, reproduced after Pred 1986: 11

In order to enable the integration of paths and projects into structuration theory, Pred regards the assumption that each constitutive institution of society does not exist apart from the long or short term projects it generates as indispensable. Thus, because institutions are project bound, and projects require human participation, "the detailed situations and material continuity of interpenetrating structuration processes are perpetually spelled out by the intersection of particular individual paths with particular institutional projects occurring at specific temporal and spatial locations. [...] Then place as historically contingent process is inseparable from the everyday unfolding and interpenetration of structuration processes in place. Place is therefore synonymous with structuration [...] processes whereby the reproduction of social and cultural forms, the formation of biographies and the transformation of nature ceaselessly become one another. Simultaneously, place is synonymous with structuring processes whereby time-space specific activities and power relations ceaselessly become one another." (Pred 1986: 10-11) This complex theoretical foundation is summarised in Pred's comprehensive schema (table 1, note the use of genres de vie here), which in itself is a valuable contribution to both time-geography and structuration theory.

The visualisation has the effect that all simultaneous relationships of perpetual becoming are clearly visible at once, whereas descriptions would struggle to capture its full complexity. The (variable) components and (according) processes of the theoretical schema are largely universal for any settled place, but their interconnectedness differs according to their (unique) historical situations. The processes and properties involved are derived from structuration, while the paths and (institutional) projects originated in time-geography and are comprised of consecutive time-space specific activities and practices. The locally present time-space resources are constraining and enabling possible activities. He strongly stresses that these fundamentals of the theory should not be seen as particularist or empiricist, but rather inform research questions for inquiries into real situations in actual settled places and regions (cf. Weber's approach contrasting ideal types against actual situations) (idem). Pred's assertions are an aprioristic way of scientific reasoning, much like von Mises' Human Action.

Towards Place as Historically Contingent Process

Institutional projects dominate their participants in a certain place in two ways. Firstly by the demands they make over time-space resources, and therefore what is doable and knowable for the participants. Secondly, they affect the daily and life-paths of specific people, influencing individual conscious development. By being dominant they structure daily paths through the priority they have over other institutional and independent projects. For its participants simply applies that by committing to an institutional project they cannot participate in any other activity at the same time in another space, neither can they do anything before or after that project, which is out of the reach in travel time, nor participate in any project that (partially) concurs with that project. Institutional processes also account for the most important path-project intersections within local structuration processes. They are the outcome and source of the most significant local structural properties and social relations due to their position in those structuration processes. Oftentimes the dominant institutional projects are related to local material production and distribution, as necessary conditions for social and economic life. Nevertheless, not in all cultures do production and distribution particularly determine social life or history (Pred 1986).

Production and distribution projects are the result of the time-space flow of structuration processes at various scales. Also, they involve a spatial and social division of labour, which is usually coordinated by a local decision-maker or any authority figure holding some power relation to the locality of labour (usually place-specific). The decisions of such power holders are not entirely spontaneous, but again dependent on their own time-space specific biographies (life-paths). They are connected to temporal and spatial details of their own participation in local structuration processes. The social division of labour manifested in the spatial division of labour is deeply rooted in the historical specific groups within a place which have enacted the practice-social structure dialectic. The way project participants will carry out such projects depends on their practical knowledge, physical skill and reflexive reasoning upon participation in other institutional projects. Eventually applies that "locational decisions are transformed into spatial distributions, while spatial distributions are transformed into locational decisions." (Pred 1986: 14) In most modern or large scale economies, local production and distribution projects are connected to the dialectic of macro-level structuration processes. This macro-level can influence the local situations by making investments, which are also dependent on the biographies and past participation of decision-makers. Despite different scalar influences in the division of labour, it is always possible that there are inflexible limits to the amount of project participants an area can support. This basically means that time-space resources restrict or enlarge the number of livelihood positions within an area, which can cause either immigration or emigration (idem). Production and distribution projects, in addition to the limitations imposed by natural time-space resources resulting from biological needs, and despite their variability in all places, are a universal conditioning at their elementary level. Such dominant projects are a requirement for biological and place specific social sustainability.

The brain and body allow enormous variety in the activities possible within a place, causing clear distinctions even within the same culture or country. Still there are always just a few dominant (production and distribution) projects or deviant cultural and social forms found within any area. Inevitably, everyday practices are constrained and enabled by the perpetual dialectic between those practices and structural properties. There is a comparatively small selection of other activities carried out among place inhabitants, which can be regarded as a complex sedimentation of other structuration processes. These activities should not be seen as historically and culturally determined, or forced by the needs of a social system. There are many, yet marginal, ways in which such structuring processes constrain and enable particular cultural and social forms expressed in a place (idem).

The first important constraint consists of the temporal resources available to either individuals or collectives at a place over any duration of time. Once the time spent on physiologically inevitable activities and on dominant projects is subtracted, only a limited number of other types of social interaction or cultural practices that can be carried out by the population of a place remain. The demand on time-space resources of other activities results in either the modification or discarding of existing activities, or the making of more time-space resources if possible. The second constraint is language. Language is culturally arbitrary and constrains and enables the activities within a place, providing a foundation for path-project intersections or knowledge-dependent individual participation, i.e. it conditions the communication of activities. Also, it is the means for intention, affecting ideologies and social domination. Its acquisition is dependent on time-space specific project participations. "Thus [...] the limits of a population's language mean the limits of their place (or the projects they can define and participate in) at the same time as the limits of their place mean the limits of their language (or the words and other linguistic elements they can acquire)." (Pred 1986: 17) The constraints language holds over place are not static, nor is the constraint of place over language, because language is in the constant process of becoming, just like the individual (idem). One can imagine other ways of communicating besides language. The kinds of human communicative activity (or Primary Message Systems) developed by E. T. Hall for proxemics may be helpful here (E. T. Hall 1959). Perhaps it would be better to say that the constraint is on the ability to communicate activities rather than to narrow it down to language, which also opens up more place specific scenes for interaction.

The constraint of knowledge acquisition is dependent on the sedimented array of cultural or social practices which determine what knowledge is available and usable locally and nonlocally. Of course, that availability of knowledge also constrains and enables new practices here. 'Not knowing' will constrain cultural and social projects at a place. Simply put, doing and knowing are dialectically intertwined (Pred 1986). As will be discussed below, this is a rather narrow concept of knowledge. It could be enriched by incorporating the more thorough ideas contained in phenomenology. Pred goes on with the economically and socially constraining and enabling position that every resident fills in relation to resources. This allows or inhibits participation in associated projects besides production and distribution. Economic and social positions are dialectically intertwined with specific dominant institutional commitments, language capabilities and knowledge; in other words, with the other constraints (idem).

Having discussed all these types of constraints, Pred says that it would actually be more correct to speak of geographically and historically specific power relations between individuals, collectives and institutions when concerned with resource based constraints and enabling conditions. Conceptualised as structural power relations, they will still be significantly influenced by practice, whilst influencing practice itself (idem).

A further essential component shaping place as a historically contingent process is the formation of biographies. Through the level of individual biography formation the material continuity of structuration processes becomes most apparent. A person's biography is where things like the acquisition of language, development of personality, a possibly articulated ideology (ideology in Pred's sense appears personalised and idealised), and consciousness develop. "The formation of individual biographies bestows continuity upon structuration because in tracing out his or her unbroken path a person neither encounters separate institutional projects nor 'independently' undertakes projects outside of an institutional context in a disjointed or unconnected manner." (Pred 1986: 18-19) The formation of individual biographies operates and progresses through time-space from project to project by two dialectics (idem).

Firstly by the dialectic between internal mental activity and external physical action: no external physical action is possible without requiring internal mental activity first. Next, external action results in internal mental activity. Subsequently, internal mental activity is intricately based on past experience, knowledge acquired through previous project participation. "External physical action always involves confrontation with specific environmental elements, personal contacts, influences or information in general, as well as emotion that otherwise would not have been personally or collectively experienced. Yet, the addition of external physical actions to an individual's path requires internal mental activity: self-reflection, the recognition of meaningful object-embedded codes, the performance of practical reasoning, the formations of intentions or unconscious goals, the imaginative creation of new project possibilities or the making of choices between new or already existing project alternatives that do not violate basic time-space constraints." (Pred 1986: 19) This extensive remark includes many complex aspects of individual decision-making and experience. Yet it is important to note that Pred directs his attention mainly to a person's history (of time-space specific project participation), which serves as a basis for all consequential possibilities. Again it demonstrates a narrow conception of the human mind and experience in comparison to phenomenology, notably Schütz's constitutive concepts (Campbell 1981, Cloke e.a. 1991). Despite this lack of phenomenological advances, he definitely infers more than proxemics could merely on the basis of observation. Although there must be the same dialectic window between physicality and sociality, only the external activity can be observed. However, proxemics presupposes that territoriality occurs through a causal relationship between actors' actions, which requires some mental assessment of the previous resulting in distance setting (E. T. Hall 1968, 2006). Pred also continues his arguments into the realm of 'independent' personal projects, which satisfy the wants and needs that can be affected by cultural disposition and socialisation (Pred 1986).

The second dialectic operates between life-path and daily path, or long term commitment to institutional roles and daily project participation or practice. All possible decisions depend on the accumulation of institutional roles and objective long term opportunities for the individual. If one adopts a different role in one's daily path than normally in one's life-path, the experiences one has at a specific time and place will open the possibilities for other life-paths and otherwise enrich oneself to better (sub)consciously choose a possible new life-path. Depending on one's personal history and other's competition, one may or may not be able to access that path. Each contribution to a person's biography cannot be attributed idealistically to one's independent personality, but results from a unique accumulation of everyday experiences affected by already existing institutions (idem).

The meanings and attachments to a sense of place are derived from path-project intersections and their underlying power relations. The same goes for social structures that come about through commonly experienced projects. "Neither personality and consciousness nor social structure arise in isolation; they are instead elements of the same geographically and historically specific processes of becoming." (Pred 1986: 21) No matter the freedom and spontaneity of self-expression in space, personality, consciousness and social structure eventually result from biographical, place specific historical, and social contexts. They simultaneously contribute to the uninterrupted becoming of biography and place. As Pred states, paraphrasing George Herbert Mead: "the objective 'me' is a social product of a historically and space-specific context, while the subjective 'I' intentionally and unintentionally produces the specifics of history and place." (Pred 1986: 21) This distinction can be made because Pred usually seems to depart from the situation that certain social and spatial structures (composing the place in which a person operates) already exist. Pred finds the continuity of biography formation essential for the contingent structuration processes, because it perpetuates institutions. "The intergenerational perpetuation of institutions requires a flow of human conduct," (Pred 1986: 22) that is a succession of path-project intersections where individuals unintentionally reproduce conditions or the momentary events of institutions, whilst forming their own biographies. This is a very insightful and important remark, although the assumption that the reproduction is 'unintentional' in this phrase seems inappropriate, especially since Pred allows his individuals self-reflection. Pred concludes that individual socialisation or biography formation and institutional or social reproduction are interconnected in the process of structuration, each constantly becoming the other, inseparably (idem).

Several very important assertions have been raised so far. This approach to concept of place basically involves the development of an all-to-all principle (cf. Hillier 2007), since, through dialectic processes, all participating elements become each other. In other words, all elements become inseparably tied together. It features a conception of individuals that borders phenomenology, but does not quite capture all the opportunities and complexity offered by such philosophies. The notion that will be most significant in the continuation of Pred's theory and eventually archaeology is based on his principal of external physical action and the way it causes interaction with the individual's environment. On this basis the concept of the *transformation of nature* is developed.

"As place-specific biographies are formed through social reproduction and as place-specific social reproduction occurs through the formation of biographies, the physical environment is perpetually transformed.[...] The transformation of the physical world is inseparable from the becoming of place." (Pred 1986: 22) This notion is extremely important for disciplines such as geography and archaeology, as it directly indicates that the becoming of a place is inevitably connected to changes in the physical environment. Pred asserts space is changed through place-bound ideology, knowledge application and action. As demonstrated above, place-bound ideology is historically constructed through project participation and personal biographies of project participants and place inhabitants. This implies that the ideology of a place influencing the way the face of the earth is transformed, is in fact a common ground of the structuring social interactions. This would be similar to the determination of the culturally set distances observed by proxemics (E. T. Hall 1968, 2006).

Changing the natural environment is not confined to (production and distribution) projects which create the visible elements of place. However, the outer nature is transformed by any project which uses human-made or natural objects (these are also resources). This entails virtually any thinkable project, caused by their internal physical logic or, sometimes, arbitrary cultural conventions. In industrialised society this connection between objects and the transformation of nature is usually less apparent. Most of our modern objects are nonlocally produced at other distinct times, rather than the time and/or place of use. The biological condition of the human body makes individual's part of nature also. Through the becoming of the place individuals inhabit, they are not only internally shaped by their experiences, but also physically transform as their paths from birth to death unwind (Pred 1986). Moreover, one can add here that through the principals of embodiment and paths (man is spatial and temporal), the physicality of the body enables physical interaction with their environment. This may essentially render the human body a type of object used for and conditioning project practices.

The dialectic processes which cause natural and corporeal transformation operate between path-convergence and path-divergence, or creation and destruction, or presence and absence, all of which deeply rooted in time-geography. People's paths are unable to move in isolation through personal and institutional projects, without touching, crossing or connecting with the time-space paths of objects (cf. the biographies of things) or natural features. No activity can be realised through the convergence of other paths (the creation of a couple), without necessitating the divergence of previous couples (i.e. destructing a prior presence, creating an absence). Vice versa, no activity terminates through path-divergence without necessitating new path-convergence, creating a new couple. The sequence that follows from this is also realised in individual movements through time-space constituting social conduct, organisation and interaction, which therefore always contributes to the transformation of nature in variable degrees. This dialectic demonstrates that all human-shaped landscape elements and objects have biographies of their own that constitute the perpetual transformation of nature depending on the history of the projects, or convergences and divergences, they were involved in. While nature is transformed, implying the structuring of local space and the attribution of new meaning, the physical development of the environment of a place is enabled and constrained by the scarcity of space, the limited packing capacity of spatial units and the time investments required for moving from site to site. Simply put, the transformation of nature is conditioned by the constraining and enabling capacity of time-space resources (idem).

Initiating new projects is only possible within the framework of transformed nature and the dominant institutional demands. The transformation of nature can only truly be understood with the identification of such important power relations. These power relations do not only specifically originate in the local social structure, relations between individuals, collectives and institutions, but are produced insofar any resource control or rules and norms of behaviour locally are playing a role. Power relations dictate to a large extent the way nature is transformed. They are said to hold the individual, society and nature together in time-space specific practices that constitute the becoming of place (idem).

Pred's dealing with power relations is strongly influenced by Foucault's philosophies of power and discipline from the perspective of the subject. In the context of place, power relations are the capacity to permit or restrict in any way time-space specific couplings of paths of possible participants into projects. They control who does what, where and when, and in terms of projects they control their content or component tasks. Also they may prevent potential participants from partaking in a project (idem).

The multiple levels of processes exercising power could be compared with Foucault's panoptism, which is an ensemble of mechanisms used in all procedures of power and takes it away from a narrow governmental conceptualisation (Foucault 1980). More specifically, Pred draws on Foucault's assertion on structuring the field of action of others. For Foucault exercising power is a way in which actions modify others, therefore power only exists when put into action (Foucault 1982). Here one should note the emphasis on action and performance, which is of paramount importance for all processes discussed up to this point. Foucault continues that power can be the result of prior or permanent consent, but by nature is not the manifestation of consensus. A relationship of power is a mode of action that does not act directly on others, but acts upon their actions. Its opposition is passivity and as an objective it must try to minimise resistance. Power functions on the basis of two principals: it presupposes an acting other, and a relationship of power will open a plethora of responses. It can result in either violence, consent or both (idem).

Freedom is a subsumed aspect in this characterisation of power. Power as a mode of action upon actions of others assumes the subjects to be free and can only extend insofar they are free. Power and freedom's refusal to submit, therefore cannot be separated. Foucault suggests that rather than analysing power relations from the standpoint of institutions (who have great influence in constructing them), we should analyse institutions from the standpoint of power relations. The fundament of the relationship is to be found outside the institution. To live in society is to live in such a way that action upon other actions is ongoing. The study of power in society is not the study of institutions, but is rooted in the system of social networks (idem). "The individual is not a pre-given entity which is seized on by the exercise of power. The individual, with his identity and characteristics, is the product of a relation of power exercised over bodies, multiplicities, movements, desires, forces." (Foucault 1980: 74) In contrast, one could add the assertions of Michel de Certeau, who holds that in participation, individuals are maximising their resistance to the system. What is observed as a conformation to power restraints is instead a form of resistance exercised in order to better cope with the system, rather than sustaining power's effectiveness (de Certeau 1988).

With this brief background on power in mind, we return to Pred's theory building. Just as in the other aspects of place-bound structuring processes, power relations are founded, reproduced and transformed by practice. This process of power relations depends on three factors. First, it is achieved by the establishment and implementation of rules necessary for project execution. Second, power relations rest on the accumulation of meaning-filled (either materially or socially recognised) resources of institution as a whole or past and present power wielders. Thirdly, it depends on the predisposition of power subjects from other projects accepting the rules and definitions of the new project, inseparable from their own biography formation. These three factors are all dependent on previous path-project intersections or time-space specific practices. In other words: the development of the biographies of those power wielders. It is this practical knowledge that will translate into institutional rules. Any type of competition expressed in activities or life-path – daily-path dialectics contributes to the securing of material and other resources for individuals with certain backgrounds rather than others. Also, the same dialectic structuration process holds here. When the factors depend on previous time-space specific practices, these practices in turn are connected to previous power relations, thus practice and social structure become one another (Pred 1986).

This also indicates that power relations are not a static concept, but prone to change. Local transformation of institutional power usually appears as a response to local or more general conflicts, resulting from any economic, political or social competition, or incompatibility of time-space resources or institutional priority claims. Otherwise they may be caused by consequential crisis situations of institutional projects that are contrary to the aims of their underlying rules and definitions. Naturally, more 'structural disjunctures' can be imagined, like consensus or external disruption to certain extents related to conflict or contradiction. However, as Pred emphasises: "power relations cannot be transformed without either the modification of already employed project definitions and rules, or the total elimination of a project and its associated content definition and rules." (Pred 1986: 28) Eventually it should be recognised that in the becoming of place the most apparent effect of power relations lies in directly or indirectly controlling what people do, say, know, and think. Simply put, when individuals participate in one project they cannot, due to their indivisibility, know directly what happened elsewhere at the same time, nor know anything that lies beyond their time-space reach associated with their participation. Through the use of unarticulated rules and habitual language in institutional projects, previous social activities with the resources facilitating those projects are obscured. Therefore, depending on whether this occurs and individuals are unaware of it, individuals will think of detailed project situations as natural rather than created by humans. Such imagined project situations thus become part of a natural, locally present ideology. This could make power subjects blind to the ultimate power being exercised over them, even when the material markers of this are recognised. This usually includes the absorption of the ideology of power wielders in regard to what is out of the ordinary, or forbidden to take place and become part of an individual's path (cf. Foucault 1980). Following Pred it must be emphasised that the historically specific way power relations contribute to the becoming of place is contingent upon the interpenetration of structuration processes of a different scope, or the extent to which local institutions and their symbol systems are based on nonlocal control and transactions (idem).

What about the Built Environment?

Pred does not explicitly mention the built environment as a principal element of his theory. Nevertheless, one does not need much imagination to see how the built environment may directly result from the concept of transforming nature, performed through individually and socially based structuration processes. Put in a concise formulation, the constant local transformation of nature through the structuration processes conditioned by time-space constraints, influenced by personal and more general histories or biographies and by the power exercised in time-space possibilities, the built environment could be conceptualised as a materialisation of Pred's place. Yet this should not be applied to the ideational significance of construction. Phenomenologically everything is constructed (cf. Ingold 2000), which includes the sense of nature or the natural environment. Hence, there is no primordial nature. In contrast, the built environment only begins at the moment constructed ideas are materialised by building activities, i.e. physical alteration of what was already there by human production. In the case of the natural environment, even though ideas about it might have been constructed before, its physicality literally should not have been touched by human beings earlier. Materialisation is physical modification or transformation, shaping the ideationally constructed world through action.

Given the details of Pred's theory, in a way now we have arrived at the other side. The other side of the spatial material record, that is. Through his time-space adaptation of structuration theory, Pred indirectly provides us a strong argumentation for individuals as builders. The conditioned processes that allow them to build are infused with individual and social meaning. In most cases the way such meaning is present in the built environment prior had to be assumed rather than reasoned. Pred himself has argued to use his theory as a model and that is precisely the value it holds. In a similar manner to the aprioristic theorising of an ideal society as von Mises did in *Human Action*, Pred's processes of becoming give us an aprioristic vantage point to understand how the natural environment becomes constructed along the performance of all individual actions generating processes.

Another important element in Pred's theory is his disguised distinction between biological aspects and social and cultural aspects. Next to the obvious requirements for the persistence or survival of each individual and the local social structure he is part of, there are the dominant projects. As Pred convincingly argues, these projects leave only a small portion of time-space resources that can be used detached from essential requirements. Place mainly comprises certain dominant projects in historically specific circumstances. The freedom that is left is still historically specific, but can deviate more freely from biological and sociological requirements. That indicates that the meaning of a place is composed of a way to deal with biology, a certain sociological ordering of the necessary projects and more individualised projects that cannot be seen separately from them.

Yet there are some aspects that remain undiscussed, overtly general or poorly conceptualised in Pred's theory of place as historically contingent process. Recapitulating, the most significant assertions made are those that focus around the generation of processes, placing the individual at their beginning. Taking into account the concept of embodiment, the spatial experience of human beings here becomes extended, not only towards understanding the world around them (as in phenomenology), but quite directly into its creation. Still, it is precisely in this concept of the individual and his decision-making (understanding through acquisition of knowledge and constructing meaning) that Pred remains vague. The freedom of his individuals is rather limited, because they are envisioned to step into already existing structured situations. Decision-making is primarily conceptualised at the level of power structures in certain institutional projects, not at the level of the individual choosing to participate or not. Although they may reflect upon their own biographies, the way they acquire knowledge of existing situations and eventually construct them is better understood through the phenomenological subject of Schütz (Campbell 1981, cf. chapter one). Individuals are strongly tied to their history (consisting of experiences contrasted against the stock of knowledge), but memory is flawed and acquisition of knowledge is selective. All this influences the way individuals arrive at an action, but is only partially present in Pred's work.

However, in the employment of action interacting with the environment, the processes conceptualised by Pred allow analysis to step away from individual particularism. Maintaining the way subjects understand the (social and natural) world through self-reference, external physical actions following internal mental activity, inherently are interacting with the environment. (Nevertheless, for this process of ideational understanding we are forced to refer to von Mises and phenomenology, since Pred affords a rather careless use of the term 'nature'.) Moreover, all elements in that environment are constantly part of dialectic structuration processes in which all become one another. The meaning of individual actions is thus understood by self-reference, but no longer to be seen in isolation. This allows for scale amplification. Archaeology, affected and limited by flawed datasets, destruction and looking at things past rather than current, is restricted to inquire upon an enlarged scale of human action. In Pred's theory the subject can be sustained as an analytical unit, placed in all-encompassing processes of becoming. All spatial units are the result of individual actions, and thus refer to underlying individual meaning, yet no spatial unit can be seen isolated from other actions and spatialities. Moreover, they will always be captured in ongoing processes.

The more individuals participate in common (building) projects, the more their experience becomes alike and the values of their biographies, leading to the decision to participate, are intertwined in the meaning buildings have. Over time, such structuration processes become consolidated in a built environment, constructed by individual actions, infused with the many individual meanings of the people performing building activities in the same project (cf. Ingold's taskscapes). This is very similar to the way local social structures come about. Even when forced to build, the choice is theirs, which is not to say that exercising power does not complicate matters. That is, the personal biographies of the ones directly or indirectly exercising the power is infused in the project also. It is for such power relations that some final comments are made.

Power relations are not the main concern here, however it is important to stress that power is not only contained in the centralised power wielders. Time-space constraints and associated decision-making are already kinds of power relations. These are prone to change as they are elements in various structuration processes. This change is not just the result of individual biographies influencing individual actions. Change may occur through imagining new projects (from original thought) or the consistent resistance against the structures and power relations locally present. Michel de Certeau (1988) argues that such resistance is present in each human action, but it may be confused with succumbed conformation of the subject. Once, through the ordinal valuation of consequences preceding the choice of action (von Mises 1998), a subject would imagine it better to explicitly act out his resistance, this could lead to a completely different situation. Alternatively, the consequence of withstanding conformist action or choosing an alternative may have envisioned better results, thus causing abstinence of action as meaningful action. For others this is an (social) environmental change, which affects their decision-making and may alter subsequent actions. Hence, through the individual decision to act in a certain way, change is coming.

In change, the micro level of individual biographies and actions becomes directly tied to a macro level tendency as well. If Pred's theory is taken as describing mainly developmental processes, his structurational adaptation can be put in an evolutionary perspective. The interconnected processes allow for seemingly unrestricted stretching over time and space. In the light of power relations and the consolidation of (social) structures in a place, change becomes the most meaningful variable in those processes. This all can be unfolded over an informing conceptual background in which place "is a process whereby the reproduction of social and cultural forms, the formation of biographies and the transformation of nature ceaselessly become one another. Simultaneously, it is a process whereby time-space specific path-project intersections and power relations continuously become one another." (Pred 1986: 31) Place has become an analytical background which informs fundamental formative processes through which empirical inquiries into specifics get meaning. Our attention is drawn to the way such elements are part of an interconnected social totality. It cannot be empirically replicated in its entirety, but it will help give inferential direction.

In order to move from here to the archaeological record and the associated interpretive aim of this study, we need to part with the socially totalising generalities assessed in Pred's processes of becoming to ideas that can also direct our focus of analysis towards specific features present in spatial datasets. Eventually those features are the building blocks upon which interpretational analysis can be based. With his theoretical outline, Pred's theory allows us the comfort of looking at the production of such datasets, the formative processes of which demonstrate how social meaning becomes invested in the built environment. Having reassessed our position and been given inferential reason, how can we get meaning out of its constitutive elements and, even more challenging, the flawed reflection of this we are confronted with in archaeology?

There are two main directions of interest that are pursued in the following. On the one hand I focus on the socially meaningful position of spatial specifics in the dataset. On the other there is the larger spatial issue of distinguishing archaeological (culture) areas. Shifting to present contributions to social geographical theory based on human action, two recent theses will be explored for their potential to further distinguish spatial features of socially inferential value. Neither one has particularly tried to arrive at better understanding of (physical) specifics, rather they are refinements of the above that significantly continue the equal junction of time and space in processes. An attempt will be made to connect their theoretical details to features of spatial datasets that might enable opportunities for theoretical treatment of materially specific issues in a socially meaningful way without losing touch with the greater scale of things.

Chapter 4 ***Theorising towards Datasets***

From Regionalisation and Culture Areas

After the level of detail involved in the discussion of Allan Pred's concept of place as historically contingent process, we ought to take a step back and make an attempt to posit it in accordance to the larger context of extended place as a region. Pred himself already emphasised that his theory is non-empiricist and socially totalising. Moreover, he asserted that in his approach to place, place could just as easily appeal to regions and larger areas. This makes place a widely applicable notion. Stretching his reasoning temporally, the contingent process of becoming is a generative process. Due to its nature a continuous generative process can be placed in an evolutionary perspective, which I argue for as a possible adaptation of Pred's ideas. So, despite the obvious possibility for the use in what Pred has alternatively called the micro-geographies of everyday life (Pred 1984, Low and Lawrence 2006), one could take his theory to inform assertions at both temporally and spatially a much larger scale. As we started from the archaeological inquiry to the development of society and its most readily available material expression in space, through Pred we may abstractly follow the development of society alongside the development of a spatial dataset. The value of such generalising aprioristic theory in disciplines which created a primary concern with empirical objectives has been recognised by scholars like Ludwig von Mises (1998, see chapter one). In the context of regions and their connection to the social, German geographer Benno Werlen takes a similar vantage point, inverting previous disciplinary analysis from space. In light of the questions we set out with and the analytical informing of archaeological inquiries, this study still seeks to create a comparable inversion (opposing discursive influences from Rapoport and space syntax) for archaeological discourse concerned with space that traditionally starts from the material record.

Although I mentioned Benno Werlen's assertion before, to appreciate it fully this chapter initially is built around some of his principal ideas. His geographical interest is mainly concerned with the construction of regions in the everyday. As with all theories mentioned so far, the foundation of his notions departs from acting man, but his analytical whereabouts are specifically situated in macro level considerations. The larger scale of his perspective connects a generative micro scale to issues of bordering, which makes such processive thought applicable to culture areas as well. He recognises that many social processes involve a spatial component with notable examples in bordering and regionalisation processes. To understand these processes and socio-spatial relations more clearly, Werlen says we should not focus on the spatial aspects of social conditions, but on the activities which constitute those socio-spatial relations, shifting from a geography of space to action, or from a geography of things to subjects. He stretches interest from describing regions to the regionalising implications of activities.

This is not the same as regional analysis, but stresses everyday regionalisations (Werlen 2005, Werlen 1998). He directly argues to change geographical discourse "from spatial description to subjective understanding and a social explanation of everyday geography-making." (Werlen 2005: 47) This is evidently comparable to Pred's concept of the becoming of place and the micro-geographies of everyday life. But Werlen specialises in regional geography, whereas Pred remains at the interface of social and historical geography, merely hinting at its potential for regions.

Werlen develops his theoretical stance upon the geographical progress from spatial science to behaviourist and behavioural geographies in order to arrive at a human geography founded on the objectives of Husserl's and Schütz's phenomenology. As generally described in chapter one, the behavioural approach gave way to phenomenology refinement, so Werlen's action theoretical approach should not be confused with its predecessors. Phenomenology made human geography focus on cognitive processes and the subjective understanding of people's behaviour. This is how phenomenology enables the addressing of a sense (meaning) of space that works towards an experiential place. Werlen holds that in order to analyse society in its spatial dimensions specifically, society should not be based on a theory of behaviour without incorporating a thorough action theory (Werlen 1998). By including a temporal element in the analysis of social space and landscape, Tim Ingold (1986) also stressed that a theory of action should be at the basis of evolutionary thinking. His take on time was heavily influenced by phenomenology as well, especially by the fundamental views of Husserl, McTaggart (see Lucas 2005) and Merleau-Ponty, who held that the passage of time was affected by people themselves through their embodiment. Merleau-Ponty distinguished the passage of time from the time entailed in human action itself. For both Ingold and Werlen the person is the participant of time and space, a direct consequence of the conception of subjects as temporal and spatial (see Ingold 2000). They intend to connect a micro scale to a macro scale and choose their perspective from the subject following phenomenological ideas, despite the fact they pursue different research goals. To add to this, Edward Hall similarly emphasised the individual (positioning the concept as axiomatic to territoriality), indicating how proxemics could contribute to the greater understanding of society. He referred to a quote from zoologist Konrad Lorenz: "Unless one understands the elements of a complete system as a whole, one cannot understand them at all." (E. T. Hall 1968: 105) This assertion could also be placed in the relational necessity of an action theory for behaviour expressed by Benno Werlen. With phenomenology subjectivity, in terms of orientating reflection and intention, is included in human action. Through personal intention the conscious decisions of other members of society are understood. Action is, as it were, the atom of the social universe, because it constitutes society as primary meaningful reality. With a better understanding of decision-making, social geography can pursue bigger and more fruitful research objectives. Such an action theoretical approach immediately results in the theoretical deviation of geography from the objectifying practices of spatial science (Werlen 1998).

On the basis of the phenomenological 'world binding' of subjects, Werlen posits the establishment, transformation or abolishment of spatial demarcations as a means of everyday activities, instead of their aim. The processes of bordering spaces are the direct result of world binding. Previous geographical discourse would itself constitute regions and spatial relations as entities by classification, acting as an observatory science (cf. culture history and social evolution). With the assertions above, Werlen counters this practice. Also he opposes starting geographical analysis from spatial phenomena to come to social phenomena, but rather works the other way around (Werlen 2005). This concurs with notions derived from postcolonial and globalisation theories. Postcolonialism challenges the ways in which colonial power and western knowledge become taken for granted by questioning its knowledge categories and assumptions (Blunt and Wills 2000). Similarly, Werlen argues against the bordered spaces imposed by observatory scientific discourse. Such discourse is what mainly defined the principal culture areas in archaeology. This has produced persistent faulty labels, visualisations and maps that are still in use and still direct research objectives. Maps, however, should never be taken as unmediated representations of the world, but rather are socially, politically or scientifically constructed meaningful realities (idem). This observation also goes for spatial science and many types of statistical 'truths' being produced in academia in general. In archaeology the culture areas were often delimited by geographical and linguistic observations instead of the social aspects employed by the society supposed to inhabit those areas. Recently the notions of transnationalism and internationalism, much due to technological advancement, have opened other lines of culturally comparative inquiry (Cheah 2003). This should be no reason to refrain from using those insights in inquiries on the past. Societies and sociality would not have taken into account academically assumed borders before these technological advancements, which allows cultural comparative analysis in archaeology to follow very similar lines of reasoning like those recent studies influenced by transnationalism and internationalism. As Cheah rightfully asks: "If comparison has always presupposed geographical or cultural areas that are a priori distinct and to be compared, how must the grounds of comparison be re-envisioned?" (idem: 2)

Turning comparative and classificatory discourse around, Cheah addresses Benedict Anderson's concept of *imagined communities* (Cheah 2003, Anderson 2006). This idea can be transferred to the academic practices that Werlen and I oppose. Many culture areas are imagined on the basis of natural environmental, linguistic or stylistic associations not established by research on the society residing there. Anderson's notions are of particular interest because if nations are imagined, thus making them inadequate bases for interpretive discourse (idem), the culture area defined by associational imposition similarly will be no good as analytical units. Cheah goes on to discuss Anderson's main arguments against the demarcation of areas: the fictional nature of maps, the investment of meaning resulting from imperial intervention and the way virtually all countries in economy and politics now are part of, influenced by, and impact global processes (Cheah 2003). In archaeology the debate on communities is still ongoing, exemplified by as many adversaries as advocates for both the imagined community and natural (statically bounded) community. This means an explicit dealing with the topic is still much in demand (Isbell 2000). Our concern here does not lie with deconstructing areas per se, but the way areas or regions are constructed in everyday practice, actually partaking of the agenda including Anderson's imagined communities. It is important to note that the areas currently dividing space are usually of scientifically imposed nature. Werlen's action theoretical approach to regionalisation may inform us how areas occur in a socially meaningful way. His phrase 'space is an element of action, action is not an element of space' has implications for the study of regionalisation and bordering processes and the wider concept of everyday geography-making (Werlen 2005).

Towards Regionalisation and Culture Areas

Shifting from space to action in geography involves both an ontological necessity and a methodological implication. Werlen holds that answers to questions on the ontology of research objects and on the analytical methodologies are relevant to one another (Werlen 2005). In contrast, the distinction of the geographical discipline on the basis of 'space' is also applicable to 'material remains' as the demarcation of archaeology. Similar to the way the status of space needs to be explained in its social ontological context in order to integrate such concept in geographical research, the same needs to be done for material remains so they truly may become the concern of archaeological investigation. This also means that in formulating a theory for such research objectives one should take into account the possibility to formulate a methodology in which the researchable objects refer to both theory and methodology. In geography space has been conceptualised as a cause for social action, as a container of the social world, and as objectified socio-cultural meaning, Werlen summarises. These have in common that space is a pre-given to human action, making the analysis of space a certain kind of socio-cultural research. This relates to a superficial view of the socio-cultural, obstructing deeper understanding of writing and speech, pertaining to an outside view in the material sense. Differing social ontologies imply or express specific modes of geography-making. What is understood by the 'spatial' depends on (changes along) specific *modi operandi* of geography-making underlying the various social ontologies (e.g. the change from a traditional modus operandi of geography-making to geography-making in the condition of local everyday life) (idem).

While the traditional modus operandi of geography involves the restraint of social interactions tied to materiality, the modus operandi of the aforementioned globalisation process opens new opportunities dissolving this restraint (idem). As also suggested in Giddens' distanciation, actors no longer need to be physically present (Giddens 1984). Moreover, Pred's higher level of locally influential power relations aims at the same (Pred 1986). Caused by the connection between the materiality of the agents' bodies and meaning, Werlen continues his account of geographical development. Traditionally, geographical analysis focused on the study of spaces and its causal power. Despite the empirical evidence, it confused (communicative) constellations and their description as spatial categories. This is how all actions received an objectified pre-given space. It legitimised the containerisation of societies and regionalisation of cultures. Still the focus remained on space and explanatory distance (agents' reach of control in their activities) as the object of study. The latest shift to geographical constellations and social ontologies demonstrates that a space-centred view of everyday life cannot be sufficient. The relation between meaning and matter was never fixed, but a changing representation of socio-cultural practices (Werlen 2005). Meaning might also include symbolism which does not coincide with the underlying rationality of its construction. This permits a direct transference on architectural objects, whose history often discloses how their meanings have undergone revisions and reinterpretations (after Werlen: Azaryahu 2001). A relation to Pred's (1984, 1986) historical contingent processes is easily made, and one can imagine the meaning searched for by Rapoport (1982) being part of it, though departing from a spatial viewpoint. Globalisation and technological developments enabled agents, emphasising local conditions and the separation of meaning, body, and material. "Under these conditions the 'real', non-substantial ontology of space becomes obvious." (Werlen 2005: 49) There is no room for continuing the view that space exists in some independent way as a container or something that (substantially) existed before social practices (idem) (cf. Ingold 2000 on the environment). So while phenomenology, postcolonialism and globalisation made Werlen realise this, social practices as the producers of space were just as much part and parcel of the past. Interpretation of space needs to take this into account.

For archaeology obtains, just as much as for geography, that for a more effective methodology of everyday geography-making we should leave the paradigmatic positioning of space (or materiality) at the centre of inquiry. Spatial problems become problems of certain types of action, involving bodies and things, corporeality, materiality and physicality. In filling in an "'action-centred perspective', and discard space as a starting point in itself, we focus on the embodied subject, the corporeality of the actor, in the context of specific subjective, sociocultural and material conditions. We adopt then a perspective that emphasises subjective agency as the driving source of action and hence of social change, while it also stresses that conditions of the social and material world 'shape' social actions, while the latter produce and reproduce social and physical conditions." (Werlen 2005: 49-50) Such processes are found in Pred's theory as well, although less coercively conceptualised. Werlen's view inhibits to see space as constituting the social world. However, because the subject is embodied, physical conditions remain relevant to actions, but actions cannot exclusively be explained by them. Therefore, in order to explain actions and interactions, physical conditions need to be systematically accounted for. Objectified space (the physical environment of the body) cannot determine actions or the actors' frame of reference. Space as a frame of reference is itself the product of actions. Space and materiality do not have a meaning in themselves, but only get meaning through interpretations in the course of interactions, in the context of intentions and social and subjective conditions (idem).

Most notions of space in geography are articulations of geomorphology, which theoretically claim a kind of independent status related to actions. This allows the notion that society finds its expression in space and that geographical space can be understood as a footprint of past social processes. The ambivalence in this research objective, despite social theoretical efforts in theorising space, consists of taking some form of representation of objects as what can be theorised. It feeds the rather eclectic debate on space, using constellations of elements of general social theories. Werlen calls Lefebvre's (1991) 'production of space' to the attention and contends that Lefebvre has not reckoned with the basic assumptions of his theory. One should be aware that Lefebvre's space is very conceptual and historical; it is not materialistically real and does not exist independently of social praxis. This means that the significance of spatialities for social practices can only be comprehended through understanding objects as constitutive elements of social action (Werlen 2005). The assumptions Werlen writes about can again be found mainly in phenomenological literature. Comparable sources of inspiration, such as those Ingold uses for his positioning of man in time and space, are paramount here, like Heidegger's existentialism and Merleau-Ponty's view on the intrinsically temporal and spatial subject (Ingold 2000). Also, the phenomenological bi-implication and the mutual perception of embodiment and the (spatial) environment appear implicitly present. The eclectic use of social theoretical space in geography allowed a position in which society is theoretically conceptualised and space is not. Therefore space needs to be conceptualised on the basis of an agency-centred analysis of society (Werlen 2005).

Since archaeology demands to analyse the socio-cultural aspects of human activities starting from a conception of space, it acts exactly the same as social geography. Therefore we can follow Werlen in saying that any adequate conception of space requires reference to the basic principles of applied social theory. Practice is not independent from space, nor does space exist independently. "'Space' does not exist outside a specific theoretical framework." (Werlen 2005: 51) Such construction of internal truth allows for plural conceptions and consequent outcomes in the treatment of space. Much like the conceptual relativism of Hillary Putnam's (1981) *internal realism*. In developing a methodology for spatial inference in archaeology we need to avoid the pitfalls demonstrated by geography. The methodological problem is that objectified space is allowed an explanatory function in actions and social structure without making its causal role and potential explicit. Also, space then usually incorporates several complementing concepts of spaces (cf. Lefebvre 1991), which complicates coherent critiques (Werlen 2005).

Werlen names Wolfgang Zierhofer as one of the few exceptions, taking space as the frame of reference of actors (idem). To an extent together with Andreas Koch, to whom we will turn later in this chapter, Benno Werlen and Wolfgang Zierhofer form a movement that goes against 'space fetishism' in geography. Researchers like Zierhofer and Werlen assert that any semiotics of space is meaningless because it could be replaced by location, distance, area, movement, etc. (Koch 2005). Zierhofer conceptualises *speech acts* as the framework for the analysis of general interactions. Zierhofer explains that the sociological tradition of action theories regards the social as constituted by interactions, and the concept of 'action' represents certain activities as intentionally structured events. An activity is an action if it follows a purpose and strives to achieve a goal. The aim is to change a situation by using a particular means to an end. Actions are intentionally structured; however, they produce intended and unintended consequences (Zierhofer 2002). Zierhofer's consistent concept of action concurs with Ludwig von Mises' (1998) human action. Actions cannot become transcendental with nonessentialist perspectives, so actions are seen as a rhetorical scheme applied by actors, making them mutually accessible or comprehensible. Zierhofer, however, sees a further distinction. He argues a difference in actions we can perform alone and actions which, like the speech act, require a partner. The latter depend on a sender and receiver to be successful. The reaction is a necessary aspect of the effectiveness of the intention of the speech act. Intention includes other actions, shaping units of interaction, thus having social activity as a result. Actions aimed at ourselves are a different class of actions than those whose success depends on other actors. Within speech acts there is a virtually unlimited diversity of actions, and new ones are also being developed (Zierhofer 2002).

Despite the usefulness of language pragmatics to illuminate such differentiation, I see little progressive advantage in it. The differentiation does not take into account the self-referential understanding subjects have of others and objects. Even in actions which we perform alone and for which we do not need a receiver, the consequence can still be(come) social. The changes it might cause in the environment are invested with human meaning, e.g. in the transformation of nature, the act being witnessed or the observed consequence. This is possible in either intended or unintended cases. In executing an action, the interaction with the non-social environment contributes to the understanding of ourselves. Such experiential knowledge will be carried into subsequent social interactions, which directly involve self-referential identification applied to our prospective partners (cf. Schütz's stock of knowledge (Campbell 1981, Eberle 1984). Because all actions (including interaction) are meaningfully understood through self-referential processes, all actions one has performed alone (or all witnessed actions of others and consequences of actions performed alone by others) will reflect in social interaction. Even though one might distinguish certain types of actions based on their characteristics, being human action performed in a world with others, actions never truly stand alone. Perceiving and acting in a world infused with the results of human actions performed (alone) by others, however potentially restricted, is indirect social interaction. Just as with language, actions with social intentions are intelligible through the assumption that they can be understood self-referentially. This process is still operating in observing the performance or consequence of isolated actions. In a way, one could argue that, without this possibility, archaeology as a social science has no ground.

Zierhofer does acknowledge that society is not built up out of speech acts alone. He holds that they structure the metabolism of society, though the biophysical work cannot be done with words. As geography deals with meaning and matter, action theory needs to take both speech acts and ordinary acts into account. Zierhofer adds to this the important notion that communication depends on physical mediators. Thus interaction (communication) provides the potential to organise or structure physical conditions, but not vice versa. Language enables everything to be represented and the argumentation that follows may regulate relevant activities. "We may regard language as a metalevel (or a reflexive sphere) of social reality, and we may take speech acts as the key to the structuration of society." (Zierhofer 2002: 1362)

Zierhofer argues his speech acts go beyond intersubjectivity. Giddens, phenomenology, and Werlen take intersubjectivity as binding the actions of different actors together. In their view the coordination of actions is the outcome of compatible subjective perspectives. It is not communication, but the experiences of interaction that structures meaning and social order (Zierhofer 2002, Werlen 1998, 2005, Giddens 1984). The characteristic of speech acts which by their intention include other actions, is for Zierhofer the only true binding of actions, hence social. Language is just a means for meaning to be transported from one person to the other, rather than generating meaning and coordinating interaction reflexively. Speech acts are binding in their demand of specific reactions. They are successful if that reaction is performed, based on a mutual acceptable interpretation of actions and an agreement on the intention of the action. Thus speech acts are constitutive of social order and, in being mediated by a physical means, this has a direct spatial implication. For Zierhofer, intersubjectivity is merely a precondition for social order, the container of meaning versus the meaning of coordination (Zierhofer 2002).

Although I appreciate the intentional binding force of speech acts, to me the differentiation passes on the insight that the performance of communication depends on the subjectivity of the sender in its formulation of the message, and on the subjectivity of the receiver to decode that message. In fact, as stated before, the understanding force of language is also an assumption on the basis of intersubjectivity. What appears as order is no less chaotic than the indirect communication established by the performance of other acts. Yet through the repetitive participation in collective projects tied to specific time-space situations and the experienced communication involved there, the biographies of subjects grow more alike and language becomes more consistently consolidated (cf. time-geography and Allan Pred). Still, both the learning and utilising processes employed are no less subjective at any stage. It seems that Zierhofer's assertions render subjects as much back into passivity as poststructuralism did before, despite incorporating reflexivity. It leans too much on assumptions of an uncorrupted (non-individual) passive learning process, like Schütz's common stock of knowledge or e.g. Parsons normative total social system. In this latter example, an actor should make conforming choices of action for the required consensus to arrive at and continue a society (Cambell 1981). The common or normative order could very well be documented and formalised, or alternatively be observed by scientists, yet knowledge and consequent meaningful actions are individually subjective. Conceptualising a requirement of such adopted passivity by subjects reduces the genuineness of choice or freedom to the success of social order. Approaches of von Mises, aspects of Schütz, other phenomenologists, Werlen and even Weber, find this rather positivistic reduction unnecessary.

The strengths of Zierhofer are present in his departure from space as a centrefold point of departure for geographical inference and his thorough conceptualisation of speech acts as a type by language pragmatics, which might help certain specialised analytical foci. Nevertheless, the hazard of many linguistic theory approaches is that they tend to prioritise language pragmatics as a paramount way of conducting analysis, not allowing lateral analytical alternatives. All is referred to as language. Speech acts are not a significantly stronger binding force, because equal transportation of meaning does not exist. The intersubjective binding in social life is also a foundation for the social inferential capacity of archaeological discourse, in which I find that interpretation is possible on the basis of researchers studying their own species, although they have been distanced in time-space. Despite the appealing alternative, I tend to agree with the continuance of intersubjectivism as contained in Werlen's approach.

Now continuing on Werlen's perspective, I will proceed with two misunderstandings in the geographical conceptualisation of space. Based on the initial Cartesian confusion of extension and corporeality, the spatial representation of physical-material entities has been confused with the idea of physical material space. Secondly, the significance of the spatial ordering of physical-material things as social practices has been blended with the idea of the spatial existence of socio-cultural facts. To avoid the consequences of tying social phenomena to physical conditions, the ontological status of space needs explication, spaces require differentiation from other spaces, and, accumulatively, space should be placed in the context of different meaningful social performances. "If 'space' were equal to extensive materiality [Descartes] it would have the status of an object." (Werlen 2005: 52) (Some related Cartesian arguments referring to agency can be found in another form in Zierhofer 2002.) This implies that it is possible to distinguish the totality of all material objects and space as an object beyond that totality, which is not the case. But for Werlen, space is neither a material object, nor a consistent theoretical object. Instead, it is a formal concept: a frame of reference for the physical components of actions and the enabling and disabling physical conditions of performing actions. It is formal because it is detached from topical aspects of objects; it is 'classificatory' in the sense that it describes an order of objects related to their dimensions. In this way, space can be used as manifold different significations in everyday actions, the meaning of which can only be comprehended in its relation to human activity and its bodily carrier. As such space becomes twofold, it both precedes and constitutes action and it is a socio-cultural construction, forming a tool for the structural relation between meaning and matter and a starting point for the social theorisation of space (Werlen 2005). The issues regarding space as an object or totality have also been addressed by philosophic sociologist Niklas Luhmann (Arnoldi 2001), in which autopoietic theory plays a large role. Some attention will be given to this later on, after having discussed some systemic notions of Koch (2005).

Werlen does appreciate Lefebvre's advancement in discerning three different kinds of connections between practice and space in social theoretical conceptualisation: first, spatial practice and perceived space; second, representation of space and conceived space; third, space of representation and lived space (Werlen 2005, Lefebvre 1991). However, Werlen stresses it is important to recognise that the social and spatial are compatible on the ontological and conceptual level. Without this notion, analysis will focus on theoretical reasoning instead of the production of everyday social practices under research. It means that action alone has the capacity to constitute social reality, and that space is only a conceptual medium of action. Depending on the character of action, space is conceptualised accordingly, which necessitates that its categorical dimensions require compatibility with actions' social frame of reference (Werlen 2005). Such compatibility also needs to be accepted for archaeology, since without it one can still focus on space divorced from sociality, which confuses the social research agenda. Separating them would not take into account the intrinsic human condition of man's spatiality and temporality, which inhibits an analytical focus on subjects. The conceptual compatibility makes the everyday social processes inseparable from the production of physical expressions (spatialities). Nevertheless, one should take care not to confuse those theoretical aspects which adhere to the subjects under study with a preoccupation of those that pertain to scientific discourse (idem), as both interests so permeate the arguments made above.

The dimensional differences of formal and classificatory interpretations of space result in according differences in the (action-based) constitution of space (expressing the interpretation). This constitution depends on the specific interconnections between the body and other situational material aspects. In table 2, Werlen recognises a three-way division:

Action	Formal Dimension	Classificatory Dimension	Examples
Rational	Metric	Classificatory	Land market (capitalist)
	Absolute	Calculation	Location theory
Normative	Metric	Classificatory-relational	Territorial state
	Body-centred	Normative	Back-/front-region
		Prescriptive	
Communicative	Body-centred	Relational	Regional/national identity
		Signification	Regional symbols

Table 2, reproduced after Werlen 2005: 53 (Cf. Koch 2005 stages of translation or structural linkages below)

Rationality, or geometry, is comparable to Weber's demystification of the world: cartographic representations, capitalist land markets and clocked labour markets are all made possible through formalised spaces. On the normative level, territorialisations are produced (cf. E. T. Hall's (1968, 2006) proxemics). The formal aspect is the geometric appropriation of extensions in a body-centred way. It is classificatory in the relation between body and material context, and the normative prescription ('where one can do what', by authoritative control also). These regulate prescriptive regionalisation by the in- and exclusion of actors and utilities. The communicative orientation of action is also body-centred, in which the body is linked to experience (stock of knowledge) and the meaningful and operational basis of subjective action. The meaning of objects depends on the knowledge and use we have for them. Symbolic meaning is thus constituted by the relation between knowledge and intention, the key feature of everyday geography-making (Werlen 2005). I would like to stress that in the appropriation of personal territorialities, experience is an important aspect also. The experience of the body in relation to its physical environment and to other actors as physical presences, is expressed in distances (that can be metrically represented) following upon actions affected by that experience. In contrast to Zierhofer's (2002) likely preoccupation with the common stock of knowledge, Werlen here talks of an experiential stock of knowledge that includes freedom of choice, selection and interpretation contained in its personal acquisition.

With Werlen's approach the praxis of everyday geography-making and its ontological and conceptual connection to space becomes the focus, with special attention to the use of spatial concepts in those everyday processes. It follows the tendency of human geography to concentrate on everyday practices, but according to Werlen most perspectives do not make consequential implications explicit (e.g. geographers such as Pred, Gregory, Thrift). Regional geography has become more sophisticated, yet the point of departure is still the region, rather than the making of and constitutive processes of regionalisation. Traditionally, regionalisation is the geographical praxis of spatial classification, while at the everyday level it is the process of appropriation and delimitation. Physical markers are no more than material representations of symbolic delimitation of normative standards. Material conditions are not social constraints: only social norms are. Therefore spatialities neither cause nor are reasons for action in and of themselves. They exist socially to the extent that they are used as a means for categorisation and symbolic representation of actions. Regionalisation is firstly a (non-spatially delimited) selective appropriation of the world. Werlen's everyday regionalisation is a form and a process of world-binding, the praxis of allocative appropriation of material objects and subjects. Regionalisation is a praxis of re-embedment, to bring the world (in spatio-temporal references) under the control of actors. This control enables the direction of subjects' own action or others' possessive practices. It is therefore "not the production of 'spaces' that is of central interest, but the use of spatial and temporal dimensions (frames of reference) for different types of appropriation." (Werlen 2005: 56)

For Werlen many of these notions have direct implications for the way we see the modern day world. Although our concern does not primarily lie with current situations, almost all of the above can be applied quite directly in archaeological discourse. It lets us appreciate the plural character of any social bordering process which has led to material expressions. It demands that we reassess our maps and the scientifically drawn borders. Due to regionalisation, the region is no longer a static concept, but rather continually changing and being produced. Like communal memberships, spatial expressions might adhere to various appropriating processes. Moreover, regions can actually overlap to various degrees. From this could follow that a culture area, if physically expressed, should pertain to many social processes of regionalisation that accumulatively coincide in some sort of material border. Unlike our highly institutionalised world now, ancient regionalisation would have emphasised other social meanings in their bordering processes. The full array of social processes at work is indicative for this. Nevertheless, Werlen also notices, following de Certeau (1988), that in practicing everyday geographies few totalising traditional regions can be sustained. The differentiation of functional, political and cultural dimensions obstructs a totalising common ground in their according spatial frameworks (Werlen 2005). With this theory we have arrived at a stage where we can reformulate our totalising and imposing analysis of space and turn it around (discursive inversion) for a nuanced, plural derivative of subjects' social appropriation and subsequent actions. Although Werlen's scheme shows some empirically distinguishable examples and forces us to approach spatialities on the basis of certain characteristics (dimensions), his theory remains general and spatially broad. It could serve as a theoretical background for big questions involving the development of culture areas on the basis of societal bordering processes.

Even though the equivalence of time and space remains strong in Werlen's contributions, for a treatment of temporalities it offers limited potential, equally so for an inferential methodology for built environments. This is probably caused by a persistent constructivist tendency in his thought. The main advantage is the processive view of everyday regionalisation, which acts in a scale exceeding manner. Now we need a further step towards spatial specifics and features in which we can find the materialisation of formal and classificatory dimensions to analyse on that basis. Although a concrete selection of spatialities or a list of features (cf. Rapoport 1982) will be hard to assemble, I think the systems theoretical interest of Andreas Koch (2005) implicitly allows more specific orientation onto certain aspects of the built environment. In contrast to Werlen, his proposals appear to have a direct relation with the mutuality of the phenomenological bi-implication. This may enforce an application to archaeological remains of built environments.

Constructing Detailed Systemisation

Before moving properly to Koch's theory, it is important to stress the difference in his point of departure from Werlen's and Zierhofer's. Koch does not agree with the socially totalising tendency in the regarding of space. He holds that the social is just as much spatially constructed as the spatial is socially constructed. Probably reacting against the particularism that may flow out of phenomenological approaches, Koch remarks that the idea that everything is socially constructed is as contra-productive as environmental determinism (Koch 2005). At first glance I would agree, since the physical world enters our perception and thus influences experience, choices and actions that follow from that moment onwards. In the light of this thought, motivated by the bi-implication of humans and their life-world, Koch's thesis that the relationship between the social construction of spatiality and the spatial construction of sociality is mutually dependent and symmetrical seems appealing (cf. Lefebvre 1991). Koch finds himself inspired by the idea of Luhmann's *autopoietic systems, systems theory* and *Actor Network Theory* (ANT). In this he stresses that systems theory replaces the social causation of space with a reciprocal relationship of sociality and spatiality, and most system theoretical approaches have failed to deal with space adequately (idem). However, he deviates from my own conviction, also present in Werlen (2005), in giving equal primacy to space as to the social. Even though Werlen and others appreciate the influence of space on our being, this influence also would only become significant through individual and social terms of experience. Koch thus sets out to equalise the positions of space and the social. Despite our nuanced disagreements, he proposes interesting ideas which may work as an incitement to guide our attention to certain features in spatial datasets which can be researched with archaeology's empirical methods.

It should also be noted that while I posited Koch initially alongside Werlen and Zierhofer, he manoeuvres himself in a position as mediator. He does not belong in the camp of 'space fetishists', but goes on with the notion that even 'space exorcists' allow a dash of meaning in their concepts of space (in terms of substance) (Koch 2005). In other words, he is prepared to take the bitter with the sweet. Through this he approaches phenomenology more than the rather constructivist viewpoints of Werlen and Zierhofer. Against that background we can evaluate his efforts. In a comparative manner, he does to notions of space in geography what Ingold does to the notion of landscape in anthropology and archaeology. Ingold suggests that a focus on the temporality of landscape "might enable us to move beyond the sterile opposition between the naturalistic view of the landscape as a neutral, external backdrop to human activities, and the culturalistic that every landscape is a particular cognitive or symbolic ordering of space." (Ingold 2000: 189) Koch holds that container space has been too easily associated with material notions of world, truth or reality, while in fact it should be seen as a representation. He proposes to replace the link of container space as the non-material background with stages of translation. World as a deliberate abstract (metaphysical) notion, including both the spatial construction of society and the social construction of space, remains unreachable in each stage. All elements remain independent (autonomous) and mutually constitutive for a representation of world. Translations imply that equating the (representative) image and the signified is inappropriate for the social process of construction, but at the same time suggest that translations are necessary to make the relationship of spatial and social constructions balanced. "All semiotics of space is embedded in a complementary circle of references to model the 'world'." (Koch 2005: 6) Container space is as real as any notion (or abstract specification) of space. From this follows that in the spatial concept of world, space achieves a dynamic and independent quality. The rules defining spatiality are different from those defining sociality. For the emergence of a hybrid world, independent properties are unavoidable. With the assumption of monist ontological differences of perception, no hybrid communities or spatialities can be imagined. To create a symmetry, Koch proposes the use of systems theory in considering spatial systems as systems in the environment of social systems (idem).

The problem with these basic assumptions is that container space is a social notion also, since such background is a perceptual conceptualisation. That means that the *spatial systems* in the (background) environment must also be a social construction. Translations are unnecessary, since through embodiment human beings are directly spatial, just as they are directly temporal through their physiological finality. Their actions as interactions are directly environmental, be they social or physical, and inherently temporal as well. All is understood through processes of perception, often following and directed by action. Hence there is no need for symmetry as such. Keeping this in mind, a conceptualisation of spatial systems in the perceptual environment of social systems could still be fruitful.

Koch's idea of a system is heavily influenced by Niklas Luhmann, who in the work of Husserl and Parsons found his inspiration, in spite of their usually opposed positions. For him the social system is an organic system capable of self-regulation, much the same as for Parsons, but he took the notion of *autopoiesis* from biology (the production and reproduction of single cells by themselves) and continued it into the social system. Autopoiesis, or auto self-creation, here incorporates a fundamental dialectic between function and structure. However, Luhmann moved away from Parsons's structural functionalism in proposing that social systems are systems of communication, not action. This symbolic communication is observing or meaning-constituting in social systems, a way of making sense of the environment (Arnoldi 2001). Such primacy of communication also allows for the narrow focus on speech acts as proposed by Zierhofer (2002), but in Koch's theory it becomes of importance by claiming that spaces can communicate (Koch 2005). Luhmann chose a middle ground between the externally placed action of Parsons and the internally placed action of phenomenological experience. Actions are external to actors, because actors are reduced to psychic systems, while actions are concerned with the social system as making sense (observing) in phenomenological terms. Luhmann does not study how actions are coordinated into action systems, nor does he describe social order through actors' experiences. He focuses on meaning-processing social systems, driven by a communicative process of making sense, i.e. how a system makes the environment intelligible (Arnoldi 2001).

Luhmann applied autopoiesis as a notion of constitution from within itself, to the context of social systems linked to self-reference. Following Husserl, he asserts that the Boolean logic of differentiation is the most basic operation through which anything meaningful or intelligible manifests itself for the observer. This logic is concerned with distinctions (e.g. this vs. the other, inside vs. outside), which are the foundation of observing and meaning. Therefore, things become intelligible. Something is distinct from something else. Such distinction-forms are centrefold to Luhmann's meaning. In communication it is exactly this meaning (distinction, so nothing else) that is communicated. This meaning constitution is not concerned with opposites (cf. structuralism), but contains its own outside (self-reference). In the event of distinction, the system itself is constituted also, hence autopoiesis. Observation constitutes the observer. So the distinction is twofold: it distinguishes this from the other, and the observer (system) from its environment (Arnoldi 2001). The strength of the autopoietic approach is the focus it lays on the constitutive process of a system within itself. In biology it has been criticised for running the risk of dichotomising positions to an all-or-nothing principal of life forms (Bruun and Langlais 2003). Yet in Luhmann's sense, autopoietic systems differentiate themselves from others, and that is also clearly recognisable in Koch's use of it.

Bruun and Langlais, however, try to establish a biological basis for action theory, without referring to socio-biology or evolutionary psychology. They also work towards Actor Network Theory as a plausible reasoning behind this. The biological theory of autopoiesis could provide a better theoretical foundation for teleological explanations of action. For this they discern two levels of agency. The first is best understood in terms of an autopoietic process of standardised environmental distinctions. Through structural coupling (a history of recurrent interaction leading to structural congruence) of two or more systems, certain features of the environment are constitutive for the autopoietic process, hence the introduction of the term *constitutive environments*. This makes the identification of the boundaries of an autopoietic system problematic, because some parts of the environment are internal to the system, i.e. the system is partially extended into the environment. Bruun and Langlais' second level of agency is understood in terms of action like perception, intention, purpose, motive and identity. Actions are context-dependent, so they have their constitutive contexts, which is not the same as constitutive environments. This division of agency should not be seen as the traditional opposition of body and mind, but as an alternative in which there is interaction between the levels. Understanding the (sub-personal) first level helps understand the personal second level. "Body and action are interdependent in ways that are significant for understanding the conditions under which human action is performed. We suggest that action is embodied in the sense that certain physiological processes are internal in relation to it, they play a constitutive role for its performance." (Bruun and Langlais 2003: 45) One should appreciate that Bruun and Langlais' research agenda is rather different from Koch's, but this bit of background may serve as a bridge from the biological and philosophical autopoiesis to Koch's socio-spatial systems.

To explain his sense of system, Koch refers to Luhmann's family as a social system and home as a spatial system (Koch 2005). This makes the abstract theory more tangible, hence the concise reproduction here. In Luhmann's social system, family is of the interaction type which consists of communication (not individuals). The relation of system elements results from linking communications. Communication is a synthesis of information, message and understanding. Individuals are linked to the communication system (family) by psychic and organic systems, systems in their environment serving as addresses to execute communication. It is an operationally closed system (having a boundary with the outside), which is autopoietic. The communication system depends on the joining of communication. When communication is not performed, the system temporarily ceases to exist. Family should not be regarded as just a social system, because it exists beyond that definition. For Luhmann it also entails the psychic (Arnoldi 2001) and for Koch the spatial systems. These are necessary for the emergence and existence of the autopoietic social system (cf. constitutive environments Bruun and Langlais 2003) (Koch 2005). Most families are spatially tied to a home, the spatial system. The required communication in spatial systems has a different contextual meaning. It is a synthesis of geometry, topology, and fuzziness. The reference of spatial systems is congruency, while for social systems it is meaning. According to the formal structure of systems theory, Koch makes an analogy of spatial and social systems.

The spatial system is made up of the congruent interplay of geometry, topology and fuzziness as opposed to material components. Without structural (material) connections, a spatial system cannot emerge and exist, thus the spatial system is tied to the structural system, called architectural system. It is insufficient to regard the spatial system as such, since it needs the architectural system to determine its congruency, but also the structural connections to the social system (family) enables knowledge that cannot be acquired without it (cf. here too the constitutive environment of Bruun and Langlais (2003) is at play). The separate perspective is sectoral, while combining them is hybrid (which is Koch's goal). Systems theory replaces causal thinking with a reciprocal relationship between sociality and spatiality. Koch holds that Luhmann's attempt to integrate space in systems theory has been unconvincing (Koch 2005).

The idea of mutuality contained in the reciprocal relationships composing a hybrid system originates quite directly in Actor Network Theory (ANT). ANT emerged from the sociological study of sciences and technology, but is most famous for insisting on the agency of non-human elements. It was primarily founded by the thought of Bruno Latour and Michel Callon, who criticised sociology for only including humans in their view of networks. Although it has been criticised itself for a poor analysis of the actor, the strength is that it takes into account the indeterminacy of the actor. The refusal of defining actors aprioristically and the introduction of non-humans freed social science from the individualist versus holist dichotomy. However, this notion makes the actor virtually indiscernible and thus ANT was said to be relativist and non-theoretical (Callon 1997). Their concept of all-encompassing action and the inclusion of non-human agency presented a break in social scientific conduct. It renders objects and actors effectively into an array of (action-based) relations, resulting from a network (Law 2000). A good application of ANT can be found in the discussion of a market by Michel Callon (1997), and a critical examination of notions resulting from it are presented in *Actor Network Theories and After* by Law and Hassard (1999). ANT differs from the post-structuralism of Foucault in offering multiple possibilities for social material ordering (Law 2000). Latour's ideas of giving non-human objects agency are slowly entering archaeological practices and theories as well. Nevertheless, many post-processualists misunderstood such writing in claiming that Latour gives objects a mystical power, while essentially the agency they have is invested by humans through long processes of negotiation with the environment (Martin 2005).

Towards Built Environments

Koch envisions his use of translational stages connected to ANT, which helps to enable an understanding of relationships between social and spatial systems as a hybrid phenomenon. Here ANT provides a conceptual approach to space that will be interpreted with systems theory. This results in mutually dependent relationships between the social construction of spatiality and spatial construction of sociality, especially the call for focus on the socio-spatial hybrid settings. A characteristic of the connections between spatial systems and social systems is a persisting autonomy of the social and the spatial. As Koch argues, for the generation of hybrid phenomena both separation and translation are needed in an oscillating process (Koch 2005). ANT and Koch's translations are similar in that they both have a complementary circle of references. ANT is a semiotics (cf. Foucault's semiotics and materiality) exploring relationality, which it extends beyond language towards all entities (cf. Luhmann in Arnoldi 2001, Law 2000, Zierhofer 2002). Applying the notion of spatiality to entities, the consequence could be that the significance of space is both spatially relational and necessarily material. Relational entails the extension of the borders of spatial entities to the relational constitutive dimension (cf. constitutive environments), while material simply refers to the fact that all entities (objects, spatialities) are irreducible to a mental state (cf. Luhmann external action based on the psychic system of the actor). He states that a semiotics of materiality is essential for entities, information and objects in general, not only for space (Koch 2005). Following Law's (2000) assertions Koch writes: "Objects emerge through their relations to other objects and create in this way manifold networks of different hierarchies and/or heterarchies. […] All entities of observation are materially heterogeneous." (Koch 2005: 8) Relations are not only social, they are also spatial, because we live and act in a materially heterogeneous world. This enforces that neither objects, nor spaces and communities can be reduced to something one-dimensional. Hybridity presupposes that the components remain distinguishable (idem).

Increasing the complexity of his theory, Koch moves onto the spatial implication of objects, which consists of their performance and inhabitation of conditions of (im)possibility. In this he still follows assertions made by Law. Spatialities and objects which perform those conditions are unconformable because they are other to one another. This produces another complementary circle of references. "Because objects are able to perform spatial conditions, objects and spaces remain mutually independent and this is expressed in multiple forms. [Topology specifies the fact that relations between objects are not universal.] Not everything is connected to everything. Different objects, spaces and communities are related to one another to different degrees and through different qualities, they are 'partially connected'. In this sense hybridity will be concrete." (idem: 8) The world is not singular, nor is it multiple; it is fractional, comprised of complex and partially connected spaces and/or times. Again I can refer to Tim Ingold, who lets the temporality of activities incorporated in the taskscape dissolve in the notion of landscape, in so doing empowering the researcher to recover the temporality of the landscape itself (Ingold 2000). This essentially produces a simultaneous, twofold understanding which could be compared to hybridity.

With this in place the notion of performativity in ANT gains importance. If objects perform spatial conditions there must be nodes with a minimum of congruency and compatibility, so that entities achieve their form as a consequence of the relations in which they are located. Vice versa, spaces also perform an object's conditions of (im)possibility. There are four complementary types of performance: 1) Objects perform spatial conditions of (im)possibility, 2) objects perform objects' conditions of (im)possibility, 3) spaces perform objects' conditions of (im)possibility, 4) spaces perform spatial conditions of (im)possibility. These can be illustrated by: 1) the geometry and topology of rooms in a house, influenced by the objects inhabiting them (function depends on size and e.g. furniture), 2) it is impossible to erect a house where a house already exists, 3) the geometry and relative location to adjacent plots influence the size shape and function of a house, 4) the relationship of the rooms in a house influence its spatial function (e.g. bedroom upstairs, kitchen downstairs). Since these are mutually dependent, overlap occurs. Performativity covers the mutual relationship of process and state, of temporality and stability, or performing and being performed, spacing and timing, space in process and space as process (Koch 2005). Koch demonstrates that a social geographical concept of space approached from ANT supports the idea that space is made, but differs from other proposals (cf. Werlen 1998, 2005, Zierhofer 2002) in its dealing with the material aspect and the process of mutuality. Creating spatiality affects objects and the social (Koch 2005).

My personal concern lies with a doubt regarding the use of performativity. The theory could suffice to say that objects and space quite simply condition (im)possibilities relationally. They are their own continual medium through their material existence. If performativity is conceptualised as an agency of objects and spaces, they must be of human or social making. Much like Koch says, space is made, so any agency concerned with (im)possibilities is made, or, better put, meaningfully constructed. This would follow Latour's original notion that the agency of objects is humanly invested (Martin 2005).

Now we arrive at Koch's notion of hybridity proper, firstly discussing hybrid spatialities. There are four ANT spaces in which the emergence, (temporal) consolidation and disappearance of hybrid spatialities could be understood. 1) Regions with clustered objects and a circumscribed boundary around the clusters (immutable immobile). 2) Networks where distance is a functional relation between elements, and difference is a relational variety (immutable mobile). These topologies are known to social theory. 3) If neither boundaries nor relations mark spatial differences, social space can behave like a fluid, hence *fluid space* (mutable mobile). 4) *Fire space*: with fluid constancy, movement is more significant than stasis. Changes and resistance that are part of fluid and fire space could be compared to the respective distinctions of de Certeau's (1988) tactics and strategy, the first being continuous while the latter is forcefully detached from its former environment. The difference between fluid constancy and fire constancy entails that fluidity is gradual and fire is produced abruptly in discontinuous movements, i.e. interventions or events affecting topological relations (e.g. changing the network), despite their internal immutability (mutable immobile). These four types of space have specific relations to each other, based on their fundamental object-space relationship. This ANT typifying of space makes it neither exclusively substantial (a definition), nor an exclusive social construction. Spatiality influences the construction of objects and communities. The relational (topology) is dominant, but the geometrical dimension is not excluded. Constituting hybrid spatialities follows a pattern of mutuality in terms of (im)mutability and (im)mobility (Koch 2005).

In my opinion, one should understand (im)mutability in terms of physically constructed spaces. These can be built land divisions, e.g. borders, houses, rooms or infrastructure. Since they are built they have a definite materialised shape which in itself cannot physically change. The (im)mobile refers to degrees of movement that can in a way also be equalled with temporality. Although I would say that the abruptness of a moment or movement in fire space is still temporal, one may imagine how this differs from the internal temporal rhythms and tempos of fluid space. Comparatively, de Certeau's strategy is less affected by temporality, while his tactics are not tied to specific space yet are constant in time. Movement in networks then consists of the actions establishing their relations tied to fixed nodes (physically constructed spaces), but maintaining a temporality in their performance. In Koch's terms: as long as people commute between two constructed spaces a topological relationship exists, forming a network (immutable mobile) (idem).

It seems that here the ANT approach does take into account geometry and materiality. Still, all of this geometry and materiality is socially constructed: the immutable nodes of the mobile network, the rooms, being its immutable immobiles as well as their spatial temporal changes, be they abrupt or gradual. The substantiality of space is thus a social conception. Moreover, one could doubt all the negating forms (immobility and immutability), since they can still change by either fire or fluid space. Again, this is not surprising when one takes into account the constitutive environments in autopoiesis, making the definition of each system in itself dependable on outlying features.

As argued for performativity before, topology is not really action, but rather remains conditioning (i.e. physical (im)possibilities). It makes the relations between objects, spaces and communities not universal. Yet hybridity is not so much composed of two separated elementary values: instead it consists of qualitatively differing degrees. Depending on constitutive features and materiality the essentially social relations between objects are mediated, affecting their character in aspects as relative distances. Nevertheless, hybridity in its entirety remains individual and, through perception and actions, consequentially social. This reinstates the notion that one cannot be detached from one's own constitution of the world. Furthermore, the geometrical dimension is itself a social construction. Disregarding the philosophical and physics debates that can be held on this topic, whether or not substantiality exists without human beings inhabiting the world, this remains either way a possibility caught in a social conception. On the other hand, the strength of this proposed hybridity is exactly the strength of ANT in the first place. It allows materiality to be part of social networks and, in the relations it analyses, it allows materiality to be tied to and constructed by sociality. Therefore space cannot be regarded as separate from the social, and is intrinsically a variable temporal affair in the continuity of its constitution. The characterisation of spaces is now tied to their relations, making it impossible to interpret isolated spaces. Placing ANT spaces in the perspective of the theoretical ideas discussed before, it concretises and specifies the bi-implication of phenomenology and through its materiality may offer potential for empirical archaeology.

Hybridity, however, is not limited to spaces, but also enters the social realm in communities, described mainly by the notion of *framed interaction*. With this concept, the dichotomy of materiality and sociality can be surmounted. Just like spatialities need to be created, the social is not readily present. Sociality is also created, "continuously emerges, temporarily exists and disappears again. This process takes place repeatedly at different places. In order for social communities to be able to exist, processes of localisation are necessary. For this, the spatial context provides the frame, it is a condition of possibility to generate interactions. Processes of globalisation are necessary so that social communities are able to persist. Again, there are material components that are necessary to make it possible, at least potentially, to link interactions. Framed interactions are, therefore, not static and not persistent, they will be created recursively through interactions and within interactions. Herewith, they provide a spatio-temporal structuring which allows for contexts within and between interactions." (Koch 2005: 10) This assertion follows Latour's concepts of local and global (which is thus not geographical), complex and complicated.

In a complex situation all variables occur simultaneously, whereas in a complicated situation variables occur successively. Globalisation refers to successive interactions allowing complicated interactions to be connected. The frame of interaction can be seen as a locality, like for instance a room in a house. Although Allan Pred does not use the concept of frame, the time-space specific localities in which he situates the (inter)actions of any project appear to pertain to a similar idea (Pred 1986). Following an individual's path, the individual moves from frame to frame (e.g. room to room, etc.) which all contextualise individuals. These frames are localisations in a spatial system (e.g. a home or building). Enabled by these frames, interaction creates sociality between individuals, but only for the time interaction is performed or individuals move. Globalisation of frames is the arrangement of where and when individuals interact. These successive contexts become integrated in a large-scale interrelation (freely after Koch 2005).

Having constituted hybrid communities in this way, allowing a community (like a family) to persist, in my view, still requires a social sense of belonging and the material continuity of the consequences of actions (like physical constructions), which is primarily based on a phenomenological reasoning. It involves processes of learning through perception and experience kept in memory. Communities are maintained by the individuals who are its members, guarding knowledge about them, recognising meaning invested consequences of actions both materially and socially. Conceptualising a community as a family in terms of a project, a family literally is a project that is upheld in that specific form as its goal, until someone deliberately breaks with social codes or dies. Specifically, the necessarily spatially framed interactions make that sociality constitutes the community and that a community is spatial too. Koch supports an intricate explication for social interaction being intrinsically spatial. Through localising and globalising processes both the spatial and the social become blurred (idem).

In his last step Koch makes an attempt at applying systems theory to spatialities. He feels that the simultaneity of independence of the social and spatial (unconformable to one another) and hybridity (partial connections to one another) can be conceptualised. He gives the following definition of his system approach: "A spatial system is an autopoietic, self-referential system that constitutes itself by being different from an environment. The constitution is based on congruency. Its elements are communications." (Koch 2005: 11) Expressed in autopoiesis, Bruun and Langlais (2003) already provided us with a great tool for the simultaneous independence and hybridity presented by the constitutive environment. A system of spatialities is tied to a system of socialities on the basis of a few constitutive features contained in the other system, which is part of its environment. The same goes the other way around. In spite of their partial dependence they remain unconformable, thus independently recognisable. The conditioning of (im)possibilities operates in the spatial and objects, distinguishing spatialities and objects as properties of the system. Here spatialities are still interrelational (and also phenomenologically differentiated). The interactions necessary for social systems are in fact spatially framed, making the characteristics of communities partially spatial. In order to constitute a spatial system, congruency of spatialities is needed. This is possible through framed social interaction and globalisation. Koch would argue for communication, implying in an ANT fashion that spatialities can communicate. I believe it would be more useful to redirect the congruency, making spatial systems to the meaningful social perception, subsequent (re)construction and use of spatialities. Eventually both Koch and I assert that the social and spatial are made.

From Koch's definition follows the rejection of a series of system theoretical approaches making spatial systems: "1) identical with a social system, 2) identical with the environment of a social system, 3) a further dimension of reason, beyond the subject, time and social dimensions, 4) solely a theme in the communication within social systems, 5) the limits of a social system." (Koch 2005: 11) In my reading of his theory a close connection with the third option is felt, although there is no longer one dimension in its direction. Deviating from systems theory, Koch's environment becomes concrete instead of an abstract notion. Autopoiesis creates its own environment, in which the environment is more complex than the system. Spaces should be constructed as systems in the environment of social systems and vice versa. Communication is twofold, making sense in social systems and congruency in spatial systems. (The main difference with my critique above is that congruency is placed in the spatial system itself, rather than its systemic nature being dependent on social interaction.) This infers that social systems are ontologically different from spatial systems, while the possibility of a structural connection between the two remains (idem). It is in the shared basis of this structural connection that I will argue a potential for empirical interpretation.

The ontological difference refers to the autopoietic status of spatial systems. Koch holds that spatial systems generate their own elements (performativity of (im)possibility), joining the elements according to the system's status entirely. Autopoiesis is related to the operational level of systems, demanding that they are simultaneously operationally closed and structurally opened (idem). This obviously differs from redirecting the spatial system to the social, in which the generation of elements is enabled and restricted by conditioning (im)possibilities, and where joining them is dependent on social interaction or communication. In contrast, Koch gives both systems their own proper communication: the social system according to information, message and understanding, and the spatial system according to networks, places and locations. Yet for Koch these communicative components are not only physical, but also social. Spatial systems come into being (i.e. create themselves) as entities emerging from the total stock of communication. The spatial system thus pertains to the complete relationship in the communication process (idem). While before we saw that Pred (1986) situated interaction as path crossings, creating (part of) a place from a location in time-space, Koch actually inverts the words and lets places be selected for interactions, which makes them localised, hence the term locations. Connecting locations in the stock of spatial communication constitutes a spatial system (Koch 2005). To avoid confusion, I propose to use frames rather than locations in Koch's theory, so the definition of location can either be geometrical or maintained as time-space specific path crossings.

The possibility for *structural linkages*, Koch argues, are mechanisms of translation, which should produce a minimal degree of 'understanding' between the systems. The levels of compatibility related to the stages of translation between his twofold communication, Koch captured in table 3:

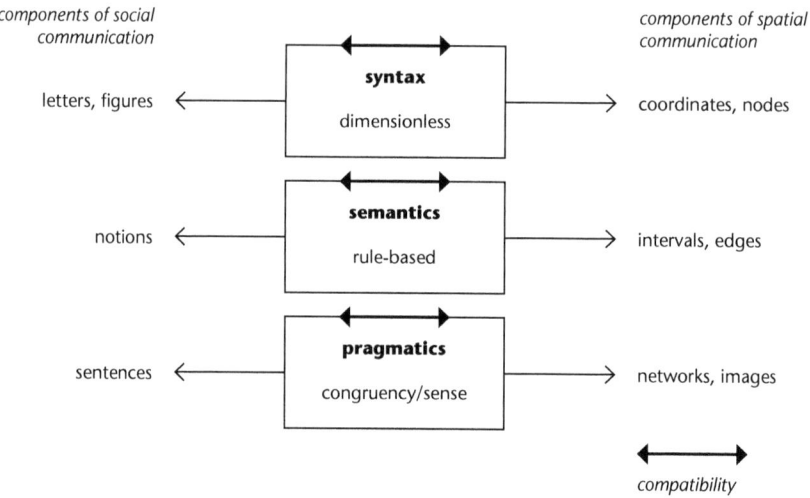

Table 3, reproduced after Koch 2005: 12

The issue that needs to be resolved is concealed in the conceptualising of the structural linkages (or translations) as recursive processes completely over all levels, leading to hybrid compositions of social and spatial components. For this to happen it is required that social features can be translated to spatial features and vice versa. Eventually communities and spatialities are in this way linked as hybrid complexes. Koch summarises, "framed interactions are executed in different spatial contexts and perform in this way the spatial conditions of (im)possibility by specifying the mutual relationships of (im)mutable and (im)mobile." (Koch 2005: 12)

Despite the great level of complexity and clever solutions provided by Koch's theory of autopoietic spatial systems, table 3 for aforementioned reasons does not represent my own views of making spatial systems part and parcel of sociality. Sociality composes a social system which has a systemic spatial counterpart. As argued before, this does not inhibit the partial connectedness and independence of both systems, whilst also taking into account the existence and continuity of materiality. Koch defies the phenomenological concept of bi-implication, and therefore departs from the subject. Therefore, table 3 should be modified to accommodate both systems, with structural linkages based on phenomenology and associated perception and (inter)action. Table 4 illustrates a possible alternative for the levels of compatibility enabling structural linkages:

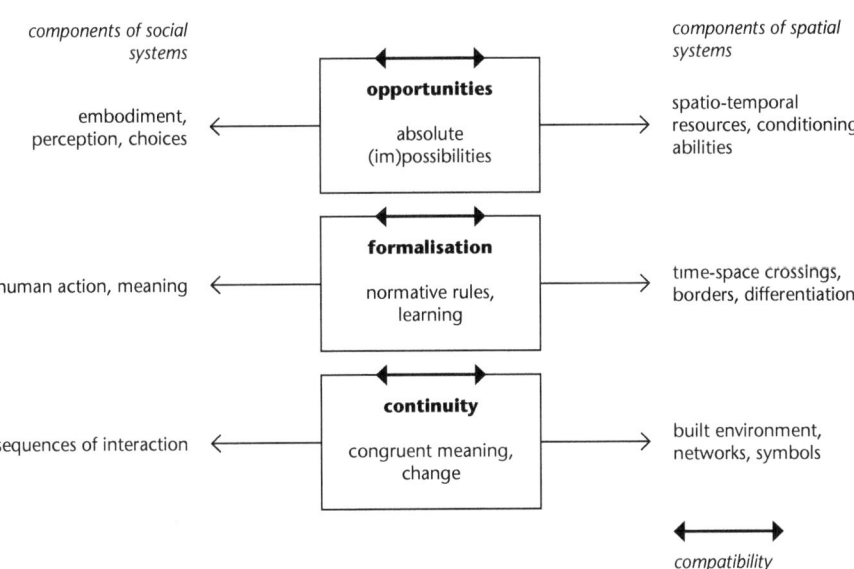

Table 4, modification of Koch's translational stages

In table 4 it is possible to appreciate the simultaneity of both systems in the acting subject. Time, space and sociality are tied together and have their respective forms and environments. The spatial system operates by grace of the social system and vice versa. This is necessary, since I do not believe that spatialities themselves can truly perform anything; rather, they impose (im)possibilities, enable, restrict, get meaning attached to them and finally, through inherent temporalities, are interconnected in itself (i.e. material continuity and associated differentiation) and to the (performing) community. Instead of 'continuity', for the spatial system one could also state consolidation on the basis of the physical construction of the built environment. Change would alter the nature of both systems, which notions of ANT fire space and fluid space may account for. Change is continuously present in the performance of actions (cf. de Certeau 1988), which in turn refers to the temporality of the event and constant present. The confusing concurrent narrow and twofold conception of communication is no longer necessary. The third level relates well to Werlen's scheme in table 2 and the connection of personal biographies in projects which transform nature (see Pred 1986). Space is not determinist, but rather a frame of reference (cf. Werlen 2005), which is related to Koch's framed interaction. Phenomenology and time-geography both offer great sets of notions which allow these constitutional levels of compatibility to remain abstract. Autopoiesis is more reserved for sociality (constituted by framed interaction), which is a hybrid complex.

Making this theory slightly more concrete, a selection of hybrid complexes would compose a place (in Pred's (1986) sense). That place would have an identity which is simultaneously social and spatial, important parts of which could be expected to be materially consolidated through the transformation of nature. Like Koch also notes, distinguishing social systems and spatial systems is ontologically possible, yet in describing socio-spatial phenomena completely futile. Hybridity thus gives us the opportunity to surmount the distinction without losing detail (Koch 2005). Although ANT offers the possibility of independence to spatialities, I think for the reasons stated above that this goes too far. I do agree with Koch that space cannot entirely be assumed to be a social construction as both are partially connected. Therefore I also agree with him that hybridity is not a symmetrical balance, but rather has multiple compositions (idem).

What is applicable to the scale of the spatial system producing regions for Werlen, is also applicable to the more specific micro scale of rooms and buildings for Koch, while Pred already recognised in his theory of place that the notion of place could be extended to regions and countries just as well. Through processes of constitution and construction, which apply both to the social and spatial, the issue of temporal scale also dissolves. In an abstract and rudimentary way, this enables us to operate on and understand from the micro scale, while addressing the big issues and themes of the macro scale (like culture areas). As stated differently elsewhere, an interrelational selection of mutually dependent social and spatial systems through framed interactions are responsible for the becoming of a socially meaningful and spatially identifiable place (cf. Pred 1986). This already bears within the selectivity we are inevitably confronted with in archaeological datasets. Therefore, we need to return briefly to the discussion on totality mentioned before.

Philosophically speaking, there is no use arguing on Luhmann's stance that in autopoiesis the system needs an environment to constitute itself. In this sense totality can only be meaningful if it contains its own distinction to its outside. Therefore totality actually becomes partial, thus a fruitless concept (Arnoldi 2001). In spite of this philosophy, when we make a selection or are inherently confronted with a selection, that selection can only be meaningful in contrast to a totality that, necessarily, is meaningful. Since our concern lies with interpreting social meaning, it could be helpful to conceptualise all sociality as an abstract totality. That totality would also be spatial, since it would need to include all framed interaction. One framed interaction's environment is the potential conditioning of another framed interaction. Then all framed interactions have a simultaneity of independence in which the environment is present, but not as a condition of such total selection. This means all (inter)acting human beings (taking into account my critique above on Zierhofer's speech acts) at any given moment framed in spatialities and temporalities, entailing all social systems. Without any outlying (excluded) interacting human beings, the environment is self-referential, which could be seen as a totality including autopoiesis. Herein the outside of totality is the fragmented world of its parts, the environment is the plethora of logically possible totalities. This definition can only be hypothesised in positing oneself as a researcher outside of the totality itself (i.e. a metaphysical position), indicating that such meaningful totality only exists in present moments in the past. On this basis, any selection of material remains representing the product of framed (inter)actions becomes a meaningful part.

Returning to the archaeological dataset of the built environment, now clearly composed of temporally specific spatialities, we may differentiate many borders, features, objects, sizes and other characteristics. Which ones will tell us most about the socio-spatial identity of a place? There is no single answer to that question, because processive outcomes are plural and hybridity has multiple compositions. Nevertheless, one can narrow down the most meaningful aspects of datasets of the built environment by regarding the consolidated or constructed features that facilitate compatibility between systems or construct the meeting place between two social systems. That is the physically constructed expression of the structural linkages between combinations of systems. Through the levels of compatibility (table 4) facilitating the structural linkages between systems, the actions and sequences of interactions establishing, crossing, exceeding, etc. the borders and boundaries of any system with another become most meaningful. Here negotiation of (im)possibilities for performing actions and eventual continuity and consolidation take place in time-space specific forms. Contrasting amongst the levels of compatibility may produce various spatial features suitable for social inference depending on the research questions.

Interpreting spatial datasets in social terms would arguably be best on the basis of features attached to aspects like public and private domains, accessibility, interrelational distance, in addition to which and the amount of spatialities crossed in interconnections (cf. space syntax). Theorisation has given us a socially significant foundation for focusing on such spatial features of the dataset, and simultaneously forces inference to be relational since all sociality and spatiality are partially interconnected. Boundaries and differentiation of objects and spatialities have become socially informed, actions and interaction are directly responsible for their meaning and often specific shapes. Yet interconnectedness does not only apply to the social and spatial: it also applies to temporalities. All spatialities are time-space specifically situated and accordingly carry specific social meaning.

The next chapter will briefly recapitulate the theoretical notions of potential importance for archaeological conduct, focusing on the concepts of the built environment, region, culture area and border. It will add to that a series of archaeological inferential issues with spatial datasets, especially the built and urban environment, which are touched upon and affected by these ideas.

Chapter 5 *Theoretical Integration for Datasets*

Some Fundamentals

The built environment has now been established as the time-space specific physical (materialised) constructions of perceiving and acting man, simultaneously constituting society. I have presented a selection of theories establishing the constitutive axes enabling man to do so: time, human action, and human space. Furthermore, I have presented theories not only describing the processes developing society, but making them inextricable from space. These theories, especially those originating in human or social geography, may advance archaeological analysis of spatial datasets regarding concepts of place, regions, culture areas and borders. Its disciplinary methodologies will be proper, yet its informing and guiding theories are epistemologically entangled with general interests dispersedly present in various disciplines, producing knowledge it cannot do without. Before moving on to some of the specific issues archaeology is confronted with in the analysis of spatial datasets and the way our acquired theoretical insights may be of aid, a brief integrating recapitulation of the most significant notions seems in order. I will do so by formulating a series of basic reasonings, specifics of which can be found in the respective discussions of theories in previous chapters.

Archaeology is a discipline that itself exists by grace of time. However, as we have seen in chapter one, for interpretive issues it is not the given of the passage of time itself that is of importance. Specifically when the social aspect of archaeological studies is concerned, notions of social time, subjective time, particularly captured in temporalities, are of paramount interest. Taking into account the passage of time which can be quantified and thus classified, and also Husserl's 'stream of internal time-consciousness' (a pre-reflexive notion of time derived from an idea of the heterogeneous continuum of time, challenging an experiential definition of time) expressed as the temporal flux (Lucas 2005), the exact position of such conceptions of time has little significance. In replacing time with temporalities it is the relative position of these interconnected temporal notions that carries meaning. My engagements with time regard the underexposed nuances of Braudel's reading of the Annales School of structural history, in arguing that the intrinsic tempos and rhythms of each timescale as well as their intricate relationships are primarily meaningful (J. R. Hall 1980). Eventually, useful notions manifesting these meaningful relationships are found in Tim Ingold's discussion of time (Ingold 1986, 2000). Following the well-known A and B-series of time from McTaggart and Husserl, Ingold proposed to approach time in terms of the real (social) time of social life and abstract time of social evolution, or, essentially, temporalities captured in taskscapes. Here human activity connects the time of social life with the development of society as a long term process in which both are socially meaningful. The timescale of events acquires a fundamental position as it becomes conceptualised as continuous stages of the present with a retention from the past and a protention for the future (Ingold 2000). This stance is comparable to the a-historicity of phenomenology. In this conceptual situation of the event, both the conduct of the archaeological discipline and human action are embedded.

Like human life is final, the performance of action is temporal. Out of the agenda of humanistic sciences emerged a series of paradigms and researchers placing human beings centrefold in their inquiries. For geography this interest has become incorporated in the broad field of human geography. The big issue of societal development in archaeology is directly tied to humanism as well. In the integrative construction of theory, it is the road established by action theories that appeals to this study. Jumping from the Renaissance to the end of the 19th century, we get to the rationality of human action conceptualised by Max Weber (Campbell 1981). What stays with me most from his influential writings is his careful use of classifications in the notion of ideal types. Although he has rightfully been criticised for the impure use of these ideal types and the many levels he arranged them in to build up his vision of society, indirectly the ideal types gave way to aprioristic lines of arguments concerned with society. Therefore it is hardly surprising that Ludwig von Mises, in building his own theory on the basis of action, both criticised Weber, whilst exclusively turning to aprioristic theoretical arguments for his perspective on the ideal society (von Mises 1998). His uncorrupted steadfast following of his own theory of human action constituting society is both impressive and persuasive. Although eventually his praxeology mainly stayed on an economic trail, the purity of his definition of human action as purposeful behaviour is taken here as a foundation to build on. Even though in later theories the realm of the mind gains significance, cognition only leads to the freely made decision to perform or abstain from acting, which then meaningfully affects environments. Von Mises' universalistic tendency in such processes is of value for their general applicability. Freedom of choice and a self-referential understanding of the world are the elements that are explicitly continued in phenomenology.

Phenomenology eventually lays various foundations for the interpretive tendencies in the subsequent theories. Although the honour of being a father to phenomenology is due to Edmund Husserl, I have chosen to replace his rather metaphysical phenomenology with the constitutive phenomenology of von Mises' pupil Alfred Schütz. This can be positioned laterally to Merleau-Ponty's existential phenomenology, influenced by Heidegger's being-in-the-world (Campbell 1981). Through such existentialism the cogent bi-implication of phenomenology is established: the mutually influencing relationship between man and world. Also, man is considered to be directly physical and temporal by the notion of embodiment, which has grown to be a favoured theme in social science. Schütz added to that the paramount reality of the individual life-world in which humans act. The temporal structures in the life-world are invariant and essential (cf. Braudel's tripartite division) (J. R. Hall 1980). In Schütz's work, the actor becomes a social subject and his social experience is analysed. Experience, however, is not a given, but intentional in the way a subject directs his attention to his environment. The environment is composed of objects and observed objects are understood by contrasting them against past experiences and acquired knowledge, which comprise experience. The attribution of meaning to objects is spontaneous, a process called apperception. All consciousness is consciousness of objects, thus individual constructs.

The experience and meaning of these objects compose the stock of knowledge. Yet Schütz also conceptualises a community or society to have a common stock of knowledge which is inherited and learned by subjects (Campbell 1981). As I have argued, this common stock of knowledge should be approached critically, as learning is individual and selective, and participation is a mutually influencing process (Ingold 2000). Schütz was no longer looking for the essences of phenomena, but instead concentrated on the processes of phenomenological reduction. In order to infer meaning in someone's actions, the empirical level of the subject's own experience needs to be maintained, though analysis can be informed by general theoretical preconceptions (Campbell 1981, Eberle 1984). Schütz was interested in discovering the elements of social life reflecting on social experience as interacting individuals, or as the intention of social life (Campbell 1981). Schütz continued von Mises' idea of a self-referential understanding of the environment, both socially and materially. This means that social interaction entails an inter-subjective understanding, indicating society can become intelligible by the analysis of various types of human action. His sense of rational activity was based on motivated lived experience. The motivation for action was conceptualised as 'in order to' (for subject's projects), whilst including ideas of inheritance, individual biographies, intentionality and decisions made on the basis of personal relevance (idem).

For the social sciences in general, and also for the discussion here, the other potent force in thought on the development of societies is structuration theory. Its relevance is already expressed well by the title of Giddens' most influential work: *The Constitution of Society* (1984). With a background in phenomenology and structuration, maintaining a focus on action, the geography of Allan Pred serves as bridge towards space from a social angle. Notwithstanding the fine contributions made by other disciplines and theorists on the interpretation of space discussed previously, as said in my commentaries, they contrarily led to inference analysing the already existing spatial product. Proxemics, being largely overlooked in archaeology, tentatively occupied a middle ground, but was not found sufficiently critical for our purposes here. Pred, on the other hand, went further than proxemics by not only tying the construction of space directly to the social, but elaborating on the establishing processes. These processes were conceptualised in structurational terms, not only taking into account the constitution of society by means of them, but also the transformation of nature.

Pred saw that people organised themselves in executing projects for themselves or with others (in institutions), and that they were both enabled and restricted to do so by time-space resources. For this he adapted notions which had been developed in Hägerstrand's time-geography. Every project participant would carry his own biography into a project, a mutually influencing relationship. Order and structure could emerge through people repetitively participating in closely related projects over time, creating biographies of experience that partially concur. Out of this power relations may emerge. Yet all elements are connected in dialectic processes of becoming each other, so this is also applicable to constituted power relations. Therefore Pred made individuals, the social and space, social reproduction, biographies and the transformation of nature all inseparable elements of perpetual structuring processes.

His processes can be stretched over large periods of time as well as vast areas, making it applicable to both micro and macro scale inquiries. Place as historically contingent process gets its meaning from individual project participants and their biographies. Those projects involving the transformation of nature can be seen as producing the built environment, which will carry meaning accordingly (Pred 1984, 1986). Pred carefully built a world of generally applicable processes, paying attention to physical constraints and enabling conditions, establishing the bridge that makes it possible to regard constructed spaces departing from the social. It is my reading of it which puts his dialectics into an evolutionary perspective, made possible by the intrinsic connection of time and space. Archaeology in particular holds the tools for studying the evolution of the transformation of nature, whereas phenomenology offers explicatory opportunities to such processes.

It is with the potential power contained in the freedom of subjects that Michel de Certeau (1988) makes his most important contribution to this debate. Pred made us understand the emergence of order, contingency and consolidation, by means of de Certeau we may reach a better appreciation of change without revolutionising it. He endowed the consumptive practices of everyday life with the power of resistance. This makes us rethink our easily assumed position regarding conformist actions, as these are no longer necessarily that. Acting is a constant reappropriation of the goods used (societal traits included), a kind of secondary production. Though much of this resistance is subconscious and silent it can also be used strategically and tactically, ways for the weak to make use of the strong. Explicitly performing resistance may cause 'incomprehensible' statistical outliers as well as account for change and periodic developments. Change thus becomes part of everyday life, instead of the extraordinary.

So far I have theoretically addressed both the development of the social and its interconnectedness with the construction of space only from general principles. Although such a theory, as Pred (1986) himself mentions, could be useful for informing and directing empirical inquiries, it will never fit empirically found situations entirely. It should rather be used as a framework. By concentrating on a particular vista of society, constituted by three main axes, I have arrived at a point which allows us to put the construction of space (or the built environment) in a social perspective. Still, archaeology as a discipline develops its methodologies around the presence, acquisition and ability to extract information from material remains. Physically constructed space, or the built environment (in Lawrence and Low's (1990) broad definition), is one of the most readily available sources of information in archaeological records. As a mediator of perception and action, constantly being reappropriated and constructed alongside the development of society, we should be able to extract social, identity carrying meaning from it. By means of interpreting the built environment in various temporalities, the spatial characteristics of developing societies should be made intelligible.

Social Positioning of Spatialities

Unfortunately, the passage of time is as much degenerative as progressive as far as the physical is concerned. In most cases archaeology is confronted with the material remains of societies that simply no longer exist. People have died, artefacts have broken, buildings have collapsed or were demolished. This results in a severe clouding of our focus, causing a loss of detail and a process of selection bound to material durability. Concentrating on spatial data, we are automatically referred to aspects of the built environment. Being an intrinsic part of social formation processes it carries considerable social meaning, yet recovering spatial data on the built environment entails an amplification of scale. Most projects of construction or durable transformations of nature are not realised by single individuals. Moreover, not all subtleties of society become constructed as spatialities. Proxemics has demonstrated that a sense of territoriality in distance setting is the most direct form of establishing a spatial identity. Such comfort zones are both personal and situational, and may relate to the various socio-spatial systems a subject participates in. If the projects executed in such systems involve the transformation of nature, this will reflect a composition of the freely made decisions to participate and act of the subjects included in the project.

In terms of the dimensions comprising spatial data, we can produce measurable representations of the constructed spatialities; at this stage preferably in the relative neutrality of data acquisition, only affected by acquisition objectives. This spatial data then represents the complicated consolidation of differentiation and bordering processes (cf. Werlen 2005), to be taken either in the large composites of the macro scale or the more readily discernable 'individuality' of the micro scale, depending on the absolute expansion of the research scope. Spatial identity markers in the spatial data are an inferential amplification of the individual when included in a socio-spatial system. Notwithstanding the unassailable unique position of the individual, which remains centrefold in analysis, there is no interpretive requirement to decontextualise single isolated subjects. The theoretically defined subject is essential for the social analysis of spatial data. Interpretation is individually humanised, whilst inextricably contextualised. The meaning archaeologists can infer from the spatial dataset is a representation of spatial identity notions of a socio-spatial system representing a community constructed by individual subjective acts, in various degrees historically contingent with subjects' perception of belonging. Thus this scale amplification is not saying that the sum of parts is more than the whole.

Now a feeling steals over us as academics that this inevitable archaeological scale amplification diminishes the significance of the individual and his actions per se. Though understandable, this is not entirely true. The way action has been conceptualised throughout this study, despite its completely individual intentional performance, fundamentally surpasses one-directional individual meaning by being interaction. Action as a bodily performance is interaction with its environment, be it social or material. Even when performed without the intention of including another individual's reaction (cf. my critique on Zierhofer's (2002) speech acts as interaction), actions are socially informative because of the self-referential understanding subjects have of their lifeworlds. Any action having a direct or indirect lasting consequence in the physical or social environment is potentially (in)direct social interaction. Even if the consequences of the actions will never be perceived by another subject, it still was a constitutive interaction with the environment, an experience in the biography formation of an individual. In this way, each interaction in a system carries an experience of all things past. So, while actions are individually meaningful on both the side of the sender and the receiver(s), the meaning their environmental consequences carry in the potential material consolidation of operating systems is not of the individual's intentional performance alone. Material consolidations are expressions of accumulated meaning, but then become part of the same still continuing processes developing, reappropriating and changing their initial meaning. Actions do not surmount the individual, but cause the individual to meaningfully tie himself to the environment he perceives and the experience he thus acquires.

Environmentally situated, action as interaction is a dialectical process, like the social acts of project participation (cf. Pred 1986). The mutually affecting nature of actions operating socio-spatial systems interconnects all constitutive elements. They are inseparable and self produced (cf. autopoiesis of Koch 2005, Bruun and Langlais 2003, Arnoldi 2001). Moreover, operating systems are in a constant state of becoming (cf. Pred 1986). In a perspective pertaining to time, actions as events are a-historical (cf. phenomenology and Ingold 1986, 2000), freely positioned in the temporal flux (cf. Lucas 2005 on Husserl), yet maintaining a richness of tempos and rhythms in their performance. Simultaneously they are historically meaningful, because of the historicity of biographies and the exchangeable overlap linking subjects' biographies in the interactions required to execute (institutional) projects (cf. Pred 1986 on time-geography). The temporal meaning they carry is constituted by the panoply of relational temporalities contained in social life (cf. Ingold's (2000) taskscapes), rather than their chronological position. The amplification of significance thus appears in the social and material environment and in time.

Temporal amplification is directly responsible for the structures and order perceived by participating subjects further affecting the systemic operations, as well as inferred by academic analysis. The closer (in geometric space and sociality) and more repetitive project participation is over time, the more affinity emerges in the experience of each subject involved. Nevertheless, this concurring affinity is partial at best. What we interpret as order is actually a closely related intricate chaotic complex of systems built of framed interactions (cf. Koch 2005). Freedom of choice is entirely sustained and individual, but as it becomes increasingly similarly influenced by acquired knowledge of comparable experiences, the process of decision-making is prone to lead to equally similar choices in most cases. As a side effect, in administratively advanced societies such equalisation of experientially influenced processes may be assigned abstracted meanings that can be formally manifested as norms, rules and laws, which are in turn often forcefully endowed by power relations (cf. Pred 1986, Foucault 1982). Archaeology, on the other hand, typically denies that common people in their everyday actions may also establish a ruling order. Yet as Pauketat tentatively argues, the formation of rules is not the consequence of political evolution, but rather a product of the structuring processes of social change (Pauketat 2000a). Formalisation should not be confused with the processes taking place in each subject or even the many operating systems in a society. No-one will act according to an exact copy of formalised rules, although subsequently the still freely made decisions will be affected by existing power relations. On the other hand, the increasing (time-space) commonality in generative constituting processes enables us to speak of a certain *socio-spatial identity* located in the material manifestation of historically contingent socio-spatial systems of a residing or settled society. This identity is essentially a composition of the social positioning of the spatialities (i.e. a kind of *spatial signature*) produced by the processes at work.

Again, such socio-spatial identity should not be regarded in an isolated way as a status quo. Socio-spatial identity is an intelligible state of consolidation which, due to the nature of its constitution, directly finds itself as a constitutive element in the continuously operating socio-spatial processes. Socio-spatial identity is contained in the built environment which is immediately perceived, used and reappropriated, and consequentially changes its meaning and potentially its specific physical shape next. Intrinsically it is a stage (temporary spatiality of temporalities) between the manifested consolidation produced by the preceding processes and the contingent processes changing it, potentially leading to a successive state of consolidation. So what I am offering now pertains to an amplification of an event, entailing a unique retention from the past and a protention for the future (cf. Ingold 2000). Without taking into account the larger temporal window internal to the socio-spatial identity contained in the built environment, it cannot be adequately interpreted socially. Spatial congruency or consolidation is thus temporal and is specifically informed by the change it embodies and the change it involuntarily facilitates.

The notion of change brings us right back to the individual's actions. Just as actions produce chaotic order, the everyday chaos bears within the potential of change. Change starts with the performance of an action which is so radically different from the actions operating the systems in its environment that they are affected by it. In other words, an action which has catalytic consequences, whether intended or not. As is to be expected, most extraordinary everyday actions are not radical enough to cause such process of change single-handedly. Perhaps the consequences are also suppressed for a period. Radical actions can be caused by original thought (creation) and the associated wish to manifest one's insights. Alternatively and more commonly, a subject will have arrived at a different valuation of the potential consequences of his actions, thus envisioning a different goal through the choice of their intentional performance (cf. von Mises 1998). Yet even more ordinary is Michel de Certeau's (1988) resistance in everyday (consumptive) practices. Although always present in any action, a strong tactic or strategic manifestation of such resistance readily accounts for change. Moreover, it makes change contingent. Interaction entails the use of mediation by the environment. Use in de Certeau's terms is a second production, i.e. reappropriation. Here it is once again demonstrated that individual meaning is the main analytical unit in the processes of sociality. It is important to note that the radical actions of change are events with their associated unique retention from the past and protention for the future.

With change we complete the theoretical spiral concretising the dialectical processes of becoming (cf. Pred 1986). The subject, sociality, temporality and (material) spatiality are all fully-fledged elements of these processes. The built environment represented by spatial data is our most readily available source of information which carries all this meaning. Now we need to get it out in such a way that an understanding of social identity comes within reach. The theory here enables us to socially inform and direct our analysis of those specific spatial features comprising the most meaningful aspects of the socio-spatial identity of a community or society. It will not do so on the basis of artefact assemblages or complexes of decorative styles, rather it does so on the basis of spatial features facilitating compatibility between different socio-spatial systems of framed interaction. This produces a perspective on the particular identifiable composition of constructed spatialities, i.e. a *social positioning of spatialities*. Rather than allowing us to know functional or cultural specifics about spatialities, it sheds light on what kind of social position a spatiality occupies related to the construction of the local community or society in a time-space specific way. A spatiality is never isolated from its sociality, temporalities and interconnectedness with other spatialities. In itself it holds little information on socio-spatial identity.

This theory may operate on both the micro and the macro scale since, spatially and temporally, interaction ties everything together, possibly into infinity. Making a selection of this all-encompassing interrelational notion, which is inevitably so in empirical archaeological research, we need to strive for inclusion of all framed interactions of sociality within the geometrical scope of inquiries. Such a selection can be socially meaningful even if it does not correspond with experience of subjects in the past (cf. commentary on Luhmann's totality (in Arnoldi 2001) in chapter four on meaningful slections). As long as this is materially manifested in a spatial dataset (or the remains of a built environment), villages, cities, areas, and regions can all be identity carriers. Geometrical and geographical spatial stretches can so become meaningful rather than just measurable. However, this entails a severe mentality shift from thinking from the spatial to thinking from the social. A shift which is implicitly present in Allan Pred's work, somewhat stronger and more specific in Tim Ingold's writing and very explicit in Benno Werlen's assertions. A shift which entails an inversion of analysis already implied and enabled by Husserl's remark that the inner world of human being should not be studied with the same methods as the natural sciences (Cloke e.a. 1991), a practice that we have grown accustomed to. In order to set out some future paths, the following will discuss what kind of methodological opportunities this theory gives us for data analysis, alongside some inferential archaeological issues that are directly affected by it.

Spatial Datasets, Interpretive Issues

The theoretical integration presented above entails several demands. Not every dataset will do equally well in providing the specific elements that can be inserted in the described general processes as the informative application of the theory. As said before, depending on the elements, the outcomes or stages of consolidation produced by these contingent processes will differ accordingly, i.e. not all identities derived from spatial datasets will be the same. However, it upholds that our main problem is the quality of the dataset. In order to infer meaning on social identity from built environments, a high degree of social relations need to have been physically constructed in a certain way at some point in time. In other words, in Pred's terms we need as much transformation of nature as possible. For that reason any use of the theory above, I think, would be most fertile in the spatial dataset of an urban environment. The choice of an urban environment is not due to an assumption of greater social complexity producing it or reaching a certain stage in teleological models of social formation (there are stages in urbanisation too, also in present day cities). Instead, the enormous degree of transformed nature, because of the historically contingent processes going on in the localities concerned, means that virtually all action then is mediated by consolidated constructed spatialities.

Furthermore, the still operating local processes were actually responsible for the production of the urban environment previously. Since it contains physical construction on most societal levels, the inferential potential of such a built environment is expected to reach great detail and enable the accommodation of research projects with a grand scope, approaching a local totality. Also, in most cases, urbanisation is at least accompanied with an equally high level of technological advancement used in construction practices for buildings and infrastructure, inhibiting many individual building projects. Therefore the material form of the urban environment reaches great detail explicitly in social relations. The presented theory should not be confused with a theory of urbanisation because of this. This methodological assertion is made to envision an idealist dataset for the theory to inform its inferential analysis. Nevertheless, some interpretive themes in the theorising of urbanisation will also be touched upon by the analytical social positioning of spatialities.

Emma Blake notes that "the archaeological concern with urbanism has been one primarily of teleology and closely linked to tracing the path of social complexity: how, when and why cities formed. The result has been an emphasis on the *functions* of cities." (Blake 2007: 238) This is indeed the case. The emergence of cities in a functional productive sense has been of paramount importance for decades. Many attempts have been made to clarify the enabling relations between city and hinterland, as well as the often assumed non-ecological production activities (e.g. administration, religion) at the core of cities (see examples in the volume by Flannery and Marcus 2003). The social dynamics centrefold in the social positioning of spatialities has not typically been the interest of (urban) archaeological inquiries.

In the context of teleology, households have been established as the smallest unit, building block, or basal feature of social organisation (Pauketat 2000b), as witnessed by the volume of Santley and Hirth (1993). Although this argument obviously refers to social formation in the realm of social evolution, we have established that such development cannot be separated from inquiries on space. Thus Pauketat makes a relevant observation in saying that "we should not assume in a teleological fashion, that household- and community-level cooperation formed the basis of social-evolutionary change. In other words, the form or function of households and communities at any point in time does not necessarily explain the evolution of society up to that point. Instead, we should consider that the forms of households or communities themselves require explanations in diachronic and historically contingent terms." (Pauketat 2000b: 16) In the social positioning of spatialities the subject or individual stays responsible at all levels, since his actions constitute any socio-spatial system. Actions constitute the households and communities composing societies, which, as an ongoing temporal stretch, also makes said actions responsible for the eventual social evolution. Similarly, urbanisation may emerge out of these dynamic processes.

Pauketat notably argues along a comparable line, judging by his words calling for diachronic and historically contingent explanations. Though not at the same level as the discussion of the smallest unit of social organisation, he continues a theoretical argument similar to mine at the level of communities, which he understands as part of an identity-formation process at local and regional scales. In order to explain the rise of any form of social complexity without teleology, he finds this positioning of community essential. At the level of community Pauketat emphasises to achieve the same detailed understanding of all social and spatial dimensions of a community in order to uncover the mechanisms (processes) by which the formation of social organisation takes place (idem). Taking urbanism as transitory stages in the formation of spatial organisation and the inseparable entanglement of the social and spatial, Pauketat's arguments are well taken care of in the integrative theory above.

As Blake justly remarks: "drawing together the fragmented piecemeal elements that constitute a city into a single coherent whole might be an oversimplification. In the framework of a city, how does the archaeologist distinguish the causative influences of intentionality or accident? Are the built features the by-products of collective action or individual agency? At the smaller scale of portable objects or single-period sites, these questions are taken for granted, while the multivalent spaces of the city demand more theorizing, at the same time offering great opportunities for interpretation." (Blake 2007: 239) In line with the statements above I naturally agree with her last point, but her initial dissatisfaction with the archaeological treatment of the urban environment can also be partially replied to. Following the social positioning of spatialities, a perspective of the city as a single coherent whole can no longer prevail. The spatialities of a city form both a complex and a complicated (cf. Koch 2005) composition that is continually developing. The theory also clearly demonstrates the interconnectedness of micro level interests and processes with the larger scale, such as in cities. Unfortunately, the question of causality or accident remains stuck in the middle. Despite the given socially challenging situation of building in a city, it cannot be presumed that constructional accidents are non-existent, leaving the problem of their distinction. Blake's second question first needs rectification of the term by-product. Building activities as the transformation of nature are part and parcel of the intentional actions constituting sociality, so by no means a by-product. Also, the term 'collective actions' is ill-chosen in the light of free subjects choosing to participate in (construction) projects. The rest of this question can in most cases be answered by the previous replies and associated technological inhibitions.

Addressing such interpretive issues in the urban environment, the pervading dichotomy of organic and planned growth is virtually unavoidable. Michael Smith nicely summarises different treatments of this dichotomy which is usually employed as a measure for classification in early cities, in which planning typically refers to grid lay-out or orthogonal coordination of the built environment. Smith rightly notes that few have made endeavours beyond this rigorous opposition and proclaims that the dichotomy cannot be maintained. There is a need for a more nuanced and detailed approach to the planning of early cities (Smith 2007). He subsequently explores three defining lines of arguments towards city planning. The first definition focuses on the deliberate actions of the builders, leading to the argument that all buildings are self-conscious in nature. This allows for premeditated planning following hierarchical power relations. However, Smith says it would be more useful to enlarge the spatial scope of this definition towards constructed areas, since we lack information on thoughts and intentions of (powerful) planners and builders. Rather, we should stick to the empirical data we have available. The second and third definitions work with empirical data, using the formal lay-outs that follow from builders' activities. The second focuses on the regularity of the city plan, not necessarily indicating pre-meditation, but construction according to specific designs. The regularity of a city plan must be discerned from comparisons with other cities. Therefore it is not possible to analyse isolated urban cases. The third emphasises the coordination among buildings. Planning is a notable formal organisation of space or group design, placing one or more buildings in relation to their surroundings (idem).

To some degree working from aforementioned approaches Smith decides to comprise his own approach along several components. The coordination amongst buildings, arrangement, formality, monumentality of lay-out, orthogonality and geometric order he puts first respectively. Secondly, he employs the standardisation among cities in terms of architectural inventories, spatial lay-outs, orientation and metrology. Smith subsequently proposes to organise cases along an ordinal scale, retaining that there are degrees of planning. The application of this scale can refer to the degree of standardisation: orthogonality involves more planning than coordination, but also can refer to the effort put into planning, e.g. the formal placement of monuments. Furthermore, it may refer to the extent of the city which is planned (in absolute and relative terms), e.g. planned centres and free residential areas (idem).

Despite the delicate balance of Smith's approach, he does not quite move beyond a classificatory method replacing the dichotomy. His approach is useful for the comparative ordering of built shapes, yet actually holds little information on the social position of such spatialities. Essentially, the debate on planned or organic growth here is not so much about emergence or growth, but rather about noticing measurable differences in physical shapes that are assumed to reflect degrees of planning. The intentionality of building activity (mentioned in the first definition) is overlooked. Moreover, as Smith himself also realises, time is largely overlooked in the discussion on city planning, obstructing comprehension of sequential changes in urban forms (idem).

The scale enlargement Smith is looking for in the approach emphasising deliberate actions could be situated in time or temporalities instead of space. An emphasis on time would also lead to a better balanced interpretation following such an approach. For socio-cultural or ideational meaning Smith still refers to the high, middle and low levels of meaning of Amos Rapoport (1982). Although Smith is not uncritical of him, in terms of meaning approaches like Rapoport's are severely restricted (see also chapter one). If one is interested in uncovering the social meaning of (degrees of) city planning, one should appreciate that in the dialectical processes of becoming in operating socio-spatial systems, builders and subsequent users become planners, while planners become users and builders. On the spatial level, that means that the organic becomes the planned, while the planned becomes the organic (cf. Pred 1986). From this follows the abrogation of the dichotomy between planned and organic growth. In the processes described in the social positioning of spatialities there is no distinction to whether a part of the built environment is organically shaped or planned. Yet all building activity is intentional, as people freely choose to participate in a building project. In addition, historically contingent project participation is responsible for the emergence of specific social order through commonality grown into experience. Out of this order rules may be formalised, which in turn may produce hierarchies of power relations (cf. Pauketat 2000a above).

Hence, through the use of theoretically defined systems the deliberate building activities producing self-conscious constructions are meaningfully informed. Those same socio-spatial systems contain the temporalities of action by which they are made operable. As desired by Smith and discussed before, processes operating in systems enable scale enlargement not only in space, but also in time. Through this, both organic and planned growth are drawn into the concern with the emergence of built spatialities per se. The relational social meaning of the emergence and subsequent historically contingent change of built spatialities in the urban environment is made intelligible. It is the relative temporal position of the operations of socio-spatial systems that allows for an informative action-based approach to urban planning.

From this also follows that our urban dataset preferably consists of several temporal layers of considerable detail, i.e. a good stratigraphy. Taking each layer as a time-space specific composition of consolidated spatialities, theory demands that we not only look at each layer separately: we should select the most significant meaning carrying spatial features of the built environment from both the preceding and, if available, successive layer. As said before, as soon as an environment is built, it is reappropriated through its use. When this reappropriation is concretised the built environment may be altered, developed or demolished, giving way to a new construction. That indicates that in our ideal dataset we require reasonably detailed dating information on both the layer containing the built environment in general and specific spatial features in particular. With sufficiently accurate and abundant dates or detailed relative chronologies stratification might not only be elucidated on the basis of superposition, but could occur horizontally also (in situations with palimpsests the previous should still be discernable). If absolute or relative dates on spatially dispersed precincts (arguably closely related to specific spatial systems) are available, significant spatial characteristics of the built environment could be compared diachronically. The mutually influencing relationship between distinct, but in function comparable parts of the same place (e.g. everyday residential spatialities, precincts) is a process which is constantly reflecting on a spatial history and (unintentionally) envisioning a possible future.

In the interpretation of spatial datasets this signifies that each feature has a past of resistance, a present resistance in its current use, while presupposing the possibility to realise resistance in a next stage of consolidation of built space. Such prospective built spatialities will facilitate new action-based resistance that differs from its foreseen functional purpose. In de Certeau's resistance, the use of planned and subsequently built spatialities is a form of consumption that resists against them as a structure of constraints. This permits experiential new ideas to be developed about spatialities, which might affect new planning of the built environment (i.e. the users become the planners). It can be expected that the use and experience of spatialities will be better articulated in newly built spatialities, thus holding fundamental information about the previous building phase. Similarly, the current built environment under study contains a previous process' newly built spatialities, which inform each other. So rather than fixing inference of stratigraphy or temporal succession in static moments of its status quo, we should envision the interpretive value of a stratigraphic layer (or temporally bound precinct) as a window including a retention from the past (previous layer) and protention for the future (successive layer). Here the methodology of archaeology adds a proper and valuable dimension to the arguments made up to now.

The proposed interpretive methodology forces us into a developmental point of view. The way growth and change occur over time, situated in their time-space specific windows, is informative for the development of the social identity we are dealing with. Being inseparably linked to the social, the construction of spatialities takes place alongside societal development. These processes forge the organic and the planned into a dialectic process, enabling the existence of hybrid forms. After all, how would one discern between those datasets which appear to be organic growth, but in fact result from planned growth, or those that appear to be planned growth, but in fact result from organic growth, solely based on spatial shapes? This could be compared to the popular belief which distinguishes natural (or organic) designs and man-made (or abstracted) designs. It bears within a similar assumption which comes down to the idea that the organic should appear disorganised, whilst the planned should be recognised as organised patterns. Biological phenomena often prove us wrong there. Instead of opting for contrasting patterns in datasets of distinct sites or places, a developmental view of periodically successive data within a site can be expected to articulate spatialities that are of social importance due to their diachronic change.

The empiricist approach of Smith partially stays with such arguments. However, the aim of the theory here is not the comparative ordinal ranking of early city planning that he attempts to reveal. Fortunately, Smith's focus means he is keen on an engagement with planning theories, of which Blake indicates there was little interest from archaeology up to this point (Blake 2007). His approach will complement the increasingly popular use of space syntax (originating from city morphology) in archaeology (for discussion see chapter one). The social positioning of spatialities does take into account the interrelational position of each spatiality in the urban environment, but functions mainly on the level of a site itself. Only when we proceed to the level of significant spatial features, enabling the interpretation of a socio-spatial identity or spatial signature of local communities or societies, could grounds for comparison be made.

Spatial Features

Most of the arguments made lean heavily on that part of the theory that is chiefly derived from assertions of phenomenology and Allan Pred's processes of becoming. As suggested in the discussion of Koch's theory, he crystallises the relationships between the social and spatial in such way that concretising them might lead us to more specific spatial features. Whereas Pred provided us with well defined processes tying both together, whilst generally including the transformation of nature as an aspect of those processes, he gave little more than time-space resources to narrow down the possible properties for inferential (empirical) analysis. The same is true of phenomenology and Ingold's temporalities, although they prevent processes and associated systems to be put in temporally secluded situations. Yet the notion of autopoiesis adds some insight to the way socio-spatial systems emerge and operate. More importantly, however, combined with ANT it leads to structural linkages between systems. The subtle mix of structurally tying processes may make our understanding of the intrinsically temporal interplay between the social and the spatial clearer. Structural linkages are facilitated by levels of compatibility (see table 4), although the significance of the structural linkages themselves depend on the perceptive meaning attributed by acting subjects in the systems. Given the spatialities that are interconnected with the operation of systems (by framed interaction), the structural linkages between systems may have a material counterpart at specific locations when system-exceeding actions are performed. Since both the spatial system and the social system are, in fact, inextricably socio-spatial systems in various degrees of hybridity, the location of the materialised structural linkage should follow from the levels of compatibility as expressed in table 4.

The elevated level of meaning in structural linkages is caused by the fact that at least two or more experiential worlds of system participants meet and are negotiated by defining the boundary (possibly with an overlap) of their respective frames of interaction. This makes them of particular interest to studies trying to establish a spatial signature of an inhabiting community or society. Just as autopoiesis requires constitutive environmental features (cf. Bruun and Langlais 2003) and imagined communities define themselves partially by understanding its outside (cf. Anderson 2006), the internal structural linkages enable a meaningful mutual definition of two or more constitutive systems in a local totality (i.e. a delimited selection of framed social interactions). At the level of opportunities such linkages probably remain mostly in the mind, while in formalisation they are normatively fixed and possibly tied to existing spatial features in the environment through social interaction. Only at the level of continuity will such facilitating properties become consolidated as parts of or features in the built environment.

The arguments here almost automatically direct us towards *accessibility*, since the compatibility facilitating structural linkages establishes accessibility between systems. Most apparent is the ever-popular relation between the public and private domain. Accessibility depends on the direct environment of framed interactions and spatialities, physical shape of spatialities and mere relative distances between spatialities. The private and public should not be seen as a rigorous dichotomy, rather there are gradations between them. One system's private may be another system's public. Also, studies on rooms in (residential) buildings, often including some type of viewshed analysis as well, appear to demonstrate increasing levels of seclusion of rooms towards e.g. the interior or sides of buildings. Archaeological studies have had definite concerns with the relation of the two domains. In the volume by Parker Pearson and Richards (1994) there was determined interest in the relation between interior space and society; in Gerstle's (1988) discussion of a possible Lenca compound in Copán, degrees of private seclusion in architectural traits were an important factor, while Burmeister (2000) argued that migrant populations would preserve their own cultural traits in the private domain, hidden behind a publically upheld façade.

Obviously most infrastructure could be determined as structural linkages between systems, radiating out of spatialities as connecting corridors or axes like a network. These infrastructural connections enable a weighed accessibility by connecting spatialities. Briefly returning to Smith's concern with planning, he recognises that "common orientation does not necessarily imply central planning because other factors such as topography or location with respect to a river or shoreline could produce the same pattern. Stronger evidence of planning is provided when individual buildings share orientations and/or arrangements through common reference to features such as avenues, plazas, city walls, a royal palace, or other urban architecture. Some of these principles of coordination are discussed by Edmund Bacon, whose 'methods of design growth' include 'axes as connectors' and 'mass as connector'." (Smith 2007: 8) In a social relational sense, infrastructure as weighed corridors or axes should be conceptualised in a similar way. Smith mentions spatialities as avenues, plazas, city walls and palaces. The degree of accessibility between e.g. a residential spatial system and the spatial system of a plaza is significantly manifested in the infrastructure, making them compatible.

This structural linkage serves as a means for communication, control, or access to ecological necessities and goods to be acquired at different frames of interaction. In Pred's words, production and distribution are dominant (institutional) projects (Pred 1986). Next to constraining time-space resources they determine the minimal requirement for local social sustainability, leaving limited opportunities for participation in other projects. Therefore it can be expected that the greatest degree of accessibility in prominent infrastructure will be associated with time-space constraints and dominant projects within a local community. With this knowledge, the advanced mathematical models of space syntax on movement through urban environments become socially intelligible. The theory here gives a clear-cut reason why infrastructure, accessibility and movement are important factors to take into account in the social inference of space. Purely on the basis of spatial data some assertions can already be made. For a more detailed understanding, however, artefact assemblages and object topologies (cf. Koch 2005) deposited in built spatialities may indicate specific functions, which gives our understanding of interconnected spaces greater detail. If through this analysis a spatiality is socially positioned within the local totality, it gets a relative sociotemporal value. Information on the function of that spatiality could shed light on the importance of various (cultural) activities in local societal life.

It should also be noted that infrastructure itself is also the material product of an operating system localised there, and therefore represents a system in itself. When this is realised we can reach more specific levels of spatial features in our dataset. The literally constructed structural linkages giving access to infrastructure or enabling access between two spatial systems without infrastructure move into focus. This pertains to doorways, windows, porches, porticos, gardens, gates, traversable or absolute boundaries etc. and whether these features can be closed off or not. All of these specific elements logically are meaningful for the degree of accessibility they enable. Edward Hall (1968) already noticed the cultural differences people felt between the accessibility between northern American homes and Latin American homes, and Amos Rapoport (1982) remarks that stylistically there has always been an interest emphasising entrances. With the theoretical reasoning presented in this study, we can now argue why these are socially significant, although such a fact sounds aphoristic. Moreover, it forces us to focus on the spatial information (e.g. measurable, size, visibility, dynamic changes as opening and closing) we have on these entrances or features of accessibility. The meeting places of systems are scenes for social negotiation, contestation and establishment, although the boundaries they represent are flexible, possibly crossable or transformational.

Due to power relations, not all infrastructural corridors or constructed linkages are reciprocally accessible. Imagine royal spatialities, where the king can get out of, but nobody not part of that socio-spatial system can get into. Also, ceremonial spatialities which are accessible to priests, but not the commoners adhering to systems outside of that socio-spatial system. Consequentially, the degree of interrelational accessibility will probably be low and it warns us not to assume that all constructed linkages are particularly meaningful for everyday life.

The spatial information derived from constructed linkages and partial generalities of infrastructure in relation to the selection of spatialities they connect, together compose the spatial signature (or socio-spatial identity) of a locally residing community or (part of) society. This opens the way to a possible alternative for pattern recognition in site lay-out, which is still the popular method for discerning cultural (societal) differences in archaeology. The alternative, social positioning of spatialities with the specific details provided by constructed linkages, is not restricted to cross-cultural comparisons between geographically distinct sites or settlements. It may apply to cases of different cultural presences in a specified settlement equally well.

Referring to Gerstle (1988), who did not adequately succeed to make such inference on the basis of the presumption of Lenca presence in the Las Sepulturas neighbourhood of Maya Copán, it can be suspected that the intra-site (cultural) differences will be less articulated. Again, within the theory this could be expected, as a consolidated part of the built environment in a greater urban environment must be a project undertaken affected by time-space, social and power relation constraints. Also, the lack of a sufficiently good reference collection of spatial data on supposed Lenca settlements (the Lenca society is chiefly linguistically ascribed to a geographical region, see chapter one) could have played a part in her marginal results based on a compound lay-out. She was able to establish differences in lay-out and accessibility routes, but eventually relied on ceramic and stylistic analysis for making her Lenca arguments. An aspect that was not adequately addressed in her study was the greater interconnectedness of the spatialities comprising the compound to (all) other spatialities in Copán. Therefore it would not have been possible to attribute significance to the spatial traits

Gerstle recognised anyway. Moreover, a diachronic analysis of spatial traits in Copán was lacking. As repeatedly noted so far, a broad time-space scope is essential for the informative theory to direct meaningful outcomes.

Some words of warning must also be devoted to the highest levels of society, authority and any type of monumentality. Due to the durability of the construction works directed and executed by elites and power holders, those buildings have been at the centre of archaeological investigation for a long time. Caused by the societal position occupied by its principal commissioners, such constructions are more prone to deviate from the general spatial signature constituted by the majority's framed interactions in everyday life. The power relations (and accepted legitimation) they exercise claim access to more material means or social pressure to force labour in order to have their building projects executed. Probably they could also employ or permit themselves access to technological knowledge more easily. Their relative independent freedom from commoners' everyday lives gives way to extravagant possibilities of construction having a public face, while most of this free extravagance will typically take place in the private domain, behind a publically agreeable façade. Such a high social position may cause excessive constructional expression, violating any rule at the formalisation level of compatibility.

Archaeologists therefore should be extremely careful in using spatial information contained in such buildings in order to interpret a spatial signature. They should be aware that those constructions, be they authoritative, ceremonial, communal, centrally commissioned or privately constructed by elites, could very well be eccentricities rather than reflections of everyday life. Even in cases which present compelling empirical indications that communal or authoritative buildings at some level copy social organisation, there is no reason to assume that in their constructed linkages they followed everyday patterning. An example of monumental architecture following social organisation are the cities of the Postclassic highland K'iche' Maya in Guatemala. Not only did every big house (*nimja*) around the plaza represent a principal lineage, there are strong indications that whole series of K'iche' terms were directly associated with houses, political buildings or principal settlements (Braswell 2003, Carmack 1981). The possibility to include extravagant constructions in spatial signatures is mainly situated in the immediate structurally linked position those buildings occupy within the local totality of a place. Moreover, they are just as much a production of the constitutive processes in the systems comprising a society. The deviating characteristics of such buildings should become apparent in their interrelational and developmental position, as well as in design or lay-out, following the same spatial features or indicators that are important for socially more competed (negotiated) spatialities.

Regarding the diachronic use of the built environment another issue emerges. As can be observed in present day Europe in particular, a considerable amount of the built environment originates from entirely different eras. People sometimes live in buildings that date well back into the medieval period, causing a kind of anachronism. In long term temporal use of the built environment, i.e. over many generations bringing forth series of occupants pertaining to various systems in the development of societies, the constructions themselves remain the same. Yet the way they are perceived will differ, just as the way they facilitate actions accordingly. Although society has changed, its processes have not changed the built environment it inhabits in all aspects. However, interconnected as spatialities are, in spite of retaining its physical shape, there will be differences demonstrated in the relations these remnant parts of the built environment have. They cause a palimpsest of simultaneous occurrence with new construction works which have taken place in its constitutive environment. With growth and environmental changes the old spatialities change their social meaning as part of historically contingent systems. The contemporaneous social positioning of such spatialities will differ according to their (period specific) possession of constructed linkages or infrastructural developments. Because the world changes its face with time, as soon as the geographical scope of the study is sufficiently amplified, a palimpsest will occur, causing meaningfully changed relationships.

Boundaries and the Macro Scale

The availability of good spatial and temporal data and reference collections for noting significant intra-site differences is definitely required for discerning cross-cultural (or more appropriately cross-societal) differences. Without considerably large bodies of spatial data, the development and differences in spatial signatures cannot be studied. When such data is available the development and differences discerned on the basis of the social positioning of spatialities are socially meaningful. We are no longer noting mere architectural, technical, or stylistic differences, but rather the differences in sociality responsible for and inhabiting the built environment. Similarly, if foreign presence is suspected within a delimited place, reference collections demonstrating spatial signatures will allow us to infer differences in historical social life instead of only observing deviating material shapes. Put into a developmental perspective it might offer the possibility of distinguishing the use of moveable objects (artefacts) or stylistic traits which have been infused by another society or strong links between places actually influencing everyday social life at that place.

Eventually the residing subjects construct their direct built environments, but the inferential significance might never be fully understood unless the directly affective macro scale relationships are considered. This may concern separated places, social relationships with foreign subjects, or the larger societal realm. Through the biographies of project participants inhabiting the systems operating at a place, such influences can seep into that local community or society. The macro scale could uncover both strong and weak ties with alien social entities. Insight in cross-cultural (or societal) relationships can be significantly altered by such knowledge. Here we are no longer talking about facets of society which can be changed at will, but processes of decision-making leading to the performance of individual actions in everyday life which continually develop and change. Our focus just shifted from the icing on the cake to the fundamental character of the cake itself. The spatial signature is the manifestation of the constitutive everyday life in hypothetically any physically constructed place, yet it is also placed in macro scale relations.

Throughout this entire thesis and confined in this account on spatial datasets, the definition of boundaries has been mentioned several times. From a social perspective boundaries have been underexposed in archaeological discourse. Again referring to autopoiesis and its constitutive environment as well as the internal definition of imagined communities, necessitating an idea about its outside, the question arises whether we should be speaking of boundaries or borders at all. Emma Blake discusses the same suggestive development of this notion. In anthropology research became more interested in border zones as interstices where conflicts between identities take place. Blake notices a tendency wherein scholars start regarding borders as representing the way identities are constructed as hybrids. Border zone activity challenges traditional territoriality. To illustrate this she concisely presents the work of Mary Louise Pratt, who "expanded the concepts of border beyond the linear boundary separating groups and the adjacent skirt of borderlands. These contact zones [...] replace the linearity of the border with the image of the liminal mosaic. [...] While borders resonate in current social theorizing, they remain under-explored in archaeology." (Blake 2007: 240)

At the core of this interest in bordering spaces we find Benno Werlen's theory of regionalisation in geography (Werlen 2005). Starting from the social rather than the spatial and regarding regionalisation as part and parcel of everyday life, Werlen develops a social perspective on regions, replacing the imposed hard lines on academically produced maps. Positioning regionalisation in everyday life, as Pred speaks of place and everyday geography making, indicates that regionalisation is not exclusively pertaining to the macro scale. Nevertheless, the more general nature of his theoretical findings make them more applicable to the macro scale than Koch's, in comparison, to the micro scale. Yet taking into account the interplay all the presented theories have, borders become not only social, but also temporal. Meanwhile they keep their fundamentally spatial character. If placed in the macro scale, the theoretical integration leading to the social positioning of spatialities provides a conceptualisation of borders in which, over geographical stretches, clear contrasts in socio-spatial identities of places are recognised. Undoubtedly these borders will never be represented by a clear-cut line. Whether a border zone or mosaic, the differences constituting the border will have a socio-temporal character that has become spatially expressed in distinct ways at both its sides. This makes the border no longer a tool handled by a researcher, but a phenomenon emerging from his inferential analysis; foremost thought of or experienced by the subjects under study.

Quickly returning to the case of the Lenca, introduced when I set out to write this thesis and cited on several occasions, what can this theory mean in terms of assigning them a socially experienced territory? What if we cannot determine a spatial signature distinguishing the Lenca from the Maya? Would it mean that we have failed? In short: no, it just means that the socio-spatial identities of the Maya and Lenca were very much alike. This could indicate that their people would not experience a spatially articulated border between the places and areas they inhabit. Given the fact that the Lenca received their name from linguistics, perhaps this is the only level on which they differ from the Maya. Communities and societies operate at a great array of strata, both socially and materially. A society could use entirely the same artefact assemblages as its neighbour, whilst adhering to a completely different socio-spatial identity. Alternatively, studying the larger spatial signatures of the Lenca and Maya might also change our perspective of the extended Maya area, discerning not two, but numerous regions delimited by socially experienced borders. Although the amount of data required could be immense, it could be worthwhile to try.

Despite the nearly exclusive focus on sociality here, one should always bear in mind that nature, geography and ecology simply condition the construction of spatialities, exercising strict inhibitions depending on technological advancements made by society. These determine (im)possibilities that projects transforming nature must follow. Essentially this is no different from the biological and somatic condition of human beings. Other dealings with nature are a matter of choice and priority. Social priorities might overrule apparent necessities from the side of nature. For the researcher it is important to take care not to exclusively opt for a one-dimensional emphasis on any inferential analysis without considering and accounting for alternatives in relation to it. In this case that means that the social positioning of socialities is partially dependent on natural inhibitions which should be taken into account. The advantage is that such awareness anticipates erroneous interpretations which could socially be possible, though are naturally confined. To give a simple example, the lay-out of a circumscribed composition of spatialities could strongly resemble a harbour area, yet without the necessary natural resources to make that work, this would be highly unlikely. Similarly, without the necessary resources to sustain a population, a residential area would probably not occur at such specific locality. If a settlement nevertheless does exist, a piece of vital information is probably still missing. This illustrates that the social theoretical angle pursued here is meant to enrich and improve inferential possibilities which generate better understanding of the continuous development and change of societies as expressed in spatial datasets. It is complementary to insights provided by natural sciences (e.g. evolution), not a mutually exclusive alternative.

To this archaeology adds empirical methodologies and perspectives which are especially fit for studying spatialities, their constitution and their contestation diachronically. Its subsequent findings may improve the theoretically inferred knowledge about materialisation and construction following socio-spatial systems and their structural linkages. The theory here has inverted analysis from starting with material remains (or space) to starting from a social point of view. The firm presence of temporalities at all levels of the theory made evolutionary reasoning truly a social endeavour. This is particularly enabled by the human geographers who connected time to their action-based approaches to space. Archaeology can cast a unique perspective on the becoming of the built environment, which makes it a dynamic concept beyond consecutive stages inferred as the status quo. Instead of time being derived from space in a kind of interpretive hierarchy, these researchers and this integration show theoretical directions that render this obstructive fashion redundant. Since the development of society is inseparable from the construction of spatialities, the transformation of nature into the built environment provides interpretive opportunities that apply to place, region, area and borders in an evolutionary context. In the realm of sociality these are expressive extensions of an experiential sense of socio-spatial identity.

It should be maintained that the theory has an informative character and allows plural outcomes in all directions. Moreover, it will need elaboration as we continue with it. Archaeology especially should contribute to future theory building and lose its fear of big issues. In this chapter I moved from the ideal type, like building blocks, to an aprioristic and idealist theory capturing socio-spatial systems in all their developmental complexity. This affects many aspects of the inferential analysis of the built (or urban) environment in archaeology, replacing interpretive dichotomies with nuanced alternatives. Although there is no prefabricated set of spatial cues which we should turn to in order to reveal the spatial signature of communities or societies in places and regions over time, there are strong indications as to which spatial features are of paramount importance in composing and temporally constituting such identity.

The empirical character of archaeology offers potent tools to concretise the relationship between space and society against the backdrop of time. It will need effective techniques to acquire spatial datasets over large areas and with great detail. Quickly advancing prospection techniques could be a solution to this end. Therefore the arbitrary border drawn between data acquisition and theorists needs to be abolished. A mutual communication will connect the direction of theoretical development with the questions resulting from improved and large spatial datasets. It enables a more deserved appreciation of the inferential possibilities retained in prospective techniques. Moreover, it will demand that technological advances will search to meet interpretive needs. It is a matter of getting together and setting the agenda. Explorations from a middle ground appear lucrative for the development of the discipline.

Finally it needs to be stressed that none of this study should be considered to preclude ecological or (biological) evolutionist archaeologies, nor does it ignore the strengths of quantitative approaches like space syntax. Rather, it exists alongside and complementary to such approaches, making the social intelligible and the quantitative meaningful.

Disputation of Potentialities

Are Things Stirring in Archaeology?

For the past couple of years there has been a convergence of archaeological paradigms. Most current research selects or integrates, according to arbitrarily changeable inquiries, the useful aspects of formerly opposing paradigms such as processualism and postprocessualism. Now the polemics are calming down there is ample opportunity for reflection. The causal relation of processualism and postprocessualism has been recognised, and consequentially both discourses are closing in on each other. This receptive attitude of scholars has obvious merits. Yet for the typical long term interests of archaeology it seems there is a reluctance to leave the accustomed paths set out by biology and positivist science. It was recently recognised that alongside this naturalist version of temporality a restored interest in history is dawning. Bearing within some remnants of culture history, these new arrivals study the processes of history. Instead of persevering in the direction of occasionally eclectic assemblages or variously integrated syntheses of traditional analyses, this archaeology of historical processes may prevent archaeological theory from growing asunder. It promises to reunite theoretical positions in archaeology. "A general willingness to reconcile disparate positions – a renewed spirit of inclusiveness – is archaeology's version of a bridge to the 21st century." (Pauketat 2001: 74) Pauketat has dubbed this potent inclination the paradigm of *historical processualism* (Pauketat 2001, 2004, Pauketat and Alt 2005).

Its distinction as a paradigm is warranted by "its relocation of the locus of social change and, consequently, […] what constitutes a satisfactory explanation." (Pauketat 2001: 74) The road towards historical processualism is paved by a theory of practice. This sharply contrasts with processualism and some neo-Darwinism which sought after the 'system' behind individuals and their material culture through the linear causality of adaptations. In practice theory people's actions and representations are generative. He continues by criticising, whilst emphasising their intrinsic elements of practice, three current theoretical approaches in archaeology: neo-Darwinism, cognitive-processualism and agency theory. Dividing neo-Darwinism in three branches, Pauketat criticises the essentialist and functionalist explanations of selectionists, though marking that they emphasise historical contingent processes in a universalistic way. Individualists are criticised for locating change only within the 'agency' of few aggrandising or charismatic individuals, thereby defying any study of historical processes. Finally transmissionism, according to Pauketat, comes closest to a non-essentialist practice theory, by focusing on the mechanisms of reproduction, transmission, and transformation of ideas at times allowing the human resources of experience and meaning.

Although variation in practices is emphasised, this occurs because the deeper meaning of the products of practices is not necessarily revealed to the performing actors. Cognitive-processualism shares this concern with variation. It concentrates on how cultural information was transmitted, emulated and transformed between specific points in time or space. Cognitive-processualists demonstrate the ability to deduce generic characteristics of ideology from material remains, however they are prone to rely on a teleological rationale in explaining social evolution. At best rudimentary human actions are broken into sequences exercising contingency on tradition, cognition or physical properties to varying degrees. The studies of technical *chaînes opèratoires* which resulted from this may help interpret technological change meaningfully on both the micro scale of practice and the macro scale of traditions. In this it has the potential to release us from behavioural essentialism and functionalist reductionism (Pauketat 2001).

By establishing an equal accessibility of human agency, social history and traditions at both the micro and macro scale simultaneously, ideas of agency entered archaeology (idem). In their article *Agency in Archaeology*, Dobres and Robb (2000b) also raise the question of the possibility that agency could be regarded as an archaeological paradigm. Due to the absence of thorough theoretical critique, agency has been quickly adopted and widely acclaimed in archaeological discourse. Therefore the concept of agency acquired an ad hoc appeal to particular issues and the problem of its meaning has been avoided. This nourishes the idea that agency is inherently sound, despite the lack of consensus on its meaning (Dobres and Robb 2000b). As Pauketat remarks, there have been faulty claims to agency. "These misguided claimants tend toward methodological individualism, often overlooking the central importance of the process of 'structuration' [...] as opposed to particular agents." (Pauketat 2001: 79) Yet because it has become broadly renowned and offers many perspectives that could profoundly affect the way we conduct archaeology, Dobres and Robb appear to conclude that agency as a paradigm could exist with the right theoretical efforts, though not in its current problematic state. Agency should be made to fit the long temporal vision and material culture centrefold to archaeology (Dobres and Robb 2000b). As a reaction to agency's theoretical ambiguity, there has been an explicit interest in practice and structuration (Pauketat 2001, Joyce and Lopiparo 2005). "However, there is no practice-theory cookbook, nor should archaeologists simply reify Bourdieu's concepts as ready-made interpretations rather than as jumping-off points for building theory." (Pauketat 2001: 79)

Archaeologists have attended to Bourdieu's concepts of *doxa* and, when associated with power relations, *heterodoxies* and *orthodoxies* (Bourdieu 1977), yet the theorisation of agency has not quite reached the point where it is rejoined with the processes it feeds and is produced by. Consequentially, so far, agency has been unable to adequately suit the long term or issues of changing material culture. Pauketat argues that a paradigm following a theory of practice, like historical processualism, can add considerable explanatory value to archaeological discourse without reduction or essentialism (Pauketat 2001, 2004). Meanwhile, the notion of history connects the micro scale to the macro scale (Pauketat 2001). The need for archaeology to directly engage with these issues through a focus on processes is felt elsewhere as well. Michelle Hegmon (2003, Pauketat 2004) proposed the label 'processualism-plus' to cover the diversity of contemporaneous theories used for common issues. Moreover, the concept of process or cultural process was recently elaborately addressed by Lyman (2007), noting that in both anthropology and archaeology there is a renewed strong concern for theorisation of the process. Lyman argues that processes should be clearly distinguished from evolution by revisiting the definitions of process in archaeology. "Future conceptualization must specify the duration of the process of interest such that the family of synchronic operational processes is distinguished from the family of diachronic evolutionary processes. Such conceptualization will require explicit definitions of operation and evolution." (Lyman 2007: 242) Lyman was also at the cradle of a polemic on historical processualism a few years after Pauketat published his paradigmatic proposal (O'Brien and Lyman 2004).

Although it is not my aim to mingle with a debate that is not mine, it seems important to mention that also in Pauketat's view, concurring with my own epistemological position (see the introduction), historical processualism does not exclude evolutionary approaches like neo-Darwinism (Pauketat 2004). Yet O'Brien and Lyman (2004) fiercely criticise the proposal and, not surprisingly, opt for an evolutionary point of view that, they argue, goes beyond historical processualism by providing an explanatory *theory* (their emphasis) specifying the causes of cultural change. This seems hardly just, because Pauketat does not set out to write a theory. Rather, he remarks a degree of consensus in archaeological theorising of the recent past and present that appears to have a tendency towards practice theory. It is to be expected that labelling a paradigm will meet criticism, but historical processualism should be seen to incorporate many theories (Pauketat 2004) and for me it is clear that a suitably adapted theory of practice has yet to be found.

Basing a Theory

My concern was never with defining a paradigm, but rather the apparent inability of the current state of archaeological theory to cope with a big issue as the development of society, for which I chose to pursue a consideration of a theory of space as the most immediate materialisation of being human. This quite naturally led me to the sub-discipline of human geography and especially (Germanic) social geography particularly concerned with the position of sociality in space. It was while exploring the disciplinary developments of archaeology and geography that it struck me that the lack of archaeological theory could be explained by the topics on which the development of geography and archaeology distinctly parted. In order to provide a context of academic history for the three axes of developing societies (constituting specific inquiries into such development as well as allowing for an epistemological merger of interests across social sciences), it became clear that with post-processualism archaeology split up in approaches following phenomenology, roughly resulting in agency and hermeneutic debates, opposing a biological or evolutionary direction; the former being overtly particularistic and arbitrarily individualistic, the latter addressing only parts of archaeological interests being reductionist to (developing) sociality. History and temporality, and thus development, did not typically enter phenomenological or agency approaches, separating agency debates from the structure it was originally introduced with (cf. Giddens 1984).

In geography none of this happened. Following behaviourist and behavioural geography (cf. the archaeology of behaviour and the cognitive turn of processualism), phenomenology in geography gave way to a rise of human geography. Simultaneously, this new direction reacted against geography as spatial science, unable to deal with real human problems. In human geography agency and structure were not separated, but theorisation continued to explore the specific relations between these two components. The disciplinary concern with space also presented a material element as a mediating and expressive third. Here I realised that what archaeological theory withheld from advancing could be provided by an adaptation of specific geographical thought. This answers a now abundant call to repair the unfortunate separation of agency and structure in archaeological theory (e.g. Pauketat 2001, Hegmon 2003, Joyce and Lopiparo 2005, Wynne-Jones and Kohring 2007).

Rather than departing from a theory of practice, geography starts with action theory. I prefer this vantage point to Pauketat's practice, simply because it takes one fundamental step further back. Action generates all practice and all materialisation, and thus all processes. By starting immediately at the level of practice, one runs the risk of once again underexposing the temporal scale of the event and logically forces an emphasis on *doxa*, power relations, and politicisation, losing a past inhabited by individuals. If one is not prepared to study the constitution of a practice it will be impossible to understand to process of continuous change operated by practices. Practices are consecutive actions, each of them a catalyst or (potentially creative) generator in its own right (cf. de Certeau 1988). As Joyce and Lopiparo say, "attention to innovation is the necessary counterpart to archaeological recognition of reproduction of practices over time." (Joyce and Lopiparo 2005: 371) I am sticking with the individual as the primary meaningful analytical unit, though neither in the idiosyncratic way of agency, nor the aggrandising players of neo-Darwinism. Rather, I use a kind of ontological individualism to understand society and a kind of methodological individualism to explain how society works. A similar stance has been advocated by the sociologist Jon Elster

(1989) (for a thorough discussion of the various meanings of methodolical individualism, see Udéhn 2002, Hodgson 2007). The everyday life of all individuals is catalytic for historical processes, mutually influencing each other. While the event of action is essentially a-historical, the relative temporal position of activities remains historically meaningful.

The immediacy of spatiality possibly makes my effort of theory building slightly more fundamental than Pauketat's concern with Cahokia pottery (Pauketat 2001). The commonality of facilitating spatial features accounts for why I repeatedly defied the possible arbitrariness of style and symbolism in this study. Nevertheless, I must stress that this should not be regarded as a functional reductionism as employed by neo-Darwinist selectionists. Not only may rudimentary spatial features actually refer to stylistic choices or conventions, furthermore it is entirely possible that style and symbolism construct structural linkages. Only I did not choose to make an argument for that kind of data, especially since it appears less directly connected to the primary contestation constituting sociality.

This is not far from the agency that Pauketat and Alt (2005) locate in a spatial feature as simple as a postmold. They hold that if all dimensions to the physicality of human agency are included, i.e. spatiality, corporeality, temporality, but also the occupation of space, affecting the experience of space and time of people, the following assertion can be made: "in the process of physical construction, people construct, de-construct, or re-construct cultures." (Pauketat and Alt 2005: 214) Their historical processual approach entails three procedural fundamentals. First they identify the variety of practices; secondly, they compare genealogies or histories of practices, distinguishing patterns (this implies a holistic perspective of empiricism, that is to say all the postmolds need to be considered); and finally connect and compare genealogical sets of evidence at various analytical scales. This involves comparing sets of practices with other practices, and tacking back and forth between the micro scale of site, place, person, or object specifics and e.g. the cultural area it resides in. The final stage is open ended, or as I would say allows plural outcomes. They recognise, but do not explicate, that this final macro scale comparison also evaluates the significance of hypothetical historical processual relationships, such as the practices constituting culture (idem).

Eventually this study of postmold variety, genealogy and comparison unsatisfactorily does not touch upon explaining the fundamental question of how cultures change. Despite the historical processual line of reasoning which would allow for different questions than cross-cultural comparisons, or as Pauketat and Alt themselves say, different from researchers typically interested in chiefdoms and states, the study does not continue into that. I think the lack of a specific and complete theory of practice is to blame. The difficulty is that historical processualism bridges over many possible theories, but stating that these will all be based on practice theory is not actually building a theory. Through this the issue is avoided or postponed and it remains obscure to appreciate any potential. Instead in this thesis both the micro and macro scale issues have been theorised, specifically for the field of studies concerned with spatialities. Following human and social geographical theory, I have sought to demonstrate the potentials contained in theorising the sociality of spatialities, which has brought me to the social positioning of spatialities.

Building a Theory

Instead of the predominant presence of Bourdieu in most archaeological cases, Giddens' structuration theory was primarily prevalent in geography. Following the lines set out in the three axes of developing societies, especially taking theories of action against the backdrop of temporalities as a means towards actively produced space, Allan Pred's work of the '80s is an ideal bridge builder. Adapting ideas of Hägerstrand's time-geography, Giddens' structuration, phenomenology and Foucault's power relations, he built a time-space specific theory of place as constructed and inhabited by individuals adhering to a community and/or society. His theory of place as historically contingent process (Pred 1984, 1986) is especially fit for archaeological purposes, because he directly includes the consequential transformation of nature in his dialectical structuring processes. The broad applicability of place connected to perpetual processes (time) allowed me to situate it in an evolutionary context, stretching it over concepts of spatialities on various scales. His aprioristic biographies, projects and processes tied into a systems theory were the perfect springboard towards current developments in Germanic social geography. Benno Werlen's moderately constructivist approach to regionalisation and Andreas Koch's phenomenologically inclined autopoietic systems have the equivalence of time and space in common. They direct the generalising ideas of Pred into specific treatments of the generative processes of borders and regions on the one hand, and detailed systemic spatialities on the other.

I discussed the possibility of using Werlen's (1998, 2005) regionalisation as a general theoretical background especially suitable for referring macro scale questions of borders and differentiation to the micro scale everyday life, while stressing that for a better understanding we should not start at a dataset, but at a social theory. This basically inverts traditional archaeological reasoning, accustomed to thinking from datasets, not towards them. Combined with a sound notion of time and temporalities the possibility of a social inference of culture areas, replacing culture historical methods, was enabled. Subsequently it was required to tie theoretical assertions to actual situations in archaeological datasets.

The rather constructivist ideas of Werlen partially obstructed this potential. Hence the autopoietic spatial systems of Koch (2005) appeared both a good basis for theoretical arguments on the micro scale and a guide to descry methodological opportunities. They implicitly concretised the phenomenological bi-implication. Though not uncritically, Koch's theory directed me to the structural linkages between socio-spatial systems which processes of sociality constitute, are entangled in, and exceed. The physically constructed localities of structural linkages, determinable through levels of compatibility between the social, the spatial and especially the socio-spatial systems find their material counterparts in some fundamental spatial features contained in standard spatial datasets. The notions of reproduction through the resistance present in everyday (consumptive) practices (de Certeau 1988) were of specific importance to argue for the reproduction of society over time in everyday life through space. Altogether it paved the road to the potential of deriving spatial signatures (or socio-spatial identities) from spatial datasets. This inferential process I termed the social positioning of spatialities, incorporating special attention to a developmental explanation.

That is not to say that this has been the first venture to socialise theorisation of space in archaeology. Foremost, the contributions of Robin and Rothschild (2002), Blake (2002) and Robin (2002) in the Journal of Social Archaeology definitely advanced archaeological awareness "of lived space as actively constructed and multivocally experienced." (Robin and Rothschild 2002: 160) Influenced by the concept of first, second and thirdspace of favoured geographer Edward Soja (1996), these efforts, being inevitably inspired by anthropology, also cause the literature of scholars like Allan Pred and Michel de Certeau to slowly seep into archaeology now. As Blake later notes, archaeology has been extremely selective in addressing spatial topics, letting archaeologists and architectural historians work in isolation in most cases. It is now that we should become aware that "space is no longer the sole purview of geography but is a thematic thread linking theoretical discourse across the humanities and social sciences. The growing currency of spatial terms is closely linked to the recognition of space's key role in the processes by which people construct their understandings of the world." (Blake 2007: 230) Connected to the call to study historical processes connecting the micro and macro scales, returning to (social) archaeology what is its strength, analysing spatialities could be a great place to start.

The need for studies of social complexity to integrate and connect scales of theoretical archaeological inquiries is also repeated by Kohring e.a. (2007). By providing a basic theoretical reasoning which on the one hand directly relates to the macro scale of constituting societies and a social understanding of culture areas or regions, while on the other hand seeking to analyse the processes producing a social identity in the built environment, I have attempted to overcome this impasse. Both ends of the theory become intelligible by the same aprioristic processive notions. Moreover, both allow plural outcomes and temporal, social and spatial hybridity in various compositions. There is a distinct repletion of an all-to-all principle permeating the theory. I have argued that a focus on processes may infinitely tie all constitutive elements into a totality. Making any selection, inevitable in conducting archaeological research, a systemic local totality of all framed social interaction, although it can be expected that both geographically and temporally constitutive environmental features will continue outside the selection. Such all-to-all principle seems also to be one of the reasons to emphasise outside space in studying associated houses or dwellings, making lived space an explicable holistic notion (Robin and Rothschild 2002, Robin 2002). What we are left with is the problem of materialisation which we are dependent on in archaeology (cf. Kohring e.a. 2007).

A Methodological Turn

The problem of the social positioning of spatialities is that its theory demands a holistic dataset. In this regard there is room for a rigorous empiricist turn for its methodological operation (cf. Pauketat 2005 on the historical processual procedure). That also presents us with the problem that in order to infer a spatial signature, preferably all structural linkages between (socio-spatial) systems need to be constructed in the built environment. So it is not for the popular misbelief that urbanism necessarily embodies a more complex or further advanced societal organisation (Wynne-Jones 2007), but because all sociality in the urban environment is mediated by built spatialities of its own making that I propose that urban datasets would be the most rewarding to look at. One of the big advantages the social positioning of spatialities entails is the introduction of a fully-fledged notion of temporalities in the analysis of spatial data. Smith (2007) and earlier Rapoport (1982), representing both a recent progression and favoured approaches regarding urban or built space, commented that there is no adequate dealing with time, change and development in the building of space.

Although I by no means presented an alternative view on urbanisation or the associated issues, there are some aspects of the archaeological study of urbanism that are inevitably affected by my assertions. Having established the way the built environment is produced and reproduced, in the dialectic processes of becoming it is unavoidable that planners become users and users become planners. Whereas Smith replaced the dichotomy of organic and planned growth with gradations, specifically Pred's (1986) theory abolishes the dichotomy altogether. Consequentially, built environments are nothing more than temporarily consolidated stages that carry a retention from the past and a protention for the future. As soon as they are realised, they are contested, possibly resulting in transformation, modification, or completely new constructions. Archaeology is the only discipline which owns the tools to make the dialectic evolution of the transformation of nature intelligible. This unique position should be further investigated an exploited in the future.

I suggest that the idea of stratification and the relative chronology it demonstrates be used in both superposition and horizontally (spatially equal pieces of a palimpsest). Analysing functionally similar parts to the dataset representing the layer or precinct built before and after the data that are under investigation, the spatial features of the built environment can both be regarded as an a-historical event of consolidation and a relative position in a historically contingent process. Also, the theory inhibits retaining a view of an urban environment as a consistent whole. It is actually comprised of inter-relational, contested, multivalent spatialities (cf. Blake 2007). This contestation in turn takes place in the structural linkages between socio-spatial systems.

Constructed forms of structural linkages can principally be seen as a kind of entrance, whether such entrance is reciprocal or not. In a way they represent borders that can be crossed, or, in other words, the punctuated boundaries of autopoietic systems in order to allow for outlying constitutive environmental features. Since there will be various degrees of overlap of constitutive systemic elements, a structural linkage has an elevated level of meaning. Constructed linkages facilitate accessibility. Infrastructure and all types of spatial features incorporating a structural linkage should be seen as corridors of accessibility connecting two or more spatialities. The observant reader will have directly compared this to space syntax and indeed it seems that the highly sophisticated quantitative method of space syntax appears to emphasise the right aspect in accessibility. Unfortunately, their accessibility is a spatial one, deprived of social meaning. I am not convinced that statistical analysis and mathematical formulas per se (cf. de Certeau 1988) hold any explanatory value for things which concern human beings. Nevertheless, they should not all be uncritically discarded either. Especially the all-encompassing quality of space syntax is potentially a powerful tool for exercising spatial analysis, despite its lawful nature. Starting research with an aprioristic theory like the social positioning of spatialities, the accessibility and frequency calculations of spatial analyses like space syntax will be informed, directed and improved. It will invest methods with social meaning that do not intrinsically carry that possibility, though the same caution applies as with questions asked to the spatial database of a GIS application. Such inferential method could move spatial datasets beyond the map.

Concluding Remarks

Born out of dissatisfaction with the reluctance of the archaeological discipline to address big issues and the seeming inability to derive extensive social meaning from one of our most basic sources of information, this study concludes in saying that there is immense potential for interdisciplinary endeavours in the social theorisation of space. With the building of a theory of social positioning of spatialities I hope to provide an incentive for theorists, methodologists and field archaeologists to continue the exploration of space. Especially the theories recently developed in social geography appear to form a cogent point of departure with the junction of time and space. It has been demonstrated that we can address big issues, while maintaining the subject at the micro scale as a meaningful constitutive force. The scale-exceeding efforts reveal a concern for processes which differs considerably from the teleological processes of traditional social evolution and civilisation and/or urbanisation. The spatial concepts that are affected by this strongly relate to the conceptualisation of place, both geographically and socially.

Place is a widely applicable notion which should be further explored in archaeology. It may refer to built environments, regions, culture areas and borders alike, whilst dialectically maintaining the inferential value of a socio-spatial identity. None of these should be regarded as a static concept, but rather as perpetually entangled in dialectic processes of becoming. It is only through such processes that spatialities get meaning. Although I envision the process to entail the interpretive potential of amplification into evolutionary perspectives, their nature is thus quite different from the archaeological process before. The prejudicial teleology is avoided by preventing pre-given sets of constitutive elements from entering the theory. Universality is only admitted in the occurrence of the contingent dialectic processes themselves.

The theoretical and epistemological assertions made in this study will not only affect the subject under study, but also our position as researchers. Whether or not there is a new paradigm dawning in archaeology, there is definite room for improving our treatment of spatialities and borders. Time and temporalities should be made an inherent part of such inquiries. The development of the built environment through the constant transformation of nature in dialectic processes is pre-eminently the interpretive potential of the archaeological discipline. There is not a ready-made path that we should follow, no clear-cut answers or fixed set of features to study, yet there are many ways to develop theories apt for pressing questions. By choosing an action-based approach and a processive perspective, the plurality of our datasets can be made intelligible without reduction. The unique temporal and material perspective that archaeology can offer may be important for our current dealing with spatialities and future city planning. Archaeology is a discipline which could and should contribute to the time-space specific theory building continuously progressing in social sciences.

Acknowledgements

Although the themes contained in this study quite naturally resulted from my own interests developed during my education, I could not have done without the general convictions underlying the academic ventures. First and foremost, I would like to express my sincere gratitude towards my father, Jan Vis, not only for his persistent support to the conduct of this research and my studies, but also for his unintentional slight indoctrination and acting as a forceful sparring-partner.

A special thank you to Jorge Zambrana, who kindly invited me into his home. The warm welcome and hospitality of him and his family are much appreciated, the conversations well remembered.

Also I acknowledge the influence of John Bintliff, who unknowingly directed me towards geographical themes, and Rosemary Joyce for elaborating on her interest in the work of Allan Pred. I thank John Hoopes for putting me on the trail to the core issues concerned with culture areas and culture history, especially exemplified by the Isthmo-Colombian area. Next I would like to thank Dominic Powlesland, whose lively conversations both inspired me and demystified archaeological theory. Thinking out of the box unconditionally becomes common coin with him. Furthermore, a thank you to several members of the Aerial Archaeology Research Group (AARG) and the International Society for Archaeological Prospection (ISAP), in particular Luis Barba, Branko Mušic, Michael Doneus and Darja Grosman. Although their efforts and the theme of archaeological prospection were eventually discarded as part of this study, a certain influence is felt throughout it. Huib Ernste is thanked for his patience and exceptional flexibility in guiding me through my interdisciplinary endeavour into action theories.

After some spirited conversations and a bit of collaboration, Jan Kolen decided to supervise this thesis. He is particularly thanked for his bravery and pivotal efforts structuring my arguments. Also my gratitude for Alex Geurds, who stirred up my interest in Central America and helped out at the last minute, preventing any further delays by accepting a role as supervisor.

Also a special thank you to Micha Meijer for the precious hours he could have directed towards greater goals, but chose to sacrifice to make a book with me. Leah Clarke is thanked for giving the text of the book the linguistic once-over.

Finally, my heartfelt gratitude for Rianne Dubois, giving me great support and being my bulwark. She indefatigably sat out all the tedious monologues that ordered my thoughts.

References

Anderson, B. R. O. 2006 [1983]
   Imagined Communities: reflections on the origin and spread of nationalism, revised edition, Verso, London.

Arnoldi, J. 2001
   Niklas Luhmann: an introduction, in: Theory, Culture & Society, 18(1): 1-13.

Azaryahu, M. 2001
   Water Towers: a study in the cultural geographies of Zionist mythology, in: Cultural Geographies, 21(3): 317-339.

Bailey, G. 1987
   Breaking the Time Barrier, in: Archaeological Review from Cambridge, 6(1): 5-20.

Barrett, J. C. 2001
   Agency, the Duality of Structure, and the Problem of the Archaeological Record, in: Hodder, I. ed., Archaeological Theory Today, Polity Press, Cambridge: 141-164.

Benech, C. 2007
   New Approach to the Study of City Planning and Domestic Dwellings in the Ancient Near East, in: Archaeological Prospection 14: 87-103.

Benech, C. 2008
   New Project on the Study of City Planning with Geophysical Maps, in: ISAP News 17: 2-3.

Bintliff, J. ed. 1991a
   The Annales School and Archaeology, Leicester University Press, London.

Bintliff, J. 1991b
   The Contribution of an Annaliste/Structural History Approach to Archaeology, in: Bintliff, J. ed., The Annales School and Archaeology, Leicester University Press, London: 1-33.

Bintliff, J. ed. 2006
   A Companion to Archaeology, Blackwell Publishing, Oxford.

Blake, E. 2002
   Spatiality Past and Present: an interview with Edward Soja, in: Journal of Social Archaeology, 2(2): 139-158.

Blake, E. 2007
   Space, Spatiality, and Archaeology, in: Meskell, L. and Preucel, R. W. ed., A Companion to Social Archaeology, Blackwell Publishing, Oxford: 230-254.

Blunt, A. and Wills, J. 2000
   Decolonising Geography: postcolonial perspectives, in: Blunt, A. and Wills, J., Dissident Geographies: an introduction to radical ideas and practice, Prentice Hall, London: 167-206.

Bourdieu, P. 1977
   Outline of a Theory of Practice, Cambridge University Press, Cambridge.
Braswell, G. E. 2003
   Highland Maya Polities, in: Smith, M. E., and Berdan, F. F. ed., The Postclassic Mesoamerican World, University of Utah Press, Salt Lake City: 45-49.
Bruun, H. and Langlais, R. 2003
   On the Embodied Nature of Action, in: Acta Sociologica, 46(1): 31-49.
Burmeister, S. 2000
   Archaeology and Migration: approaches to an archaeological proof of migration, in: Current Anthropology, 41(4): 539-567.
Callon, M. 1997
   Actor-Network Theory: the market test, (draft) published on-line by Centre for Science Studies, Lancaster University, Lancaster, www.lancs.ac.uk/fass/sociology/papers/callon-market-test.pdf, downloaded 04-12-2008.
Campbell, T. 1981
   Seven Theories of Human Society, Clarendon Press, Oxford.
Carmack, R. M. 1981
   The Quiché Mayas of Utatlán: the evolution of a highland Guatemala kingdom, University of Oklahoma Press, Norman.
Certeau de, M. 1988 [1984]
   The Practice of Everyday Life, University of California Press, Berkeley.
Chapman, R. 2003
   Archaeologies of Complexity, Routledge, London.
Chapman, R. 2007
   Evolution, Complexity and the State, in: Kohring, S. and Wynne-Jones, S. ed., Socialising Complexity: structure, interaction and power in archaeological discourse, Oxbow Books, Oxford: 13-28.
Cheah, P. 2003
   Grounds of Comparison, in: Culler, J. and Cheah, P. ed., Grounds of Comparison: around the work of Benedict Anderson, Routledge, London: 3-20.
Clarke, D. L. 1968
   Analytical Archaeology, Methuen, London.
Cloke, P. e.a. ed. 1991
   Approaching Human Geography, Chapman, London.
Constenla Umaña, A. 1991
   Las Lenguas del Área Intermedia: introducción a su estudio areal, Editorial de la Universidad de Costa Rica, San José.

Corbey, R. A. H. 2005
> The Metaphysics of Apes: negotiating the animal-human boundary, Cambridge University Press, Cambridge.

Cosgrove, D. 1985
> Prospect, Perspective and the Evolution of the Landscape Idea, in: Transactions of the Institute of British Geographers, New Series, 10(1): 45-62.

Dobres, M.-A. and Robb, J. ed. 2000a
> Agency in Archaeology, Routledge, London.

Dobres, M.-A. and Robb, J. 2000b
> Agency in Archaeology: paradigm or platitude?, in: Dobres, M.-A. and Robb, J. ed., Agency in Archaeology, Routledge, London: 3-17.

Dunning, E. and Krieken van, R. 1997
> Translators' Introduction to Norbert Elias's 'Towards a Theory of Social Processes', in: The British Journal of Sociology, 48(3): 353-354.

Eberle, T. S. 1984
> Sinnkonstitution in Alltag und Wissenschaft: der Beitrag der Phänomenologie an die Methodologie der Sozialwissenschaften, Haupt, Bern und Stuttgart.

Eliade, M. 1959
> Cosmos and History: the myth of the eternal return, Harper Torchbooks, New York.

Elias, N. 1997
> Towards a Theory of Social Processes: a translation, in: The British Journal of Sociology, 48(3): 355-383.

Elster, J. 1989
> Nuts and Bolts for the Social Sciences, Cambridge University Press, Cambridge.

Erwin, D. 2000
> Macroevolution is more than Repeated Rounds of Microevolution, in: Evolution & Development, 2(2): 78-84.

Flannery, K. V. 1972
> The Cultural Evolution of Civilizations, Annual Review of Ecology and Systematics 3: 399-426.

Flannery, K. V. and Marcus, J. ed. 2003 [1983]
> The Cloud People: divergent evolution of the Zapotec and Mixtec civilizations, Percheron Press, New York.

Fletcher, R. 2006
> Materiality, Space, Time and Outcome, in: Bintliff, J. ed., A Companion to Archaeology, Blackwell Publishing, Oxford: 110-140.

Fonseca, O. M. and Cooke, R. G. 1993

El Sur de la América Central: contribución al estudio de la región histórica chibcha, in: Carmack, R. M. ed., Historia General de Centroamérica, Vol. I: Historia Antigua, Edicionas Siruela, Madrid: 217-282.

Foucault, M. 1980

Questions on Geography, in: Gordon, C. ed., Power/Knowledge: selected interviews and other writings 1972-1977, Harvester Press, Brighton: 63-77.

Foucault, M. 1982

The Subject and Power, in: Dreyfus, H. L. and Rabinow, P. ed., Michel Foucault: beyond structuralism and hermeneutics, second edition, The University of Chicago Press: 208-226.

Gerstle, A. I. 1988

Maya-Lenca Ethnic Relations in Late Classic Period Copan, Honduras, UMI, USA.

Giddens, A. 1984

The Constitution of Society: outline of the theory of structuration, University of California Press, Berkeley.

Hägerstrand, T. 1970

What About People in Regional Science?, Presidential Address, Ninth European Congress of the Regional Science Association, Papers in Regional Science, in: Journal of the Regional Science Association International, 23(1): 6-21.

Hall, E. T. 1959

The Silent Language, Doubleday & Company Inc., Garden City, New York.

Hall, E. T. e.a. 1968

Proxemics [and Comments and Replies], in: Current Anthropology, 9(2, 3): 83-108.

Hall, E. T. 2006

Proxemics, in: Low, S. M. and Lawrence-Zúñiga, D. ed., The Anthropology of Space and Place: locating culture, Blackwell Publishing, Oxford.

Hall, J. R. 1980

The Time of History and the History of Times, in: History and Theory, 19(2): 113-131.

Hallin, P. O. 1991

New Paths for Time-Geography?, in: Geografiska Annaler, Series B, Human Geography, 73(3): 199-207.

Hallowel, A. I. 1955

Culture and Experience, series: Publications of the Philadelphia Anthropological Society, University of Pennsylvania Press, Philadelphia.

Heidegger, M. 1972

Sein und Zeit, 12th edition, Niemeyer Verlag, Tübingen.

Hegmon, M. 2003
  Setting Theoretical Egos Aside: issues and theory in north American archaeology, in: American Antiquity, 68(2): 213–43.

Hexter, J. H. 1972
  Fernand Braudel and the Monde Braudellien, in: Journal of Modern History 44: 480-539.

Hillier, B. and Hanson, J. 1984
  The Social Logic of Space, Cambridge University Press, Cambridge.

Hillier, B. 2002
  A Theory of the City as Object: or, how spatial laws mediate the social construction of urban space, in: Urban Design International, 7(3, 4): 153-179.

Hillier, B. 2006
  Space Syntax: the language of the museum space, in: Macdonald, S. ed., A Companion to Museum Studies, Blackwell Publishing, Oxford: 282-301.

Hillier, B. 2007
  Cities and Urban Societies: the role of endogenous factors, paper given at the 7th Mesoamerican Urbanism Conference, Leiden University.

Hodder, I. 1986
  Reading the Past: current approaches to interpretation in archaeology, Cambridge University Press, Cambridge.

Hodder, I. e.a. ed. 1998 [1995]
  Interpreting Archaeology: finding meaning in the past, Routledge, London.

Hodgson, G. M. 2007
  Meanings of Methodological Individualism, in: Journal of Economic Methodology, 14(2): 211–26.

Hoopes, J. W. in press
  Cultural Chibchas del Litoral Caribe: explorando las conexiones Precolombianas entre Colombia y Costa Rica, in: Gnecco, C. and González, V. ed., [title forthcoming], ICANH, Bogotá.

Hoopes, J. W. and Fonseca Zamora, O. M. 2003
  Goldwork and Chibchan Identity: endogenous change and diffuse unity in the Isthmo-Colombian area, in: Quilter, J. and Hoopes, J. W. ed., Gold and Power in Ancient Costa Rica, Panama, and Colombia, Dumbarton Oaks, Washington: 29-90.

Ingold, T. 1986
  Evolution and Social Life, series: Themes in the Social Sciences, Cambridge University Press, Cambridge.

Ingold, T. 2000
  The Perception of the Environment, Routledge, London.

Isbell, W. H. 2000
: What We Should Be Studying: the 'imagined community' and the 'natural community', in: Canuto, M. A. and Yaeger, J. ed., The Archaeology of Communities: a new world perspective, Routledge, London: 243-266.

Johnston, R. J., Gregory, D. and Smith, D. M. ed. 1994
: A Dictionary of Human Geography, Blackwell Publishing, Oxford.

Joyce, R. A. and Lopiparo, J. 2005
: Postscript: Doing Agency in Archaeology, in: Journal of Archaeological Method and Theory, 12(4): 365-374.

Knox, P. L. and Marston, S. A. 2003
: Human Geography: places and regions in global context, second edition, Prentice Hall, Pearson Education Inc., New Jersey.

Koch, A. 2005
: Autopoietic Spatial Systems: the significance of actor network theory and systems theory for the development of a system theoretical approach of space, in: Social Geography, 1(1): 5-14.

Kohring, S. e.a. 2007
: Materialising 'Complex' Social Relationships: technology, production and consumption in a Copper Age community, in: Kohring, S. and Wynne-Jones, S. ed., Socialising Complexity: structure, interaction and power in archaeological discourse, Oxbow Books, Oxford: 100-117.

Kolen, J. C. A. 2005
: De Biografie van het Landschap: drie essays over landschap, geschiedenis en erfgoed, academisch proefschrift, VU Amsterdam.

Kowalewski, S. 2003 [1983]
: Differences in the Site Hierarchies below Monte Albán and Teotihuacán: a comparison based on the rank-size rule, in: Flannery, K. V. and Marcus, J. ed., The Cloud People: divergent evolution of the Zapotec and Mixtec civilizations, Percheron Press, New York: 168-169.

Laporte, J. P. 2003
: Architectural Aspects of Interaction between Tikal and Teotihuacan during the Early Classic Period, in: Braswell, G. E. ed., The Maya and Teotihuacan, University of Texas Press, Austin: 198-216.

Last, J. 1998 [1995]
: The Nature of History, in: Hodder, I. e.a. ed., Interpreting Archaeology: finding meaning in the past, Routledge, London: 141-157.

Law, J. 2000

Objects, Spaces and Other, published on-line by Centre for Science Studies, Lancaster University, Lancaster, www.lancs.ac.uk/fass/sociology/papers/law-objects-spaces-others.pdf, downloaded 04-12-2008.

Law, J. and Hassard, J. 1999

Actor Network Theory and After, Blackwell Publishing, Oxford.

Lawrence, D. L. and Low, S. M. 1990

The Built Environment and Spatial Form, in: Annual Review of Anthropology 19: 453-505.

Lefebvre, H. 1991

The Production of Space, Blackwell Publishing, Oxford.

Ley, D. and Samuels, M. S. ed. 1978

Humanistic Geography: prospects and problems, Maaroufa Press, Chicago.

Low, S. M. and Lawrence-Zúñiga, D. L. 2006

Locating Culture, in: Low, S. M. and Lawrence-Zúñiga, D. ed., The Anthropology of Space and Place: locating culture, Blackwell Publishing, Oxford: 1-47.

Lucas, G. 2005

The Archaeology of Time, series: Themes in Archaeology, Routledge, London.

Lyman, R. L., O'Brien, M. J. and Dunnell, R. C. 1997

The Rise and Fall of Culture History, Plenum Press, New York.

Lyman, R. L. 2007

What is the 'Process' in Cultural Process and in Processual Archaeology?, in: Anthropological Theory, 7(2): 217-250.

Meinig, D. W. ed. 1979

The Interpretation of Ordinary Landscapes: geographical essays, Oxford University Press, New York.

Mises von, L. 1998 [1949]

Human Action: a treatise on economics, The Scholar's Edition, The Ludwig von Mises Institute, Auburn.

Martin, A. 2005

Agents in Inter-Action: Bruno Latour and agency, in: Journal of Archaeological Method and Theory, 12(4): 283-311.

Montmollin de, O. 1989

The Archaeology of Political Structure: settlement analysis in a Classic Maya polity, series: New Studies in Archaeology, Cambridge University Press, Cambridge.

Moore, J. D. 1996

The Archaeology of Plazas and the Proxemics of Ritual: three Andean traditions, in: American Anthropologist, New Series, 98(4): 789-802.

Murray, T. 1999

Time and Archaeology, series: One World Archaeology 37, Routledge, London.

O'Brien, M. J. and Lyman, R. L. 2004

History and Explanation in Archaeology, in: Anthropological Theory, 4(2): 173-197.

Parker Pearson, M. and Richards, C. ed. 1994

Architecture and Order: approaches to social space, Routledge, London.

Pauketat, T. R. 2000a

The Tragedy of the Commoners, in: Dobres, M.-A. and Robb, J. ed., Agency in Archaeology, Routledge, London: 113-129.

Pauketat, T. R. 2000b

Politicization and Community in the Pre-Columbian Mississippi Valley, in: Canuto, M. A. and Yaeger, J. ed., The Archaeology of Communities: a new world perspective, Routledge, London: 16-43.

Pauketat, T. R. 2001

Practice and History in Archaeology: an emerging paradigm, in: Anthropological Theory, 1(1): 73-98.

Pauketat, T. R. 2004

[comment] Archaeology without Alternatives, in: Anthropological Theory, 2(4): 199-203.

Pauketat, T. R. and Alt, S. M. 2005

Agency in a Postmold? Physicality and the archaeology of culture-making, in: Journal of Archaeological Method and Theory, 12(3): 213-236.

Pellow, D. 2007

The Architecture of Female Seclusion in West Africa, in: Low, S. M. and Lawrence-Zúñiga, D. ed., The Anthropology of Space and Place: locating culture, Blackwell Publishing, Oxford: 160-183.

Pluciennik, M. 2005

Social Evolution, series: Duckworth Debates in Archaeology, Duckworth, London.

Powlesland, D. 2003

The Heslerton Parish Project: 20 years of archaeological research in the Vale of Pickering, in: Manby, T. G. e.a. ed., The Archaeology of Yorkshire: an assessment at the beginning of the 21st century, Yorkshire Archaeological Society, Leeds: 275-292.

Powlesland, D. 2006

Redefining Past Landscapes: 30 years of remote sensing in the Vale of Pickering, in: Campana, S. and Forte, M. ed., From Space to Place, 2nd International Conference on Remote Sensing in Archaeology, BAR International Series 1568, Archaeopress, Oxford: 197-201.

Pred, A. R. 1977

The Choreography of Existence: comments on Hägerstrand's time-geography and its usefulness, in: Economic Geography, Planning-Related Swedish Geographic Research, 53(2): 207-221.

Pred, A. R. 1981

Social Reproduction and the Time-Geography of Everyday Life, in: Geografiska Annaler, series B, Human Geography, 63(1): 5-22.

Pred, A. R. 1984

Place as Historically Contingent Process: structuration and the time-geography of becoming places, in: Annals of the Association of American Geographers, 74(2): 279-297.

Pred, A. R. 1985

Comment in Reply: Unglorious Isolation or Unglorious Misrepres(s)entation?, in: Annals of the Association of American Geographers, 75(1): 132.

Pred, A. R. 1986

Place, Practice and Structure: social and spatial transformation in southern Sweden: 1750-1850, Polity Press, Cambridge.

Putnam, H. 1981

Reason, Truth and History, Cambridge, Cambridge University Press.

Rapoport, A. 1982

The Meaning of the Built Environment: a nonverbal communication approach, Sage Publications, Beverly Hills.

Read, D. W. 2006

Cultural Evolution is not Equivalent to Darwinian Evolution, commentary on: Mesoudi, Whiten and Laland, towards a unified science of cultural evolution, in: Behavioral and Brain Sciences, 29(4): 361-362.

Renfrew, C. and Bahn, P. 2000

Archaeology: theories, methods and practices, third edition, Thames and Hudson, London.

Richardson, M. 2006

Being-in-the-Market versus Being-in-the-Plaza: material culture and the construction of social reality in Spanish America, in: Low, S. M. and Lawrence-Zúñiga, D. ed., The Anthropology of Space and Place: locating culture, Blackwell Publishing, Oxford: 74-91.

Rindos, D. e.a. 1985

Darwinian Selection, Symbolic Variation, and the Evolution of Culture, in: Current Anthropology, 26(1): 77-78.

Robb, M. H. 2007
   The Spatial Logic of Zacuala, Teotihuacan, in: Proceedings 6th International Space Syntax Symposium Istanbul 2007, 062, published on-line: www.spacesyntaxistanbul.itu.edu.tr/papers%5Clongpapers%5C062%20-%20 Robb.pdf, downloaded 10-12-2008.

Robin, C. 2002
   Outside of Houses: the practice of everyday life at Chan Nòohol, Belize, in: Journal of Social Archaeology, 2(2): 245-268.

Robin, C. and Rothschild, N. A. 2002
   Archaeological Ethnographies: social dynamics of outdoor space, in: Journal of Social Archaeology, 2(2): 159-172.

Rodman, M. C. 2006
   Empowering Place: multilocality and multivocality, in: Low, S. M. and Lawrence-Zúñiga, D. ed., The Anthropology of Space and Place: locating culture, Blackwell Publishing, Oxford: 204-223.

Samuels, M. S. 1979
   The Biography of Landscape: cause and culpability, in Meinig, D. W. ed., The Interpretation of Ordinary Landscapes: geographical essays, Oxford University Press, New York: 51-88.

Sanderson, S. K. 1990
   Social Evolutionism: a critical history, Basil Blackwell, Oxford.

Santamaria, U. and Bailey, A. M. 1984
   A Note on Braudel's Structure as Duration, in: History and Theory, 23(1): 78-83.

Santley, R. S. and Hirth, K. G. ed. 1993
   Prehispanic Domestic Units in Western Mesoamerica: studies of the household, compound, and residence, CRC Press, Boca Raton.

Schiffer, M. B. 1987
   The Formation Processes of the Archaeological Record, University of New Mexico Press, Albuquerque.

Shanks, M. 1992
   Experiencing the Past: on the character of archaeology, Routledge, London.

Shanks, M. and Hodder, I. 1998 [1995]
   Processual, Postprocessual and Interpretive Archaeologies, in: Hodder, I. e.a. ed., Interpreting Archaeology: finding meaning in the past, Routledge, London: 3-29.

Smith, M. E. 2007
   Form and Meaning in the Earliest Cities: a new approach to ancient urban planning, in: Journal of Planning History, 6(1): 3-47.

Soja, E. W. 1996
   Thirdspace: journeys to Los Angeles and other real-and-imagined places, Blackwell Publishing, Oxford.

Thomas, J. 1996
   Time, Culture and Identity, Routledge, London.

Thomas, J. 2001
   Archaeologies of Place and Landscape, in: Hodder, I. ed., Archaeological Theory Today, Polity Press, Cambridge: 165-186.

Thrift, N. J. 1983
   On the Determination of Social Action in Space and Time, in: Environment and Planning D, Society and Space, 1(1): 23-57.

Thrift, N. J. and Pred, A. R. 1981
   Time-Geography: a new beginning, in: Progress in Human Geography, 5(2): 277-286.

Tilley, C. Y. 1994
   A Phenomenology of Landscape: places, paths and monuments, Berg, Oxford.

Trigger, B. 1998
   [review] The Rise and Fall of Culture History by R. Lee Lyman; Michael J. O'Brien; Robert C. Dunnell, in: Journal of Field Archaeology, 25(3): 363-366.

Tuan, Y.-F. 1976
   Humanistic Geography, in: Annals of the Association of American Geographers 66: 266-276.

Tuan, Y.-F. 1977
   Space and Place: the perspective of experience, University of Minnesota Press, Minneapolis.

Udéhn, L. 2002
   The Changing Face of Methodological Individualism, in: Annual Review of Sociology 28: 479–507.

Werlen, B. 1998
   Thesen zur Handlungstheoretische Neuorientierung Sozialgeographischer Forschung, in: Sedlacek, P. and Werlen, B. ed., Texte zur handlungstheoretischen Geographie, Vol. 18: 85-102.

Werlen, B. 2005
   Regions and Everyday Regionalizations: from a space-centred towards an action-centred human geography, in: Houtum van, H., Kramsch, O. and Zierhofer, W. ed., Bordering Space, Ashgate, Aldershot: 47-60.

Willey, G. R. 1971
   An Introduction to American Archaeology, Vol. II: South America, Prentice-Hall series in anthropology, Englewood Cliffs.

Wynne-Jones, S. and Kohring, S. 2007
 Socialising Complexity, in: Kohring, S. and Wynne-Jones, S. ed., Socialising Complexity: structure, interaction and power in archaeological discourse, Oxbow Books, Oxford: 2-12.

Zierhofer, W. 2002
 Speech Acts and Space(s): language pragmatics and the discursive constitution of the social, in: Environment and Planning A, 34(8): 1355-1372.